Architecture Highlights

Architecture Highlights

Hubertus Adam und Jochen Paul
With a Foreword by Prof. James Wines (Ed.)
Texts by:
Hubertus Adam, Oliver Elser, Markus Golser,
Dietmar Kölbel, Andrea Mende, Jochen Paul,
Sebastian Raedecke, Manuela Schubert, Ulrike Schulze,
Sebastian Schwarzenberger, Chris van Uffelen.

Contents

HIGHLIGHTS OF WORLD ARCHITECTURE

FOREWORD BY JAMES WINES

The majority of buildings illustrated in this book are remarkably enduring. For example, a number of them are still in active use after eight to ten centuries and some have survived for over three thousand years. In summary, there is an undeniable track record of what is now called "sustainable architecture."

Shifting focus to the present day, sustainability and a respect for the natural environment are among the most important issues of the 21st century. The construction of human habitat currently consumes nearly two thirds of the world's natural resources. This has apocalyptic implications in terms of diminished energy supplies and increased global warming. While there is a marginal green design movement today, most of the luminaries of contemporary architecture are totally oblivious to ecological responsibility. In fact, there is an almost belligerent anti-green attitude among some advocates of high-tech construction, who aggressively demonstrate their indifference by showcasing such obscene generators of toxic waste as titanium and aluminium, or contributing to a seemingly endless proliferation of massive walls in glass and concrete.

The questions revolving around this topic of sustainability are infinitely complex. Some of significant features of longevity are:

- Epochal significance - This term refers to the capacity of a building to capture the most influential social, psychological, and religious forces shaping an era. This information must then be converted into a highly communicative imagery, which can successfully weather both the physical tests of time and the erratic inconsistencies of changing tastes.

- Environmental awareness - Many great structures from the past paid little attention to what we now label as "ecological responsibility." It is also important to remember that their intrusions on nature were limited by a lack of fossil fuel technology. On the other hand, architecture was frequently used to thank beneficent gods and celebrate gifts of fertility.

- Cultural values - Without the presence of a continuously evolving culture, no great architecture can exist. If a nation lacks this seminal impetus, the entire mission of sustainability fails. People will never want to keep culturally inferior, or boring, buildings around, no matter how exemplary their use of green technology or resource conservation.

From a cultural perspective, it is interesting to evaluate a few significant historical structures and communities, just to demonstrate how their epochal dynamics have contributed to the history of sustainability.

It is difficult to determine why and when certain ancient civilizations decided to abandon circular themes of Neolithic culture and convert to geometric grids and erect massive rectangular structures. What we do know is that this decision set the course of egocentric and power-driven civilizations thereafter. The Great Pyramids of Giza, the Hatsheptut Temple at Dier el-Bahri and Persepolis in Persia, all gave expression to the dominance of the state and the imposition of societal unity, based on economic, religious and territorial gain.

The Roman Empire represented the first civilization to aggressively advance the notion that nature is here for Man's convenience and then use engineering skills to reap the benefits. Unfortunately, this great metropolis also set the stage for most of the wasteful indulgences of contemporary life through its corrupt politics, barbaric entertainment, pathological greed, and imperialist exploitation of colonies.

During the Middle Ages, Renaissance and Baroque periods in Italy and France, the Catholic Church expanded on the notion that nature exists to serve humanity and added the doctrine that Man is conceived in God's image. The most persuasive aspect of this commitment - and the key to early religious buildings' importance as sustainable architecture - is the concept that the walls tell the story. The narrative mosaics of the Galla Placidia and Sant' Appolinare Nuovo in Ravenna, the sculptured facades of Chartes Cathedral, and the Giotto frescos in San Francesco in Assisi, each attest to the value of using buildings as society's primary means of communication – rather like the Internet of their time.

In contrast to Christian buildings, the 17th century AD Buddhist temples and gardens of Japan embodied a fundamental belief that terrestrial existence is only a transition point, en route to a heavenly garden in the after life. The great Horyuji Temple complex in Nara and the Ryoan-ji Gardens of Kyoto were built as microcosms (or borrowed scenery) in anticipation of the ultimate paradise. Zen became one of the earliest organized religions to relate architecture to its natural context and grasp the value of humanity's custodial role in the protection of nature.

Moving to the 19th century and the advent of the Modern World, one can witness the beginning of the end of sustainable architecture. The great International Exposition of 1889 in Paris launched the world's love affair with the Industrial Revolution. Structures like the Eiffel Tower and Hall of Machines introduced the latest technologies and encouraged architects to reject the superfluous architectural decor of the past, in favour of seductive new materials and a functionalist ethic.

By the early years of the 20th century - with the exception of architects like Gaudi, Sullivan Wright and a few others - the concept of longevity shifted away from the notion of buildings as physically enduring monuments and respectful extensions of nature. With movements like Modernism in Europe and Constructivism in Russia, the goals of architecture became almost the opposite. The sociological and economic agendas of the Industrial Revolution advocated a constant renewal of products. Under the new definition of sustainability, people's quality of life and job security would presumably improve as manufactured items were designed, built, discarded, and replaced in the endless continuum of consumer culture.

Buildings like the Villa Savoie (Le Corbusier's model of "the machine for living in"), Rietveld's Schröder/Schräder House in Utrecht, and the work of the Russian Constructivists, Chernikov and Melnikov, all but eliminated the last residuals of 19th-century architectural imagery. The birth of abstract art was a Godsend to architects in the 1920s because, instead of having to depend on a traditional kit of parts derived from Neo-classicism, or the Beaux-Arts, they had an opportunity to invent the future on their own terms.

Moving to present, the motivational influences today are not that different from those of the Modernists and Constructivists. The works of Frank Gehry, Rem Koolhaas, Peter Eisenman, and Daniel Liebskind, all display considerable debt to the pioneers of the early 20th century. These contemporary architects' brilliant formal strategies are obviously different from those of the 1920s. Furthermore, their work is more technologically advanced through the conveniences of computer-aided design. Still, their primary influences - the celebration of industrial methods and materials and the layering and warping of form (via Cubism and Constructivism) - remain linked to the past. The re-cycling of familiar sources can be seen as one category of preservation - but this is probably not the kind of sustainability we should be talking about in a world of shrinking resources.

We are now in a new Age of Information and Ecology. The most challenging goal now is to find an appropriate architectural language that advocates sustainability and expresses the spirit of a post-industrial era. Whereas the Modernists and Constructivists were inspired by the physical presence of a new industrial technology, designers today must question how building design will change to represent the similarities between the unseen components of digital communications systems and the interactive processes of nature. If this direction expands its influence over the next decade, the result may call for a future "Highlights" book on invisible architecture.

JAMES WINES

On the Sense and Purpose and the Inevitable Limitations of a Kaleidoscope of World Architecture

The perception of contemporary architecture has been subject to change in recent years. The public at large no longer sees architects as irresponsible planners who erect stereotypical housing silos somewhere out on the city's periphery, but rather more and more as the creative designers of buildings that help cities, regions and even countries establish new identities. In the period of transition from the 20th to the 21st century, architecture is faced with one overriding task in urban conglomerations – whether in Europe or the USA, Mexico, China or Japan: the transformation from industrial to a postindustrial society. Factory sites become available for new uses, and all over the world waterfront zones receive new attention. Whether in Hong Kong or Chicago, Rotterdam, London or Genoa, where ships once unloaded their cargo, new residential areas, media cities and leisure facilities are being created. Culture plays an important role in this conjunction; museums have come to attract great public attention and serve as generators of urban development. They play the same role as major housing developments did in the 1920s, and skyscrapers in the 1960s, i.e. the leading type of architecture. In the late and postmodern period, the Centre Pompidou in Paris and the Staatsgalerie in Stuttgart became the key works in the museum boom in Europe. In the meantime, the United States is catching up. According to a report in Newsweek, there were plans for the construction or renovation of no less that 25 museums in the United States in the spring of 2001. Almost all of these projects have been designed by architects who are known and who work all over the world: Daniel Libeskind in Denver, Tadao Ando in Fort Worth, Zaha Hadid in Cincinnati, Renzo Piano in Chicago, Santiago Calatrava in Milwaukee, Norman Foster in Boston, Herzog & de Meuron in San Francisco and Minneapolis.

Just like the spectacular skyscrapers that are intended to help the skyline of London find a new profile, after its having declined over decades to visual banality, museum managers in recent years have turned to architecture as an image-maker, and this with no small measure of success. The Guggenheim Foundation established new criteria; Frank O. Gehry's museum in Bilbao put this northern Spanish city on art-lovers' maps for the first time. And now the attempt is being made in New York to take this success a step further with a building by the same architect. At the same time, the important contemporary architectural theoretician, Rem Koolhaas, is erecting an exhibition hall for the Guggenheim on the terrain of "The Venetian Hotel" in Las Vegas, in conjunction with his Rotterdam "Office for Metropolitan Architecture."

That museum operators are not simply concerned with creating an attractive setting for their works, but rather are also aware of the importance of architecture, seems at first positive. However, the development toward architectural offices that operate worldwide and which market all of their products under one label, raises the concern that many potential builders may be more interested in "big names" than in a real dialogue with architecture. Internationally famous architectural offices guarantee quality, or at least public attention. The famous architectural offices have, of course, better chances of realizing new ideas, because of the public interest, than newcomers who are known only in local circles. Jacques Herzog from the Bassle office of Herzog & de Meuron is right when he claims that in the future only star architects with have the opportunity of realizing their designs in a relatively intact condition. Caught in between general and overall contractors, confronted with clients who are not willing to take any responsibility, often change on a yearly basis, and are even sometimes simply replaced, there is little room for real architecture to unfold. All over the world trained architects play an ever more minimal role in the production of buildings. Even in the rich industrial nations, special building tasks, like hospitals, are now usually delegated to specifically trained planning specialists who know their way around the jungle of norms and codes without really comprehending that architecture can mean more than simply fulfilling certain demands. And in the construction of single-family housing in Europe and America the market is dominated by pre-planned catalogue models that become the norm on the characterless periphery, which is neither urban, nor rural.

The blame for qualitatively substandard and aesthetically unsatisfactory building practices is therefore not always to be placed on others, not always the fault of "the bigwigs," it is also possible to create examples of culturally significant building in a private context. Architecture, that is worthy of the name, does not have to be more expensive than a project planned and realized with little thought. It does, however, demand that the future users are prepared to give account of themselves with regard to their own needs, desires and expectations, and it demands the willingness to enter into a dialogue. Unfortunately, however, there are very few clients who are willing to enter into that sort of a dialogue with the architect. Hence, although it appears that contemporary architecture has become more attractive, this turns out to be a myth that misrepresents the real state of affairs. However, culturally important architecture has always accounted for but a fraction of all building. An architectural historian, who studies the temples and pyramids of the Egyptian pharaohs, discovers very little about every day life in that age. That reveals itself only to the archaeologist who identifies the remnants of simple wooden housing posts in discolored soil and analyses burial grounds or the contents of latrines. Most of the buildings, that have come down to us over time, were used for religious purposes or to demonstrate power. They were valued by later generations, or sometimes they were only used by them because of the indestructible nature of their construction, and now they determine our view of architectural history: temples and theaters from antiquity, churches, monasteries and palatinates from the Middle Ages, villas from the Renaissance, castles from the Baroque period, museums and parliamentary buildings from the 19th century.

What seemed decisive in the conception of this book was the consideration that architecture, because of its three-dimensional quality, demands – more imperatively than painting – that we enter into a direct aesthetic confrontation with it. Therefore, only buildings that are still in a condition that allows visitors to perceive how they originally looked were included in the catalogue of 180 buildings. Structures that can only be reconstructed by ethnographers or archaeologists were not considered here. That meant that pre-historic cultures as well as buildings from Polynesia had to be excluded. The fact that the present-day condition of some buildings is the result of a reconstruction process undertaken later, and in which the period in which it took place is reflected (for example Knossos) or the fact that some can no longer be seen at their original location (like the Ishtar Gate of Babylon or the Pergamon altar, which were dragged off to Berlin by their discoverers in the 19th century) was accepted in individual cases, because of the importance of the structure. There was also no consideration given to the urban context, although it often has a determining influence on the architecture.

The buildings that were chosen are not presented in radically chronology order, which would have meant that the Taj Mahal would have been placed somewhere between Inigo Jones's London Banqueting Hall and S. Andrea al Quirinale. It seemed to make much more sense to organize the buildings roughly in terms of their cultural context, whereby, with regard to the Western tradition in architecture, the stylistic categories of art history were also applied, with date of construction as a subordinate criterion within the chapters. For the 19th and 20th centuries the decision was made to refrain from using stylistic categories – since the Age of Enlightenment architectural history has stood more or less at the disposal of every architect and could be employed at will, depending on the task at hand. Hence, for some building projects Karl Friedrich Schinkel submitted designs in more Classical and in more Gothic styles, and the Karlsruhe Architect, Heinrich Hübsch, introduced eclecticism by posing the question: "In which style should we build?" Before the dawn of the 20th century a countermovement was established, under the influence of English reformers, that put an end to the confusion of styles with the call for "functionalism." The "Modern Movement" in the 1920s, known since the famous exhibition in 1932 in the Museum of Modern Art as "International Style," furthered this tendency to simplify forms and developed its own aesthetic canon, which still has a great influence on architecture today. However the pendulum still swings back and forth between a strict, rationalist concept of design and a free and expressive stylistic vocabulary. At present so much is going on simultaneously: Deconstructivism alongside "new simplicity," High-Tech architecture alongside Neo-Traditionalism, the call for more craftsmanship alongside computer-aided design. Within less than a decade the computer has changed the work of designing in architectural offices completely; there are indications that in the future this will lead to an architecture that will differ fundamentally from what has been know up until now. As yet the potential inherent in the more complex programmes, and the possibilities of realizing them, have only begun to be perceived.

The most important criterion for the order of the buildings within the chapters was generally the date the building was completed, and sometimes the period of a building's most notable building phase. However, a publication that intends to provide a survey of world architectural history cannot dispute the fact that there are very few buildings that are "uniform in style," and hardly any feature their stylistic characteristics in programmatic purity. Gothic cathedrals, for example, were built by generations over centuries and many of the big churches, among them the cathedral in Cologne, were only completed in the wake of a romantic nineteenth century nostalgia for the Middle Ages. The ideal Gothic cathedral, the perfect Baroque palace, the Greek temple par excellence can only be found as drawings in textbooks of architectural history. They do not really exist, reality is far more complex.

Hence, it had to be decided where in the order to put buildings that were built over a long period of time. The criterion was generally the building phase that contributed most to a particular building's importance in terms of architectural history. The Reichstag in Berlin was not dealt with as the work of Paul Wallot within the context of the architectural history of the 19th century, but rather introduced with the renovation and the dome by Norman Foster as an example of a new form of representational architecture in the old and new German capital after the fall of the Berlin Wall in 1989. While the Reichstag represents a mile stone in German architectural history, the current international perception of the building is colored by the prominent dome, that one can walk up into, but which the architect originally never intended to build. The concept with which he won the competition foresaw spanning an enormous roof over the entire historical building, but it is not considered here. The only buildings presented here are ones that were actually completed, no models, drawings or alternatives. The illustrations were supposed to be given a lot of space, and to concentrate on the most pregnant views of the buildings.

Temporary buildings, such as those found at fairs and exhibitions, also had to be excluded, even though sometimes in such contexts more daring architectural projects are realized than in permanent architecture. The Netherlands Pavilion, erected by the Dutch avant-garde architects MVRDV under the title "Holland makes space" was justly considered the real landmark of the Expo 2000 in Hanover and, in addition, it was a building that was just as programmatic as it was ironic, marking an fundamental position in current architectural discourse. However, the structure was torn down after the exhibition and no longer exists.

A look at the table of contents reveals a deliberate disproportionality that was consciously accepted in the conception of the book. The architectural eras, and the cultures that are dealt with, are not equally represented. The emphasis lies clearly on the 20th century, and determined by a European and North American perspective. This should imply no claim to the superiority of Western culture; on the contrary, the intention is simply to make readers familiar with masterpieces of architecture from the perspective of their cultural horizon. If this book has a goal, then it is to make people more aware of the built up world around them.

Since in contrast to the fine arts or music, architecture is unavoidable and inevitable. No one is forced to view paintings or to go to a concert; but one is permanently confronted with architecture. We spend almost all of our time in surroundings that have little to do with their natural state. They are the result of conscious planning processes. Our environment is made up, for the most part, of built up surroundings in which examples of important architecture are like pearls in a sea of banality. Therefore, a panorama of almost 5000 years of architectural history can have only one objective: to provide the reader with criteria that will help to view the surroundings in daily life with a sharper eye.

The buildings presented in the following form a kaleidoscope. There is not necessarily any connection between the individual buildings, even when they appear consecutively within the book. Yet it is still hoped that the whole thing will mean more than just the sum of its parts.

Hubertus Adam

Egypt, the Near East and Ancient Architecture

Egypt, the Near East and Ancient Architecture

What is now perceived as ancient Egyptian architecture is but a small part of what once existed. Similar to other early high cultures, only a small portion of the residences and palaces of ancient Egypt have survived the ages. The Nile, the universal artery of life supplied the sun-dried mud brick of the buildings and woven plant materials and reeds. What remains are the tombs and temple complexes built of stone. Our impression of ancient Egypt is therefore deceptive and fraught with clichés. Monumental stone architecture existed in the Old Kingdom (ca. 2635–2155 BC) as early as 2600 years BC, beginning with the King Djoser's tomb in Saqqarah. Stone, as a building material marked the beginning of a technological revolution. The pyramids, originally reserved for the Pharaohs alone became the ideal form of Egyptian funerary architecture. Their formal development was rapid, evolving from the step pyramid through to the classic ideal, seen in the Cheops pyramid. The tradition of building royal pyramid tombs in the Old Kingdom came to an end with the decline of Memphis. The funerary architecture of the Middle Kingdom (ca. 2150–1550 BC), of which Thebes was the centre, followed new paths. This was seen in the terraced temple of Queen Hatshepsut. In place of the walled graves, there were increasingly more tomb shafts. In the New Kingdom (ca.1550–1070 BC), these axially arranged cult sites with towering columns and pylons became dominant. Procession Temples represent the epitome of Egyptian temple architecture. Enormous walled temple complexes, like those in Karnak and Luxor, determined the architectural appearance of this period. Always constructed in the same manner, their entrance was flanked by pylons with monumental statues and obelisks in front of them. One entered a courtyard surrounded by columns and walked through a vestibule to another large columned hall. At the end of the halls and chambers was the shrine. This pattern enabled the creation of enormous temple complexes by simple addition. The Temple of Abu Simbel followed the same laws of construction. Egyptian architecture originated in the profane structure built for the population at large and was contrived neither mathematically nor technically. That was why the forms of Egyptian columns are usually inspired by the lotus, papyrus or palms, paying more attention to the context of the cult than to questions of load and support. The temple of Edfu marks the end of a tradition that went all the way back to Imhotep, the architect of the Djoser's step pyramid. In close contact with Egypt, Minoan culture blossomed in the

Aegean region (3000–1200 BC). The most important centre was Crete. The Palace of Knossos was built without fortifications. On the Greek mainland, Mycenaean culture developed a number of centuries later (1500–1000 BC), with the castles in Mycenae and Tiryns as the most important buildings. In 1200 BC, the Doric people moved south destroying the monuments of Mycenaean and Minoan culture and adopting only the megaron, which formed the centre of Mycenaean palaces. It slowly evolved into the form on which the temples of Greek and Roman antiquity were based. After 800 BC, a pan-Greek identity began to emerge and was reflected in more uniform architecture. During this development, masonry, forgotten since the Mycaean period, experienced a renaissance. The techniques had to be learned again. They had been guarded secrets in the previous high cultures. In the Greek antique period this knowledge was formulated in a system of mathematical laws. From then on knowledge of construction was freely available and this facilitated the spread of a uniform temple style throughout the entire Mediterranean region. The basic scheme of temple construction was the same everywhere although the second temple front was discovered in Corinth and the Ionic order of columns was looked upon as characteristic of the city states in Asia Minor. The Parthenon on the Athens Acropolis is still the most prominent example of a Greek peristyle temple and is generally seen as the prototype of its age. Greek antiquity also offers other examples like the Doric temple in Paestum or the diminutive Athena Nike Temple built in Ionic style and set in front of the Propylaeum of the Athens Acropolis. With the death of Alexander the Great, the Classical Age of Greece drew to a close. In the opulence of Hellenism that followed, the clarity of Classical forms gradually disappeared and architecture conveying more drama began to spread, particularly with the increasing number of profane buildings. The beginning of Roman architecture can be traced to the buildings of the Etruscans, who presumably came to Northern Italy from Asia Minor and were the first to unite Rome as a polity. After the victory over the Etruscans, Rome extended its sovereignty over Southern Italy, Greece and Asia Minor from 200 BC onward, taking over everything that Greek culture had to offer, until it was ultimately subsumed by Roman culture in the Augustan period (31 BC–14 AD).

Saqqarah (Egypt)
Stepped Pyramid of King Djoser
around 2650 BC, Imhotep

left:
The oldest surviving monumental building in the world constitutes, with its six-stepped design, a link between the traditional block tombs of the Ancient Egyptians and the true pyramid. Erected by Imhotep as the centre of a large funerary area (544 x 277 metres – 1,785 x 909 ft.), this construction is set upon an over-sized square-plan mastaba, whose individual ashlars were inclined gently inwards for structural reasons.

Imhotep was a scholar, astronomer, doctor and at the same time a brilliant master builder of antiquity. He is generally considered to be the true inventor of stone architecture. His reputation has not simply outlasted the centuries; in 700 BC he was even raised to a god of scholars and writers because of his wisdom that was widely praised. Mastaba is the Arab word for the obligatory flat stone bank in front of the Egyptian house. Similarly the graves of the first Egyptian kings were rectangular mud bricks buildings, with a flat roof and several aboveground and underground rooms. However, on Djoser's burial chamber Imhotep placed five other, increasingly smaller rectangular blocks in two stages. Finally through that, a symbolized "sky stairway" was created upon which the dead king should ascend to the other side. The stepped pyramid, over 60 metres high (66 yds.) measuring 119 by 141 metres (131 by 155 yds.) at its base, is the principal item of a complicated stone grave arrangement similar to the secular building works of the king's residence in Memphis. In contrast to this, however, it consists only of false buildings. It was originally designed and begun as a disproportionately large square Mastaba. Only later, after lengthy testing of the construction possibilities, did Imhotep arrive at the rectangular form of the pyramid foundation constructed from stone blocks. He shifted the stone blocks of the six-stepped pyramid with low inclination to the central axis. Because it was constructed without any bonding agent, this contributed to the greater rigidity of the building. Every step retreats about two metres behind the previous one. The step heights vary between 8,40 metres (9.24 yds.) and 10,50 metres (11.55 yds.).

The stepped pyramid of Djoser is the first monumental structure in the world that was constructed from hewn stone. It is not actually a pyramid in the classic sense, but an increasingly enlarged mastaba on a rectangular layout. The tomb is fascinating due to its simplicity and pellucidity of construction by the severe, but simultaneously simple silhouette of the step edges, and by the dynamism of the ascending edifice. However, the elevated static character of the structure is still maintained.

Gizah (Egypt): Pyramids of Cheops Chephren and Mykerinos
around 2500 BC, Hemon

Opposite Cairo, the city of millions, on the west bank of the Nile, the most famous pyramids of the world rise close to Gizah. The triumvirate of the pyramids of Cheops, Chephren and Mykerinos with their temple structures and adjoining pyramids appeared within only a few decades, from 2500 to 2465 BC. The three pyramids distinguish themselves by a regular geometrical form and, unlike the stepped pyramid of Djoser in Saqqarah, they have a square layout. Cheops was the first pyramid to be built. With an original height of 146,5 metres (161 yds.) and an edge length of 230 metres (253 yds.), it is the biggest of the Egyptian pyramids and

still the most gigantic stone construction in the world. It determines the harmony of the whole ensemble of the pyramids of Gizah, the temple constructions and the impressive sphinx of Chephren (with a 73,5 metres / 80.1 yds. length which is the most monumental statue of ancient Egypt). It is the oldest and, furthermore, only surviving building of the Seven Wonders of the Ancient World. The proportions of the Cheops pyramid are based on the golden section. But also the location of the building and its position relative to the stars are thought through to the smallest detail. However, whether the pyramid was ever used as a burial place is open to doubt

Of the three pyramids built on the edge of the Libyan Desert during the Third Dynasty, the Pyramids of Cheops
(146.6 metres, or 481 ft.) and of Chepren (143.5 metres or 471 ft.) stand out particularly as the largest tombs of
Antiquity. Against them, the Pyramid of Mykerinos (66.5 metres or 218 ft.) is quite modest in size. The sphinx set
at the base of the Chepren Pyramid as the guardian of the funerary area is the largest sculpture of Ancient Egypt.

since even the identity of its royal owner remains
shrouded in mystery today. Additionally, the construction
process has escaped intellectual analysis, although the
pyramid has been extensively investigated. Most of all,
the logistics remain a mystery: Approximately 2,300,000
limestone blocks with an average weight of 2,5 tons
were used.

It is not known to this day which principles of
technology were utilized to move the hundreds of
thousands of limestone blocks and granite ashlar
weighing up to 40 metric tons. For the lower half of
the building various ramps were undoubtedly used.
Archaeologically there is only proof that an inside
ramp was built that cut deeply into the construction. However, the solution to the problem for the
transportation to the higher sections of the pyramid
is still completely unknown.

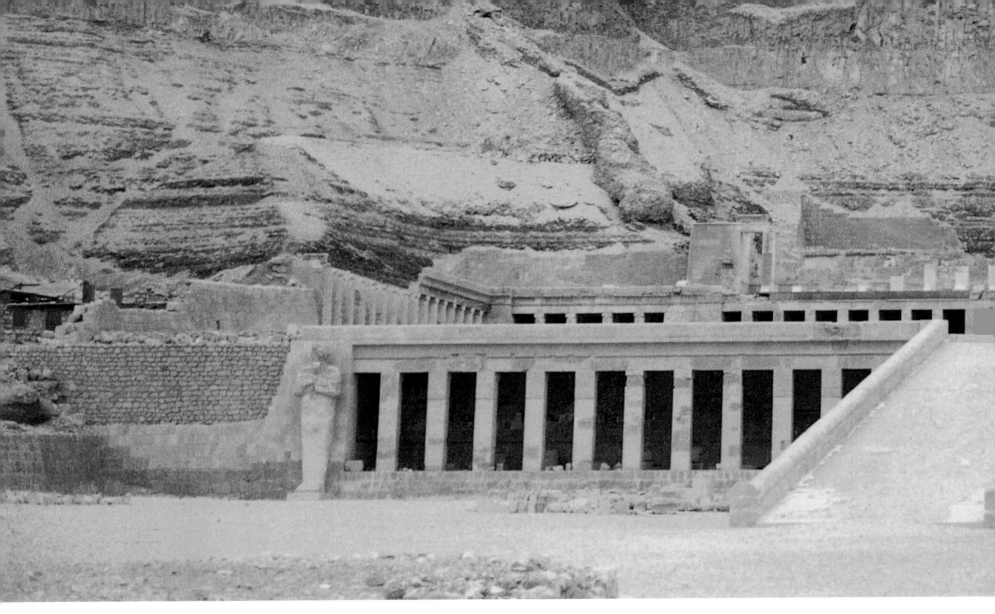

Deir el-Bahari (Egypt):
Terraced Temple of Queen Hatshepsut
around 1500 BC, Senmut

The monumental funerary temple of the Pharaoh Hatshepsut lies opposite the old capital of Thebes, on the western bank of the Nile. The terraced temple ascends in double steps and lies in harmony with the more than 500 years older temple of Mentuhotep II, from the 11th dynasty, situated directly beside it. Senmut, the master builder and favourite of the queen, created one of the most willful cult constructions of Egypt. Carved out of the soaring mountains, it extends gradually over more than three terraces connected by gently rising ramps. Harmoniously adapted to the ground inclination, it forms an extremely successful symbiosis of landscape and building. The aesthetic impression resulting from it represents something completely new in Egyptian style. The constructions align to the temple axis of the Amun sanctuary in Karnak, presumably to illustrate its close attachment to queen and god. Sphinx avenues, water basins, and pylons hemmed this long route as well as sacred persea tree rows. Column halls existed around both lower terraces. An enormous hall of pillars stood behind a forest of Osiris pillars occupying the high terrace. These were decorated with reliefs dedicated to the imperial history and life of the queen. No less lavish were the rest of the sculpture arrangements of the

above:
After Mentuhotep II had his tomb and a monumental mortuary temple erected in a basin-shaped valley near Thebes around 202 BC, Hatshepsut followed suit more than 500 years later. With its three-step construction, this terraced temple, dedicated to the gods Amon, Hathor, and Anubis, fits harmoniously into the surrounding countryside.

building. For example, intricate crowned the pillars of the Hathor chapel situated at the south wing of the temple. By comparison, the triple sanctuary that was hewn into the cliff was more mediocre. The division of this burial chamber of the funerary temple is one of the fundamental innovations in the architecture of the New Kingdom.

The building of monumental temples in Thebes was accompanied by an intense development in the field of sculpture. However, since they were intended to be viewed from a distance, the statues were mostly carved in simple forms. Only from the reign of Queen Hatshepsut did new innovations appear. The artists aimed at portrait representations, although they used canonized sculpture types. The degree of individualization depended on where they were to be installed.

Luxor (Egypt): Amun/Mut/Chons Temple of Amenhotep III

1402 – 1364 BC, Amenhotep, son of Hapu

left:
This temple, erected around 1400 BC under Amenophis II, is above all dominated by the monumental colonnades that form the 16 metre (52 ft.) tall columned walk, and the harmonious proportions of the colonnaded court. All that was completed of the latter was the 52 metre (171 ft.) long central aisle with its seven twin columns.

The Karnak temple in the north and the Luxor temple to the south, were the cornerstones of ancient Thebes. Processional streets lined with sphinxes connected them and this simultaneously formed the axis of the city. Amenhotep III had the temple of Luxor established in the style of the Chons temple in Karnak. Amenhotep, son of Hapu, is considered to be the master builder, and a namesake of the Pharaoh. The temple of Luxor is situated close to the bank of the Nile in a long north-south expansion. Like the Amun temple in Karnak, this temple building is also an example of the expansion of the whole structure in chronologically reverse order. The colonnade, second court, column hall and inner temple containing the Barken sanctuary and holy of holies, are buildings dating from the time of Amenophis III. Under Ramses II the pylons and first court were added. Consequently, the temple axis was severed and the new temple facade established along the processional route to Karnak. Colonnades characterize the architectural appearance of the temple. For example, a colonnade of 74 papyrus pillars surrounds the pillar court of Ramses II. The central colonnade remained unfinished and only the 52 metres (57 yds.) long centre aisle with seven pairs of almost 16 metres (18 yds.) high pillars was completed. Behind it lies one of the most beautiful rooms of ancient Egyptian architecture. The court of Amenophis III. The architraves of its papyrus-bundle pillars need only carry the sky as a roof. Six colossal figures of Ramses II once stood before the enormous pylon. Of the two obelisks made of red granite, the west obelisk was donated by Mohamed Alis to Paris and in 1836 they were erected at the Place de la Concorde after an adventurous ship passage.

The Luxor temple was established as a "harem" for Amun who once a year celebrated the holy wedding here, during the Opet festival. At this place the earth mother Amenophis III. was impregnated by the god-king Amun-Re. There the king and god-king enter into a direct affair. In mythological respect it is thus the birthplace of the temple of Thebes and simultaneously the prototype for the processional temple.

Karnak (Egypt): Amun Temple
1304 – 1224 BC

left:
This is the largest sacred site in the world, at the point where the Egyptians localized the origin of the Earth. The first pylons were also constructed here, with massive masonry narrowing upwards. Large supports arose here, with a diameter of up to 4 metres (13 ft.) through the colossal bell capitals.

Karnak is not a temple in the original or schematized sense. Neither is it a planned and subsequently implemented structure, but rather a gigantic temple conglomerate in which all kings from the Middle Kingdom up to the Romans extended, altered or built over. The monstrous temple city thus lacks a certain logic and symmetry. Only the basic plan of the Amun temple is clear and orderly despite its 2000 years of construction history. The centreline extends from the holy of holies in the right corner of the east, to the Nile in the west. The temple gates and pylon are chronologically aligned to this coordinate from the inside to the exterior. These play an especially crucial role in determining the date of these significant buildings. To a certain extent they are characteristic milestones of separate construction epochs, because they were built by different pharaohs. What presents itself today as a complex temple work, is none other than the stereotyped succession of portals leading to the core area, the holy of holies. With the extension of the structure, the courts were transformed into pillar halls between the pylons of the east-west axis. Together with this is the large hypostyle of Karnak, which represents the biggest room of Egyptian architecture with its 134 pillars and a base of 5,500 square metres (6,575 sq. yds.).

Despite this, the many plant pillars lend it a floral lightness and make it appear more elegant in spite of these enormous dimensions.

The construction history of the Amun temple was concluded during Ptolemaic times with the establishment of the first pylon – 2000 years after the first building period under Thutmosis I. It was planned to be the biggest temple gate of Egypt with a width of 100 metres (110 yds.), but was never completed. The Amun Re temple forms a cult unity, with the northerly complex of the Mont temple, the Mut temple in the southeast, and the 2,5 kilometres (1.6 miles) distant Luxor temple, to which it has been connected since the time of Amenhotep III by an avenue of sphinxes.

Abu Simbel (Egypt): Rock Temple of Ramses II.
around 1250 BC

left:
The seated statue of Ramses II in front of the temple in Abu-Simbel is testament to the immense economic upturn Egypt experienced under his rule. The temple itself was constructed using the tunnelling method and reaches 60 metres (197 ft.) deep into the rock.

With the establishment of temples, the master builders always had to solve a whole variety of difficult tasks: from the arrangement of the interior to the problems of lighting and colouring. This task was still more difficult, when one turned to the establishment of rock temples whose façades were made from the sculptural restructuring of the cliff face, while the adjoining rooms were driven into the cliff. Accordingly, this special form of temple architecture is applicable to the building of the Ramses temple by Abu Simbel. Entirely driven into the standing cliff, it simultaneously represents a novum and climax of Ramses' building in Nubia. No other building of ancient Egypt has such perfect form, embodying a synthesis between architecture and sculpture. In spite of all its uniqueness and peculiarities, this building also shows all "normal" elements of Egyptian temples. The façade of the big temple has the stylized form of a pylon tower with sloped walls, round bar and fillet. As usual, four 22 metres (24 yds.) high giant statues of Ramses II, carved from the rock, guard the gate. The subsequent pillar court functions as a 17 metres (56 ft.) deep hall, which is flanked, by Osiris pillars. Leading off this is a four-colonnaded pillar hall followed by the sanctuary. In Abu Simbel two buildings form a uniform ensemble: the big temple consecrated to the pharaoh and three gods – Amun, Re-Harakhte and Ptah, and the small temple dedicated to the goddess Hathor, who appears in the form of Ramses' wife Nefertari. Nowhere before in Egypt had a woman appeared on a temple façade and in no other Ramses temple was the queen entitled to such a rank.

The temples of Abu Simbel originally lay in the cliff face of the Nile valley. Today they stand 64 metres higher and 180 metres inland – above the "Nubian sea", which is the name of the dam stretching from Aswan 500 kilometres (312 miles) to the south. The shifting of the temples, which began in 1965 and lasted three years, was one of the most spectacular projects of the 20th century.

Edfu (Egypt): Temple of Horus
around 237 – 70 BC

left:
The temple constructed for the god Horus in Ptolemaic times is considered the best-kept building from Antiquity. The extensive court is bordered by 32 columns with composite and palm capitals, with wall plates depicting reliefs between them. A sculpture of Horus guards the entrance to the vestibule.

After the conquest of Egypt by Alexander the Great in the year 332 BC, a close contact was set in motion between Egyptian and Greek art, and the Ptolemaic dynasty developed an active building project. With the designing of the temple layouts, Egyptian traditions predominated. The new sanctuaries were consecrated to old Egyptian gods: Isis on the island of Philae, Hathor in Dendera, Sobek in Kom Ombo, and Horus in Edfu. The Horus temple was begun under the regency of Ptolemy III. At that time, the construction period probably took more than 150 years. Although only the excavation works of the 19th and 20th centuries again exposed the building to daylight, it is in a strikingly good condition and almost entirely preserved. Agitated early Christians systematically smashed only the faces, hands and feet of all persons represented. The pylon, Egypt's second largest, is 64 metres (211 ft.) wide and 36 metres (119 ft.) high and generally decorated with monumental reliefs. They depict Ptolemaic kings sacrificing before their gods, and in battle. In the white court in whose centre an altar originally stood are 32 composite and palm columns. They draw the eye to the portico where a horus-falcon is enthroned as a guard as seen in front of the entrance pylon. Six pillars connected by barriers flank the entrance to the pronaos which is supported by lotus columns and papyrus pillars. To cross this threshold, even the king as a high priest, had to undergo special rites. In the following pillar hall, all available surfaces are decorated with relief pictures. Through the sacrificial table hall and the hall of the "god of rejuvenation" one reaches the sanctuary where the scenario of the pictures follows the usual patterns.

The history and form of the temple are integrated into a tradition extending back for millennia: The Temple of Horus breaks the basic rules by being lying parallel to the Nile. Ancient Egyptian temples are supposed to be located at right angles to the Nile. In the pellucidity of its layout it serves as the classic example of a late Ptolemaic Roman pylon temple.

Babylon (now Iraq): Ishtar Gate
605 - 562 BC, Nebuchadrezzar II

"Marduk, wisest of Gods, proud prince! ... I vow to make no other city more magnificent than your own, Babylon." Herodot attests to the fact that King Nebuchadrezzar II kept this promise, seen in the form of an inscription on a building, in his enthusiastic descriptions of the city of Babylon, dating from 460 BC. The legends concerning the tower of Babel, which was a part of the temple dedicated to Marduk, also seem to support this view. With the destruction of the city of Nineveh, the centre of power in Mesopotamia had shifted to Babylonia, and Nebuchadrezzar II (604 – 562 BC) was one of its most important kings. He had a new city built on the banks of the Euphrates. Its streets were laid out geometrically and connected the most important religious sites with the palaces. The Ishtar Gate, actually a double gate, spanned the 20 metres (ca. 66 ft.) wide and 250 metres (820 ft.) long Processional Way that led from the Marduk Temple to the king's palace. What was unusual about this structure were its tremendous size and the fact that it was built of brick, which had to compensate for the lack of stone in the alluvial basin of the Euphrates. The outer gate was smaller than the inner one. The north, or inside façade was decorated with colourful glazed brick reliefs that display a loping steer and

the dragon Tiamat (a demonic creature that was a cross between a snake, an eagle, and a scorpion, with the paws of a lion) on a background of light and dark blue. These first motifs on brick were said to have been borrowed from tapestries. They were applied to the bricks before they were cut into pieces, fired and finally reassembled in situ.

In 539 BC, Cyrus conquered Babylon and, later, the remains of the city, that was about 100 kilometres south of present-day Baghdad, was used as a quarry. Today, some parts of the gate have been reconstructed and can be seen at the Vorderasiatisches Museum in Berlin.

left:
The Ishtar Gate is one of the most important remaining pieces of evidence of Late Babylonian art. It is currently in Berlin. A gold-coloured relief of striding bulls and snake dragons against a dark blue background are shown by the glazed tiles covering its walls. Ornamental forms arranged in a frieze-like manner frame the figurative depictions.

Knossos (Greece): Palace of King Minos

2000 – 1400 BC, Minos

left:
The seat of King Minos and the setting of the saga of Theseus and Ariadne was already the site of a first palace complex in 2000 BC. After their destruction during an earthquake in 1700 BC, the buildings were quickly re-erected. Arthur Evans began excavating the remains of Knossos, the most important of the Minoan palaces, in 1900. On the basis of his researches, he was able to reconstruct a complex grouped around a rectangular central court, which was laid out in a highly confusing and cluttered manner.

The palace of Knossos is the most famous monument of Cretan architecture. It extends along the flat Kefála hill and measures approximately 150 metres (165 yds.) from west to east and 200 metres (220 yds.) from south to north. Its construction history begins at the end of the 3rd millennium BC. Already in its later dimensions of 50 by 25 metres (165 by 82.5 ft.) the central inner court, which extends approximately in a north/south direction, was built first. The first palace appeared around 2000 BC. After an earthquake the second palace was established around 1800 BC on the ruins of the first one. Already existing dimensions were partly adopted, but on a larger and more complicated scale. The houses now had two storeys. After repeated destruction and reconstruction, two centuries of the highest development in architecture and interior decoration followed, starting around 1750 BC. Probably as a result of the invasion by the Mycenaean Greeks or another earthquake – the volcanic eruption of Santorini around 1500 BC had already destroyed much of it – the palace fell victim to a large fire around 1400 BC. Knossos is the most extensive and important of the palaces during the bloom period of Cretan culture. As opposed to ancient Egyptian monumental artworks with their severe symmetry, the layout of the Knossos palace adopts different principles of form. They manifest themselves in a loose order of single rooms and room-systems around a central court. As the core of the structure, it is important for the axial relations of the rooms, halls and corridors that open freely onto one another and in several directions. One section is built on the same level as the court; other sections are lower or two to three floors higher. This interrelation between interior and exterior, from limited space to extended landscape is the true principle of form behind Minoan architecture.

Excavations have taken place in Knossos since 1900 under the English archeologist, Arthur Evans. His restoration and reconstruction works, although not undisputed, have nevertheless been to his credit that the enormous palace complex is today again to be experienced as an architectural creation.

Mycenae (Greece): Treasury of Atreus
1400 – 1300 BC

left:
Outside of the Bronze Age castle of Mykene, which was excavated by Schliemann, a number of elaborate tholos tombs had previously been constructed during the 16th century BC. The largest of these is called the Treasury of the Atreus. Prior to the building of the Pantheon in Rome, this was the largest room of Antiquity to be spanned by a single vault.

The grave of Atreus – the designation "treasury" clearly indicates how richly the grave accoutrements must have been – belonged to the last group of altogether nine dome graves to the west and southwest of the Acropolis of Mycenae. In accordance with their special characteristics they are chronologically divided into three groups. To the last group, built between 1400 and 1300 BC from carefully treated, rectangular stones, belong the graves of the geniuses, the treasury of the Atreus, and the grave of Clytemnestra. They belong to the most perfect architectural examples of this epoch. An enormous Dromos leads into the grave of Atreus measuring 36 metres (40 yds.) in length and a width of 6 metres (20 ft.). On both sides, the grave has a façade as high as 11 metres (33 ft.), hemmed by obliquely rising walls. The magnificent entrance façade was originally adorned with geometrically ordered white, red and green stones. The gate was 5.40 metres (17.8 ft.) high and 2.70 metres (8.9 ft.) wide, and tapered as it projected upwards by about 30 cm (12 in.). This was finished by a wooden doo in two parts ornately decorated with bronze. On the right and left were relief-decorated pilasters of green marble. The door facade and the area above the lintel – formed from two enormous monoliths, of which the inner one continues its form along the dome curvature – was once richly decorated. The dome that has the form of a beehive has a diameter of 14.50 metres (16 yds.), a height of 13.20 metres (14.5 yds.) and is comprised of 33 parallel-running ashlar stones of conglomerate rock. In the west side of the vault an open entrance leads into a square room hewn into the cliff containing the burial chamber.

For centuries right up to the establishment of the Pantheon in Rome, the treasury of Atreus was the biggest unsupported interior of antiquity. To this day it is an impressive example of monumental architecture of the time. The grave was already robbed in antiquity, although Dromos was buried underground after his funeral.

Paestum (Italy): The Temples of Paestum
5th - 4th century BC

left:
Three Doric temples have been preserved from the heyday of the Greek colony. The first to be built was the "Basilica" (540 BC), shown here in the bakkground. According to the evidence of excavated votive offerings, this temple was dedicated to Hera, as was the falsely termed "Poseidon Temple" which can be seen in the foreground. Built around 450 BC, this temple gives a very clear impression of the severity and harmony of Doric sacred buildings.

Between the 8th and the 6th centuries BC the Greeks founded many colonies and trading settlements in the Mediterranean area. Often, cities took the initiative in the establishment of these settlements. This was true of the Archaic colony of Paestum, called Poseidonia in Greek, which was established by citizens from Sybaris on the Gulf of Tarent, south of Naples, in the 7th century. Three well-preserved Doric Temples still to be found there form a unique ensemble. The "Basilica" (ca. 540 BC) is an Archaic peripteral temple with 9 rows of 18 columns and the Temple of Neptune (around 450 BC) is a classical peripteral temple with 6 rows of 13 columns. Sacred offerings found in the temple have led to the assumption that they were both dedicated to Hera (hence they are referred to as Heraion I and II). The third, the Athena Temple (also called the Ceres Temple), dates back to roughly 500 BC. It lies somewhat to the north and is particularly interesting because there seems to have been some intention of creating an interior room at the core of the temple. The Doric building style is complimented by the Ionic decorative elements used inside. In addition, this is the first time that columns arranged in 6 rows of 13 are found. It would later become the rule in Greece. In all three of these buildings Greek architecture and Etruscan influences are blended harmonically. In Paestum, better than anywhere else, one sees the original austerity of Doric architecture and the stages in which it was relaxed by the admixture of Ionic elements.

The German writer Johann Wolfgang von Goethe saw the Temple of Paestum twice during his trip to Italy in 1787. On his way to Sicily he was surprised by it and found the "mass of blunt, funnel shaped and densely arranged columns bothersome, even horrible." Two months later, however, he describes Paestum as "the greatest idea that I will take northwards with me in its entirety."

Athens (Greece): The Parthenon
447 - 432 BC, Ictinos, Callicrates

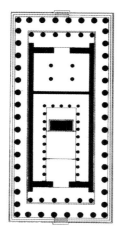

left:
This place of worship to the virgin Athene was built 447–432 BC as a Doric peripteral temple: the cella is surrounded by 58 columns. The sculpted ornaments, which now are scattered throughout world, depicted on the entablature mythological and historic scenes of battle. Outside of the cella was a 160 (525 ft.) long frieze in relief, which depicted the Procession of the Panathenaea (British Museum, London).

Thucydides, a major opponent of Pericles's (495 – 429 B.C), the most powerful statesman in Athens, charged the latter with decorating the city of Athens "like a whore wearing precious stones, statues and temples costing thousands of talents." Ultimately, Thucydides was banned for his critical attitude and Pericles unrelentingly pursued his costly plans for a holy mount overlooking Athens. The building projects that he initiated led to the creation of some of Greece's greatest architectural treasures. History may have proved Thucydides right, to the extent that the monies Pericles spent on Athens were sorely missed by the Delian League, contributing to the decline of their military prowess. The history of architecture, however, celebrates other heroes. In 447 BC, Phidias began overseeing the execution of building plans drawn up by Ictinos and Callicrates. The latter was also to go on to design the Nike Temple on the Acropolis. By the year 431 BC they had built a temple for Athena Parthenos that is quite singular in its clarity and monumentality. A Doric frieze measuring 160 metres (525 ft.), designs on the gables and 92 painted metope fields served to decorate this building already stunning in its perfectly harmonious proportions. They also serve to underline the importance and the ambitious intentions of this, the largest, temple on the Greek mainland.

The statue of Pallas Athena, created by Phidias, was made of gold and ivory and found its way into art history as Athena Parthenos. Athena is Zeus's daughter and the goddess of victory, as well as the patroness of the City of Athens. The sculpture, which was 11 metres (36 ft.) tall, was displayed in the Parthenon, more precisely within its cella. Many architectural historians see this place as an important precursor of the modern concept of interior space.

Athens (Greece): The Temple of Athena Nike
425 - 421 BC, Callicrates

left:
The Ionian Temple of Athena Nike, built around 448–421 BC by Callicrates on the edge of the Acropolis (on the Nikepyrgos) is laid out on the amphiprostyle plan. This type of temple repeats the open hypostyle hall in the façade of the simple prostyle temple once more at the rear. The decorative relief on the entablature depicts a group of gods and the battles of the Greeks against the Persians.

The small Temple of Athena Nike stands on a bastion on the south western corner of Athens Acropolis, outside of the Propylaea. A sacred wooden statue of Athena Nike the bringer of victory, stood in the middle of the cella (the wingless Nike Apteros). Her wings were removed so that she could not flee from her shrine in Athens, thus ensuring that her powers of victory would interminably serve the city. As early as 449 BC, after Athens victory over the Persians, Callicrates drew up his first plans for a so-called Illios Temple on the site of his altar for the Goddess. However, the Peloponnesian War delayed the construction, and the temple which was made of pentelic marble, a building material often used at the Acropolis in Athens, was only completed in 421 BC. The Nike Temple had a determining influence on the Ionic style in Attica and is one of the most important examples of an amphiprostyle temple, having prostyle porticos supported by four columns in Ionic order on both the eastern and the western sides. Decorative imagery was found in the form of a frieze over the architrave depicting a gathering of the Gods, as well as battle scenes, some of them against the Persians. After Alcibiades victory over the Peloponnesians he had a Nike balustrade erected around the temple in 410 – 09 BC, the marble reliefs of which show Nike preparing a sacrificial offering (steer).

Pericles (495 – 429 BC) led Greece to new heights. This was manifested architecturally: in the Acropolis dominated by the Parthenon and the Nike Temple and the Erechtheum and the Propylaea. The power of these buildings reflects their turbulent history, full of destruction and new beginnings.

Epidauros (Greece): The Theatre at Epidauros

3rd century BC, Polykleitos the Younger

left:
This, the best preserved of all the theatres from Grecian Antiquity, was constructed in the early 3rd century BC as an extensive sacred quarter. The rows of seats set into the natural slope faced the building that bears the stage. This consisted of a hall reached at both sides by ramps, and decorated with Ionian half-columns, which were used to suspend the changing stage sets.

Theatre attendance was a civil obligation in ancient Greece and enduring performances lasting from morning to evening, sometimes even day after day, was - at best - "rewarded" with a loss of income. In Greek, the word tragedy means "goat-song" and indicates that the origins of theatre are found in the Festival of the Dionysian Cult, which itself was rooted in prehistoric ritual practices. In Epidaurus, south of the city of Mycenae on the Peloponnese, this structure from the 3rd century BC, bears witness to the special forms of Greek theatre. The singing and dancing chorus were at the centre of the circular orchestra at the Dionysian altar. After the 6th century BC individual actors and speakers also appeared. These actors were all men and all of them wore masks, usually representing some form of hero. Behind the chorus stood the two-storey stage structure with a proscenium in front, where stage backdrops could be installed. In front there were the seats for the audience, originally arranged in 34 rows for 6,500 visitors. After the 2nd century BC another 21 rows were added for a total of 14,000 seats. In contrast to the way they built temples, the Greeks strove to blend architecture and nature in building theatres. Functional considerations played an important role in this context as the first wooden theatres had often collapsed, and hollows in the slopes of mountains were used to provide seating on solid ground.

The Dionysus Theatre in Athens was begun under Pericles, but was only completed 100 years later. Its form was destined to become the model for theatre construction for the following millennia. Yet even in antiquity, the Theatre at Epidauros was already seen, for example by Pausanias, as a building that was perfect in its harmony.

Bergama (Turkey): The Altar of Zeus
Pergamon (Pergamum), 180 - 160 BC, Eumenes II

"In Pergamon there is a tremendous marble altar, 40 feet in height and resplendent with the most captivating sculptures, including a Gigantomachy." Taken from the report by Roman author, Lucius Ampelius, in his "Liber memorabilis." The altar is undoubtedly one of the most important works of decorative construction. The almost quadratic (36 x 35 metres - 118 ft. x ca. 115 ft.) altar platform, with a wide stairway (30 metres or ca. 98 ft.) leading up to the upper part of the structure, is decorated with a figural frieze measuring 120 metres (ca. 400 ft.) in length and 2.3 metres (7.5 ft.) in height. Upon the platform there is a hall of Ionic columns with an altar court.

In its drama, the sculptural frieze depicting the Gigantomachy is one of the most important works of Hellenistic art. The source of the Gigantomachy is Hesiod's epic relating the gods' struggle against the giants, "Theogony." This theme may have been chosen to celebrate King Eumenes's victory over the Galatians. Shrines and sacrificial altars were not necessarily located within the confines of temples. On the contrary, temples were reserved for the gods and ceremonies were conducted on altars built outside. The Pergamon Altar, which was probably dedicated to Zeus and Athena, is one of the most monumental examples of an altar on which offe-

above:
The monumental altar has been in the Pergamon Museum in Berlin since 1878. It was constructed under Eumenes II from 180–160 BC as a centre of a religious district dedicated to Zeus. A 118 metre (387 ft.) figure frieze depicting the fight between the gods and the giants extends around the square substructure. There were further mythological depictions on the superstructure surrounded by Ionic columned halls.

rings were burnt. When acts of sacrifice were performed they were only visible to a chosen few behind the curtain of columns.

Pergamon was at its peek for only about 150 years. This period (283-133 BC) is related to the Attalid dynasty, which succeeded in defending the kingdom from encroachments by both Macedonia and the Seleucid Kingdom. Pergamon was one of the economically and militarily most important major cities in the province of Asia. The Pergamon Altar has been reconstructed, with some pieces substituted, and can be seen at the Pergamon Museum in Berlin, located on the "Museum Island".

Pompeii (Italy): The Menander House

2nd Century BC

left:
The city was settled from the 7th century BC until AD 79, when it was completely buried by the eruption of Vesuvius. Excavation work began in 1748, revealing an antique city that was almost completely preserved. A city in which not just sculptures were preserved, but important evidence of Roman fresco and mosaic art too.

Graffiti and various inscriptions bare witness to the lives of the inhabitants of the house, almost like a newspaper pasted on the wall. On one wall inscribed: „I directed the chorus," indicating that one of the family members was active in the theatre. On others we read: „Romulus in heaven," „Hail Popidius Rufus, he is worthy of the office," and then „Menander. He wrote the first comedy." Because of these lines, written under the portrait of the playwright, we now call it the „Menander House.". This typical Pompeian house looks like a fortress from outside. A narrow entrance leads into the atrium that has an open roof and drainpipes under which rainwater was collected in a basin. Smaller rooms and a garden were located off the atrium. In more luxurious houses there were also colonnades and a room for gatherings. The portrait of the playwright, and other theatre motifs used in the remaining wall decorations, are mainly in fourth Pompeian style, for example "The Victory of Troy." Works from older phases, like the mosaics and murals over the triclinium, the largest in the city, were executed in second Pompeian style. The bath, which is luxurious for a private house, measures 2.3 x 3.7 metres (7.5 x 12 ft) and even has its own caldarium, a room for hot baths. This almost 1.800 square metre (6.000 ft) complex was continually inhabited for over 300 years, in the end by Quintus Poppaeus and his family.

Pompeii is near Naples in Southern Italy. The city had just finished rebuilding after an earthquake, when they were surprised by an eruption of the nearby volcano Vesuvius. A few Pompeians were able to flee, but most of them died in their homes. It was a unique event in human history to find a city buried from one day to the next. As a result, numerous documents of architecture and every day life were effectively preserved.

Orange (France): Triumphal Arch
around 30 BC

left:
The subdued architectural arrangement sinks clearly into the background of the rich, decorative reliefs. Their pictorial program focused on the victorious battle of the Romans against the Gauls. While various implements of war are depicted above the side arches and in the lower section of the attic, the actual battle scenes are located on the pediments along the narrow sides and the central façade bay of the upper attic region.

The Triumphal Arch of Orange is considered to be one of the most beautiful and best preserved of its time. With its monumental structure, also frequently referred to as the Arch of Tiberius, it is probably one of the earliest extant triple arches. They are especially known from the later triumphal arches of Septimus Severus (203 AD) and Constantine (315 AD) in Rome. Two lower ones on either side flank an accentuated big passage in the centre of the gate. Above that rises a multi-profiled double parapet. Four faded Corinthian pilasters divide the front. The central arch and four pilasters on the narrow sides each carry triangular gables of equal size. The architectural arrangement is rather understated and, consequently, the sculptural adornment with relief work is all the more sumptuous: all four sides are extensively decorated. Above both lateral gates as well as the lower parapet the representation concentrates upon military equipment, while the central projection of the top parapet, depicts battle scenes which undoubtedly portray the battle between Gauls and Romans, leaving little doubt as to the outcome of events. The original purpose of the gate is still open to different interpretations. The rich adornment with sculptures largely excludes the possibility that it could have been a city gate. More likely is that the building was a bearer of a political statement.

Fundamentally, triumphal arches were established only on the Forum Romanum in Rome. Therefore the structure can probably be interpreted more as a founding arch of a town which signaled Rome's universal claim to power in one of the most important street connections of Gaul. Like most buildings of its time, the gate has an exciting history. In the Middle Ages, for example, The Count Baux converted the gate into a small fortress, which was only cautiously dismantled again in the 19th century.

Nîmes (France): Pont du Gard
End of the 1st Century BC

left:
The 49 metre (161 ft.) tall bridge was part of an aqueduct that provided the city of Nîmes, which was founded by Augustus, with water from the source of the Eure, 50 kilometres (31 miles) away. The Pont du Gard is an airy construction that spans the steep gorge of the Gardon. Surmounting two tiers of broad, elongated rounded arches is a third arcaded storey that bears the water conduit.

The Romans are known for the trouble they took to supply their towns with water by means of mile-long conduits. These aqueducts often had to overcome deep gorges, meaning that mighty bridges had to be constructed. With three tiers, a height of 49 metres (161 ft.) and 64 round arches covering a length of 275 metres (902 ft.), the Pont du Gard is one of the masterpieces in this development in Roman architecture, which is termed the rational functional mass style. The Pont du Gard is part of a roughly 50 kilometre (31 mile) long aqueduct that was aimed at channelling water from a spring near Uzès to Nîmes. The greatest technical achievement here was not the construction itself, but rather the surveying work involved in the overall project: the builders had no more than an abacus and a straightedge combined with a water level (chorobates) at their disposal. With a drop in height of just 17 metres (56 ft.), the inclination of the aqueduct had to be a mere 34 centimetres per kilometre (13. 4 inches per 0.62 miles). Even today, mastering a task such as this is anything but the norm. The efficiency of the structure enabled each of the around 40,000 inhabitants of Nîmes to consume up to 400 litres (423 quarts) of water a day. The bridge is built of blokks of heavy seashell limestone weighing up to three tons a piece, which in some cases had to be heaved up to a height of 50 metres (164 ft.). For this the Romans developed lifting cranes with rope winches and large wooden wheels to drivethem. The master builder introduced interesting irregularities into the measurements of the 64 arches, in order to give the clear, strict logic of this functional construction greater aesthetic appeal. Consequently, the diameter of the rounded arches in the lower two tiers diminishes as they progress towards the bank. Each stone had to be exactly calculated and cut, because the masonry of the vaults consists of large blocks that have been placed together without the use of mortar or iron clamps.

Rome's dominion and urge to expand was founded on the achievements of its engineers. The most exemplary constructions for demonstrating power and superiority were those that served its infrastructure. For this reason the engineer Frontin, who was responsible for Rome's water supply at the dawn of the 2nd century, described "the aqueduct (as) the main testimony to the greatness of the Roman Empire."

Nîmes (France), Maison Carrée
End of the 1st Century BC

left:
This structure from the Augustan Era on its high podium is an example of the so-called pseudo-peripteral temple. In contrast to the surrounding periptery, which is ringed all around by free-standing columns, the Corinthian columns only stand free from the cella at the front end, while the engaged half-columns on the longitudinal sides merge into the walls.

This temple is assuredly the most elegant construction left behind by the Romans in the south of France. Although it is relatively small, having a height of 17 metres (56 ft.), a width of 15.55 metres (51 ft.) and a length of 26.40 metres (86.6 ft.), its sensitively balanced proportions and fine décor make it a masterpiece of antiquity from the Augustan Age. In addition, it is exceptionally well preserved. This is due to the fact that it has been kept in constant use since antiquity, with frequently changing purposes that were not always totally appropriate. The current name of the temple and its actual date of origin are by and large unclear. According to an inscription, it was dedicated "to Gaius Caesar, Son of Augustus, Consul, to Lucius Caesar, Son of Augustus, Designated Consul, the First of the Young." These were the emperor's two prematurely deceased grandsons, which would allow the building of the temple to be dated from the first years AD. This theory is supported by the style of the architectural ornament on the capitals and cymatia, which are characteristic of Augustan Classicism. In addition, the temple has nothing in common with its Hellenic counterpart. The Maison Carrée is little less than the prototype of the Roman temple built on a high podium, the pseudo-peripteral temple, in which the semblance of a surrounding periptery is created by means of Corinthian half-columns. Consequently, the temple does not convey a three-dimensional effect, nor was it conceived of as an autonomous building. Rather, it was part of a larger architectural ensemble, which determined the angles it was viewed from. This explains its extremely pronounced frontality. Leading up to the front façade with its richly decorated timbers is a broad stairway that extends across its entire width.

Since 1823, the Maison Carrée has been home to the Municipal Museum of Nîmes. Sadly, important details of the temple, the whole of the interior, the entrance door to the cella, and the coffered ceiling in the porchare are no longer in their original state.

Rome (Italy): The Colosseum
70 AD - 80 AD, Vespasian

left:
The three lower storeys of the Colosseum are decorated on their outer walls by the theatre motifs characteristic of Roman architecture, such as are also found on the Theatre of Marcellus or the Tabularium. A mighty arcade of piers is clad with a colonnade of engaged half-columns, which vary from story to story from Doric to Ionian to Corinthian at the top. These motifs were later to become widely used in Renaissance and Baroque architecture.

"There was land here a minute ago. You cannot believe it? ... In a short time, you will say: There was an ocean here a minute ago." Some of what we know about what went on in the Colosseum in Rome has been passed on to us in the epigrams of the Roman poet Martial. The arena could be completely flooded, so that battles at sea could be staged, as well as battles on land and, naturally, fights involving animals and gladiators. Countless people lost their lives for the entertainment of others. To ensure that as many visitors as possible were able to view the spectacle, a new form of architecture was developed in Italy that combined the theatre with the stadium, or circus – an amphitheatre in which an oval arena was surrounded by seating arranged in terraces. The building is 50 metres high and offers space for roughly 50,000 people to view the events staged at the centre in comfort. Every seat could be reached quickly, food was lowered on ropes, and sailors, brought in especially from Naples, hoisted a sail to provide shade from the sun when it was needed. The last gladiator fight took place here in 404 AD, the last reported fights with animals in 523 AD. The Amphitheatrum Flavium, as the structure was called in Antiquity was begun under Emperor Vespasian between 70 and 76 AD. Its opening was celebrated in 80 AD with

a festival that went on for 100 days. Each of the first three storeys had 80 arcades' arches, the uppermost level was enclosed using Corinthian pilasters and was added after 80 AD.

The weight of the building, including that of the corridors with their barrel and groin vaulted ceilings rested on 560 travertine columns. The skeletal structure of the building was technically quite innovative and seemed to anticipate modern construction methods. After the pyramids, the Colosseum is the largest structure dating back to Antiquity that has been preserved to the present day.

Rome (Italy): Pantheon
about 118 – 125

left:
The interior of the Pantheon shows a two-zoned wall construction. Its lower zone has remained Antique in character, with rectangular niches opened by column colonnades. However, the aedicule sequence of the upper zone is the result of redesigning in the Renaissance. The room is developed from a sphere and receives its light exclusively via the opening in the peak of the coffered dome.

This symmetrical building, which is certainly the most impressive of its kind in antique style, is also the most completely preserved structure of classical Rome. The Pantheon rises from the site of a temple, which Marcus Agrippa had already erected in 27 BC as a pantheon dedicated to the descendants of Julius Caesar (burned down in 80 AD). Even at the beginning of his reign, Hadrian decided upon a completely new structure in a massive rotunda style. In reverent memory the inscription on this structure by Hadrian mentions only the name of the first founder, Marcus Agrippa. The central structure forms a brick rotunda, with walls over 6 metres (20 ft.) thick. A mighty dome, whose vertex of 43,3 metres (48 yds.) corresponds exactly with the diameter of the rotunda, overarches this. Thus, the interior is developed through a sphere inscribed in a square. The marble-clad interior walls are of a layered construction. The lower zone is characterized by rectangular niches, each containing two Corinthian columns, and flanked by fluted pilasters. The attic zone has a row of low pilasters, interrupted only by "blind" rectangular windows. This structure was changed during the Renaissance. A circular opening nine metres (ten yards) in diameter pierces the centre of the coffered dome. The only source of light for the interior is through this opening. The exterior structure is limited to console cornices, which divide the walls into three zones. The rotunda was furnished with a portico, whose original pediment, decorated with relief, was supported by Corinthian columns.

Pope Boniface re-dedicated the Pantheon to the church "S.Maria ad Martyres" in 609 AD. This conversion to a Christian centre of worship is also the reason for its excellent state of preservation. The dedication to the mother of God and all saints introduces the pantheistic destiny of this formerly heathen temple. In the following century the henceforth Christian Pantheon served as an example to several St. Mary's and Martyr's churches constructed as rotundas.

Tivoli (Italy): Hadrian's Villa
118 – 134, Emperor Hadrian

left:
The so-called canopus dates from the second and last period of construction of Hadrian's Villa, built between 118 and 134 AD. The dining hall, which is designed as a grotto, was erected in an enlarged hollow in the form of an open semi-dome construction. Set before this is a channel terminating in a semicircle, which is bordered by elegantly placed columns. The alternating sections of entablature and round-arched arcades used here anticipate a motif that was later much favoured, especially under Mannerism and the Baroque.

The Villa Hadriana, situated on terraced and hilly terrain at the classical Villa Tiburtina, was built as Hadrian's country seat during 118 to 134 AD. The emperor chose the environment of the Sabina Mountains, which provided recreation for the citizens of Rome, even during antiquity. The largest preserved residential complex of Roman Antiquity is assembled through various groups of buildings, loosely arranged around spacious courtyards, merged through skilful utilization of different levels. The unique elegance and delicateness of the architecture is expressed in particular in the maritime theatre, built on a man-made island, or the so-called "Canopus". Here, elegant columns that have partly been replaced by caryatids border a canal, which ends in a semicircle to the north. Later, the rhythmic succession of arcades and architrave pieces became widespread as the so-called Palladio-motif in the architecture of mannerism. The complicated spatial arrangement and the abundance of varying perspectives are also expressed in the reconstruction of the so-called Piazza d'Oro, which was designed as a spacious courtyard with surrounding porticoes and southern nymphaeum.

Whereas the villa in the first instance described an agricultural establishment, the "villa urbana" was adopted to describe the summer seat of the upper classes during early imperial times. These structures, oriented towards Greek residential buildings, became increasingly more complex and grouped around lavish gardens and terraces. The wings of the buildings and colonnades of the "villa maritime" could extend right into the adjoining ocean through porches. Next to Hadrian's villa in Tivoli, the villa of Maximianus in Piazza Armerina resorts under the Roman country seats.

Trier (Germany): Porta Nigra
Early 4th Century AD

left:
Porta Nigra was built at the end the 2nd century as the main gate. It consisted of two tower-like wing buildings enclosing a transverse rectangular central block with round arches. A comprehensive structure powerfully combines the individual building units into a unit. In front of the close sequence of round arched windows is a sculptured half colonnade. The ledges of the windows encircle the building unit and tie it up, so to speak.

In the course of the governmental reorganization in Gaul under Augustus Caesar, Trier (Augusta Treverorum) was founded around 16 BC at the crossroads to several major highways and waterways. Around 180 AD, the city was enclosed by a wall, of which remnants are still to be found on the estate of the Cloister of St. Irmine. The Porta Nigra was the northern city gatehouse, through which the arterial road to the Rhine led to the German Provinces. The construction is 36 metres (118 ft.) in length, 30 metres (98 ft.) tall, and has a depth of up to 21.5 metres (70.5 ft.). It consists of a central structure with two carriageways, flanked on either side by a tower. The two towers jut out in massive curves on the sides facing onto open fields, this eliminating any blind when firing at invaders. Four storeys can be seen from the outside of the towers, and originally these loomed above the central building. This merely has two upper storeys, and encloses a courtyard for weaponry, the landwards side of which could be closed off by means of a portcullis. The gateway was planned not only for defence, but also as a symbol of Roman might and power. The heavy, hewn sandstone blocks were originally fitted together without mortar, and remained in place simply by virtue of their weight. Later they were joined using iron clamps with lead plugs. These were torn out during the Middle Ages, when there was a shortage of metals, leaving deep gashes in the masonry. Since the palace-like building was never completed, the masonry remained unplastered. The fact that the Porta Nigra Still stands is undoubtedly, because it was transformed into two chuches located one above the other durind the Middle Ages under the auspices of the Collegiate of St. Simeon. This close alliance was only sundered in 1749, when the French Revolutionary Troops occupied Trier.

Centuries of weathering, soot and dust turned the sandstone black, thus lending the building its name. As with many later Roman buildings, this is a copy of older models from the Roman Empire. The enormous gatehouse is regarded as one of the most impressive monuments of Roman architecture on German soil.

Early Christian and Byzantine Architecture

Early Christian and Byzantine Architecture

Early Christians met to worship together in private buildings (Dura Europos). It only became possible for an independent form of Christian architecture to develop after Emperor Constantine I (313 AD) had consented to tolerate the practice of Christianity. The most important ecclesiastical structures were basilicas that adopted the same basic form as Roman markets and court buildings. These had a nave and two (or more) aisles with roofs that were staggered in height, as in the case of (the old) St. Peter's Basilica in Rome (after 320 AD). The altar area with a semi-circular apse was sometimes expanded, even at this early date, by ambulatories or transepts. Towards the end of the 4th century, smaller buildings were created for religious communities or monasteries in which, in addition to basilicas with a nave and two aisles, like S. Maria Maggiore in Rome (after 432 AD), there were also simple hall churches. In addition to these laterally orientated buildings, there were also already central plan churches with a variety of floor plans, which in individual cases, for example San Lorenzo Maggiore in Milan (353 – 372 AD), could be highly complex. They often served as baptisteries or as monuments, like the Mausoleum of Theoderic in Ravenna, and often had an ambulatory separated by colonnades. After the dissolution of the Roman Empire (395 AD) an independent form of architecture gradually developed in the Eastern Empire that was eventually to give birth to Byzantine architecture. In this conjunction the gallery basilica was to become dominant after the middle of the 5th century. An example of this is the Áyios Dimitrios Basilica in Thessalonica. Constantinople played a leading role in the ornamentation of buildings, and just when it was flowering during the reign of Emperor Justinian I (527 – 565), Byzantine architecture embarked on a course of development that was entirely different from that of early Christian building practices in Western Empire. Under the auspices of the emperor, large, clearly structured, domed buildings began to be constructed. These combined central-plan and longitudinal floor plans. Three different types can be identified: the domed basilica, like the Hagia Sophia in Constantinople (now Istanbul), the domed central-plan church with an ambulatory, like S. Vitale in Ravenna, and the cruciform domed church, like the St. John's Basilica in Ephesus (550 – 564). The latter were buildings that had a nave and two aisles and were built on a cruciform floor plan with separate domes over each of the spatial compartments. This type later became the model for medieval churches in regions that were beyond what was still considered the Byzantine Empire, but which stood in contact with it. Examples of this are S. Marco in Venice and the domed churches in Aquitaine. In the 8th and 9th centuries the Iconoclastic Controversy led to a considerable stagnation in the development of Byzantine architecture. It was only under Basil I (867 – 886) that it experienced a resurgence. The cruciform domed church came to play a dominant role in middle and late Byzantine architecture after the beginning of the following century and was to change very little thereafter (Hosios Loukas Monastery). Examples of variations on this basic form are the eight-column building and the church with an ambulatory at the Pammakaristos Monastery in Constantinople (1310). The exterior began to be structured with an increasing degree of plasticity and enlivened by alternating layers of brick and squared-stone masonry, as in the Chora Church in Constantinople (11th – 14th century). When Constantinople, the centre of Byzantium, finally fell into the hands of the Ottomans, architecture in the former Roman areas in the west had already reached the end of the Gothic period. The Renaissance that followed was also destined to make its mark on the Eastern European architecture that had evolved from the Byzantine (for example the St. Basil Cathedral in Moscow).

Ravenna (Italy): Tomb of Theoderic
6th Century (1st quarter)

Already during his lifetime, Theoderic the Great, who died in 526, erected a magnificent tomb in order to document his reign. The building is most unusual in its structure. Around a two-storey polygonal central construction a heavy column arcade encloses it in the lower zone, reminiscent of the substructures of Roman buildings. Here the core building is only visible through the round-arched openings and reveals a rich arrangement in the upper levels. The wall arrangement over the developing recess (with semicircular compartments) was sometimes analysed as preparation of the curvature of an original gallery. But probably one can detect in the preserved projections from the wall the remnants of a former sequence of shell niches. Over a simple cornice the ten-angled structure becomes rounded. The large, seamless ashlar construction of the entire tomb culminates its monumental ascent at the peak. Thus, a 12-handled monolith adorns the shallow dome of the building. The crack penetrating the huge block most probably occurred when the 230-ton stone was originally laid on it. The interior of the basement clearly reveals it to have been laid out as an oratory and has the form of a cross comprised of equal arms. The round upper level housed the porphyry sarcophagus of the ruler of the goths.

In the introduction to his artistic biography, first published in 1550, Giorgio Vasari dismissively used the term "Gothic" to describe the monstrous and barbaric architecture of the northern Alpine late Middle Ages. In writing this, he was less mindful of the historical facts than his personal antipathy to the Gothic building customs as represented in France and Germany. The tomb of Theoderic, however, is one of the rare examples of "Gothic" architecture in the literal sense.

Ravenna (Italy): San Vitale
dedicated 547

The exterior building is divided solely by the flat lesenes and buttress-like corner reinforcements, reflecting the architectonic structure of the octagon surrounded by a two-storey deambulatory. The narthex in the west, which has moved out of its axis, is unique in architectural history. In the east, though, there is an impressive staggering of building units, which are polygonal, semi-circular or rectangular in their ground plan.

Construction of the Church S.Vitale was begun about 525/530 on commission of the Bishop Ecclesius. He replaced an earlier Christian building, which was erected during the 5th century on the site where St.Vitalis is said to have suffered his martyrdom. The commencement of the eastern Roman rule over Ravenna coincided with the construction period, which ended with its dedication in 547. This explains the clear connection of its architecture and furnishings with the Justinian imperial house. This memorial church was built as a central-plan structure with a complex ground and elevation arrangement. The eight sides of the octagonal domed structure curve like apses up amongst the pillars into a double-storey gallery. Triple arcades divide these exedras, both at the lower level and at the height of the gallery. On the west side a presbytery is separated from the gallery, which is interrupted at that point, by means of a similar motif. A circular apse, flanked by pastophories is linked therewith. In the west a narthex is positioned with a peculiar shift of the axis in front of this octagonal building. The short sides of the narthex end in semicircular apsides. The exterior structure is limited to fillets and buttress-like reinforcement of the corners. The overall design is clearly oriented towards examples from Constantinople. This

close relation is also apparent in the quality capitals, which are most probably imported artefacts made in Constantinople.

Mosaics and frescoes formed definite components of interior design in early Christian and Byzantine ecclesiastic buildings. Of the mosaics preserved in the presbytery of S.Vitale, the portrayal of Justinian and his wife Theodora with their current entourage is worth mentioning.

Istanbul (Turkey): The Hagia Sophia
532–537, Anthemius of Tralles, Isidorus of Miletus

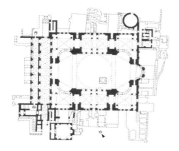

left:
The enormous building of the Hagia Sophia is dominated by the main dome, which is illuminated by numerous windows. Its four powerful pillars can be seen from the exterior building thanks to their buttresses. The four minarets were constructed when the early Christian church was converted into a mosque.

"A church, the likes of which have not been seen since the days of Adam and will never be seen again." Emperor Justinian I (527–165), who is noted for re-instituting Eastern Roman rule in Italy and for fighting heathenism and classical philosophy, had a church built in just five years that is still considered one of the most monumental structures in the world. In selecting a design for the church in Constantinople, Emperor Justinian broke with Western tradition and called in two scientists and mathematicians, Anthemius of Tralles and Isidorus of Miletus, from Asia Minor. His role as the spiritual head, as the "thirteenth Apostle," is reflected architecturally by the integration of various elements of palace architecture in the design, particularly in the treatment of the interior walls. Just a few figures illustrate the monumentality of the building. The church, which was dedicated to Sophia, Divine wisdom, has a rectangular floor plan measuring 80 metres (ca. 90 yds.) in length and 70 metres (ca. 80 yds.) in width. The space under the cupola measures 55 metres (60 yds.) from the floor to the highest point, and the dome spans 33 metres (36 yds.). There are mosaics extending over a surface of 15,000 square metres (16,400 yds.) and the building costs of 360 hundredweight in gold indicate that the interior

furnishings were hardly humble. The construction of the Hagia Sophia marked the departure from the traditional basilica, with a main vessel varying numbers of aisles, as the predominant type of church architecture. Here the traditions of longitudinal and central plan architecture are combined in an innovative manner and, for the first time, the cupola was the element that dominated the space. With the exception of the Pantheon in Rome, cupolas had only been built over baptisteries and mausoleums. The most important building in Byzantine architecture was destined to make a lasting mark on the tradition of domed architecture and to contribute to the cupola's emergence as a dominant interior element.

The Hagia Sophia, along with its hippodrome, golden hall, thermal baths and palace guard's quarters was an extensive building complex that can be roughly reconstructed on the basis of excavations. The shape of the former hippodrome has been preserved to this day in the At Meydani (Horse Market) in Istanbul.

Thessalonica (Greece): Hagios Demetrios
Mid 5th Century

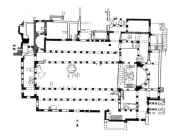

left:
Although the exterior building of the St. Demetrius Church is mostly the result of post-1945 reconstruction, the façade still mediates an impression of Early Christian architecture. In this way, the masonry of the narthex placed in front of the façade exhibits the characteristic transition from cut stone ashlars and clay brick bands typical of Byzantine architecture. The windows ordered into groups of three (trivalent) and their lattice-like subdivision (transcendent) is also a widespread motif in this cultural area.

In the year 306 Demetrios was martyred during the course of the last Christian persecutions under Maximianus in Sirmium. From there his cult was soon transferred to Thessalonica, where the first church dedicated to this saint was built, as early as Constantine's time. A 55 metres (60 yds.) long basilica replaced the latter towards the middle of the 5th century. Having been set on fire under Heracles during the early seventh century, the building could to a large extent be restored to its original form. This was also accomplished after the fire in 1917, which subsequently necessitated complete reconstruction after the Second World War. This early Christian church was built as a five-nave basilica with a transept, semi-circular apse and extensive crypt. The galleries above the side aisles of the nave extend over the western narthex. The five naves are separated by four rows of Corinthian columns, which are interrupted by four square pillars towards the central nave. Division of the space by four approximately square bays provides a rhythm, which finds late followers in Ottonian architecture, e.g. in Hildesheim and Gernrode.

After the division of the empire in the year 395, an increasingly independent architecture develops in the East-Roman Empire. This later leads to Byzantine architecture. The basilica with its gallery, showing the predominant style, was the first to become widespread. Other examples are the Studios Church in Constantinople, the churches of Acheiropoietos and Hagios Demetrios in Thessalonica. These only materialized in isolated cases in the West-Roman Empire.

Hosios Loukas (Greece):Church of Theotokos
begun End of the 10th Century

left:
The exterior of the katholikon, which dates from the early 11th century, shows the rich variety of materials and stone masonry that typifies Late and Middle Byzantine architecture. The irregular masonry in the lower sections gives way in the upper section to interplay of wide belts of dressed stones and narrower layers of brick. The ashlars at the corners, which in some cases are exactly cut, are spoils from buildings of Antiquity.

The monk Loukas who was born in Stiris originally founded this monastery. He predicted King Romano's liberation of Crete from the Bulgarians in the year 941. The fact that this prophecy was indeed fulfilled two decades later resulted in the canonization of Loukas, who had died in 946, as well as the complete reconstruction of the monastery. This founding phase reveals the remains of a trapezium. Two directly adjoining churches form the centre of the complex. The church of Theotokos, situated to the north, was built towards the end of the tenth century in the form of a domed cross, with square naos and wide narthex. Its walls, built as interplay of dressed stone and brick are decorated with characters and reliefs typical of the time. During the early eleventh century the larger and more impressive katholikon was added to the south. The naos is in the form of an octagon, where the central dome is supported by eight pillars, amongst which the nave opens up to the cross-vaulted aisles. Under these the bema is raised in a domed space. Splendid internal decorations were preserved in this church, including marble floors and panelling, mosaics and frescoes. This corresponds with the diversity of the mixed masonry of stone and brick of the external structure.

Building plans were already drawn up in the 9th century for the "palace church" Basileios I. in Constantinople, which today is known only from descriptions. These plans were almost obligatory in the middle and late Byzantine ecclesiastical architecture: the cross-vaulted church. Its square naos contains a further square, comprising four pillars, which support a pendentive dome. Tunnel-vaulted spaces extend the dome's volume into a Greek cross. This building style, which was adopted in the Theotokos Church, had many variations, including the octagon form of the katholikon.

Venice (Italy): San Marco
begun 1063

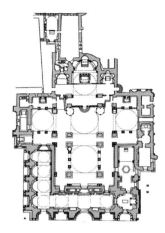

left:
The west façade of San Marco's church was designed as a monumental five-portal complex. Originally, the façade was unadorned. In the 13th century it received its mosaic decoration. The columns of the portal jambs, which were added in the 14th century, represent a reduced form of contemporary figure portals of French cathedral Gothic. This is also the case with the tympana mosaics, which project the north Alpine relief decoration on the surface.

The Church of S. Marco, which served as palace chapel to the doge, rises from the remains of a 9th century structure whose design closely followed the example of the Justiniatic Hagii Apostoli in Constantinople. After the doge Pietro Orseolo, one of his successors of office restored the early Byzantine predecessor of this building, Domenico Contarini decided upon a complete reconstruction, which began in 1063. The church was built as a cross-shaped central-plan structure. At the lower levels the domes of the four arms are supported by aisle-like corridors, which continue through the crossing pillars that are segmented by arcades. The individual dome volumes are separated from their galleries through bridge-like double or triple arcades. Galleries extend all the way above these arcades. The extremely opulent decorations and furnishings determine the appearance of the interior. Thus the gold-based mosaics of the domes and upper walls display an extraordinary splendour, which is enhanced by the multicoloured mosaic floors and marble cladding of the lower level. Of the numerous quality exhibits, the Pala d'Oro in particular is worth mentioning. The 83 enamel plates and 137 enamel medallions of this gild antependium originate from the 10th and 14th centuries.

The close relations between the increasing trading power of Venice and the Byzantine Empire is also reflected in the Church of St Mark. Its design as a cross shaped building with five domes clearly points to the church of Holy Apostles that was built in Constantinople under Justinian. Half a millennium later this building plan became the model for the Aquitanic dome church of the Romantic period.

Islamic Architecture

Islamic Architecture

The development of Islamic culture between the 7th and the 18th centuries can be classified in three basic periods, each of which produced characteristic styles of art and architecture. The first period is characterized by the Caliphate of Umayyads (661 – 750). During this period the sphere of Islamic influence extended from Damascus in Syria all the way to Spain. The middle period was concurrent with the reign of the Ábbasids (750 – 1258), who founded Baghdad in 762 and opened their realm to the east. This dynasty existed until it was conquered by the Mongols (1258) and was particularly famous for supporting culture that was dominated by Iranian art forms. The third period is the Ottoman (around 1300 – 1922). Within these periods myriads of stylistic influences emerge in areas under the control of subordinate rulers, like the Fatimids, under whom the construction of the el Ashar Mosque in Cairo was begun in 970, or the Safavids (1502 – 1722), who built the Shah Mosque in Isfahan. With Islam's expansion under the Umayyads it not only developed as a world culture, its architectural canon was also notably augmented. The spectrum of profane architecture developed continually and the proverbial Oriental opulence and luxury became characteristic. The Alhambra, near Granada in Spain, the residence of the Nasrid rulers, can be seen as the prototype of Islamic palace architecture. It belongs to the same tradition as the government buildings of the Ábbasids in Samarra and Topkapi Palace in Istanbul. Just like Alhambra in the West, the Taj Mahal is an architectural icon of Islam in the East. Although the teachings of Islam actually forbade the construction of artistic mausoleums, they were nevertheless constructed for representational purposes. Along with the mosques and palaces they are the most ingenious buildings in Islam. The pre-eminent sacred structure in Islam is the mosque, which is modelled after the House of the Prophet in Medina. In this sense, a mosque consists of a prayer room (harem), of which the back wall (kiblah) on a longitudinal axis, is orientated toward Mecca and marked by an apsidal prayer niche (mihrab). Absolute necessities were a closed courtyard with a fountain for the ritual washings and a minaret from which the muezzin called believers to prayer. Originally this was relatively squat and stood alone, as at the mosques in Samarra or the Ibn Tulun Mosque in Cairo, only later did it become more slender and lance-like. There were also regional variations on this common concept. When the Muslims conquered

Syria in 636, they took over many of the churches built in the early Christian period and transformed them into mosques. These basilicas were long buildings and often had two aisles, in addition to the main vessel, and flat roofs. Asia's mosques also have a style of their own, particularly the pavilion and the staggered roof mosques in China and Southeast Asia. The type of domed mosque that was built in the Ottoman empire is a relatively recent development and limited for the most part to Asia Minor and Anatolia. The layout is basically the same as that of Byzantine churches, particularly of the Hagia Sophia. Süleyman I's mosques in Istanbul and Selim II's mosques in Edirne are classic examples. They mark not only the high period of domed mosques but also mark the high point of Islamic architecture. Chronologically they coincide with the Renaissance in the Occident, in which domes also played an important role in architecture, albeit for different reasons. The name Sinan – the master builder at the court of Süleyman I – is closely associated with the concept of the domed mosque, as it became obligatory in the Ottoman Empire in the fourteenth century. In contrast to the Christian churches of the day, it was not just a question of creating a dramatic impression, but rather one of clearly defining space. The interior of the mosque therefore displays none of the intricacy in its external structure found elsewhere. All of Sinan's work is involved on the stylistic dialogue with the Hagia Sophia. This leads, on the one hand, to almost all of his mosques seeming, at first glance, to be identical, and, on the other hand, to the once largest church in Christendom hardly being recognized as a church today. The construction of mosques is also not only a matter for architectural history. In every Islamic country there are new mosques, more or less worthy of note. Outstanding examples in this century are the Bhong Mosque in the Pakistani province of Punjab, completed in 1982, and the al-Ghadir-Mosque in Teheran, which is the most important building in modern Islamic architecture.

Samarra (Iraq): Great Mosque with Minaret
848 – 852

left:
The spiral-shaped ramp winding around the building gives the minaret its characteristic shape. The exceptional form of this brick construction was probably inspired by the Ziggurat of Chorsabad, which was still in existence in the 9th century. The 55 metre (180 ft.) tall minaret towers above the Great Mosque, and once afforded a view of the whole of the capital of the Abassid Empire.

It was said to have accommodated over 100,000 of the faithful at any one time: the fortress-like construction was the largest mosque of its day, but now it is in a state of virtual ruin. The building of the administrative town of Samarra in the desert near Baghdad commenced under the Caliphate of the Abbasids in 839. The work was continued until around 883, but never completed. A complex of buildings surrounded by walls, and covering 175 hectares (approx. 430 acres), was built inside the town, and contained not only administrative buildings but also the mosque. This Shiite tomb mosque incorporated numerous elements of Sassanidian architecture from Persia. These include a hall covered with a barrel vault, the so-called iwan, which opened onto an inner courtyard. Four such halls set one on each side of a square courtyard created the basic form of the madrasah. It acted initially as the Koran School, the place where religious instruction was performed in the mosque. The emergence of dome construction in 11th century Persia led to the founding of the tradition of the four-iwan court mosque. A visually prominent element of the mosque is the spiral minaret done in brick masonry. It towers to the north of the mosque – in line with the building's middle axis – 55 metres (180 ft.) above the ground. Its

shape presumably draws on the ziggurats of Babylon in ancient Mesopotamia: massive temple towers of mud-bricks consisting of several steps, with a shrine at the apex that could be reached by a stairway that encircled it outside. Several other free-standing minarets exist apart from the spiral minaret of Samarra: the minaret of the Ibn Tulun Mosque in Cairo, and several Southeast Asian versions. The best-preserved court mosque with minaret from the early Islamic period is the Omajja Mosque in Damascus (705 – 715), which was built around an older Christian basilica.

Minarets probably go back to the Syrian tradition of marking the four corners of a building with short towers. Our picture of them is dominated, however, by the image of slender, needle-shaped minarets that are integrated into the main body of the building, and are particularly known from the Ottoman tradition of mosque building.

Córdoba (Spain): Mosque
786 – 990

left:
The spatial impression of a huge hall can still be obtained at the sides, even though a large Christian cathedral was constructed in the same-shaped naves of the mosque in the 16th century. Two arches made of sand and brick in alternation were attached. This was because the 600 monolithic columns (spoils from Roman and Visigoth buildings) were too short.

In the 9th century, Islamic architecture developed the full range of its true expressive possibilities. Abd al-Rahman I founded an independent kingdom in Córdoba and donated the Umayyad mosque at the centre of the city. Building work on the mosque, which was modelled on the so-called third wonder of the world, the Great Mosque of Caliph Al-Walid in Damascus, commenced in 786, during the classic period of Islamic architecture under the rule of the Umayyad and Abbasid caliphs. A first building was finished ten years later, but this was followed by 200 years of major expansion, so that the mosque can only be regarded as completely finished by around 990. The building is testimony to the 300 year-long competition between Córdoba and Baghdad to become the most important cultural centre of Islam. Unique here is the combination of elements of both Islamic and European art. The famous Horseshoe Arch, for instance, was adopted from the western Goths. A highly unique feature, on the other hand, is the two-storey system of arcades. The pattern of the columns draws on elements from Egyptian palaces and temples, as well as from the apadanas, the multi-columned halls of Persia, which probably served as audience chambers. The mosque, built on the Syrian scheme, provided space for 30,000 people. In its day it was among the largest mosques in the world, and represented one of the highpoints of Umayyad architecture. The alignment of the prayer wall or mihrab deviates 17 degrees from Mecca, because the ruined walls of an old cloister were allowed to remain there.

The impression of space and the semblance of infinity in the mosque are quite overwhelming. The rhythm of the columns produces vistas that give the illusion that one can see the horizon. The feeling of wide distances in the room is often linked with nomadism and the experience of the desert expanses. After the reconquest of the city by Ferdinand III, the mosque was consecrated in 1236 as a Christian cathedral, and later various church fixtures were installed.

Cairo (Egypt): Ibn Tulun Mosque
876 – 879

Simplicity, quietness, and a feeling of the sublime: the mosque is impressive not only due to its size, but even more so to its contemplative and hallowed atmosphere. It is enclosed on three sides by an almost square, 19 metres (62 ft.) wide courtyard, designed as a shell to keep out distracting noises. The construction has almost no columns, just simple pillars that bear the arches and support the vault. The walls, both inside and out, lack almost any ornament. This similarly applies to the 19 pairs of inner and outer portals. The pairs are set opposite each other, and constitute the sole divisions in the exceptionally long stretches of wall. Rising up at the centre of the courtyard is a domed pavilion containing a fountain. The interior is likewise bare, and merely divided up by niches decorated with plaster carvings and panels bearing Kufic lettering. Five parallel rows of columns each with 17 arcades lend form to the prayer hall. Its décor consists solely of an ornamental band along each side and a frieze of arabesques made of sycamore, at least 2,000 metres (6,562 ft.) in length, that is set below the ceiling. A similar, uninterrupted frieze runs around the arcaded courtyard. With its pattern of lozenges, triangles and straight bands with circles, it is one of the earliest examples of a geometrical arrangement in Islamic art. Whereas the mosque was constructed from fired bricks, the minaret is made of cut limestone. It is 4,044 metres (132.68 ft.) tall, and has four storeys set on a square base. The outside stairway makes more than one counter-clockwise turn before reaching an octagonal kiosk.

Ahmed Ibn Tulun, the first independent governor of Egypt was only nominally bound to the Caliphate of Baghdad. His mosque was similar to the mosque of Samarra, although only half as large, with a ground surface of 26,318 square metres (283,290 sq. ft.). It became the third largest mosque in the world and is also the oldest mosque in Egypt after the Amr Ibn El-As Mosque in Old Cairo, dating from 642 AD.

Granada (Spain): Alhambra
13th – 14th century

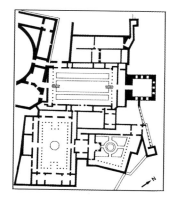

left:
It was only after 1362, under Mohammed V, that the Patio de los Leones, or Court of Lions, received its present form. Rooms with jutting stalactite vaults are attached to it laterally. The Romanesque Lion Fountain (ca. 1060) might be from the predecessor building destroyed in 1090.

"Woman, give him (the beggar) alms, for there is no worse punishment than to be blind in Granada": this sentence is written on the ruined castle of Alcazaba (11th century). This was once the home of Mohammed I, the founder of the Nasrite Dynasty, who chose Granada in 1246 as the capital of the Nasrite Empire, and with that created the right conditions for such an outstanding building as the Alhambra. The castle at the foot of the Sierra Nevada forms the heart of the last Moorish Empire on Spanish soil, in the region around Granada, Malaga and Almeria. The region only fell in 1492 to the Reconquista led by the Catholic monarchs Isabella of Castile and Ferdinand of Aragon. Mohammed I not only created the conditions for the future buildings on the political level, but also in quite practical ways: he saw to the water supply on the Alhambra hills and commenced building the defensive wall that encloses the city. The name Alhambra refers to the colour of the walls: "Kalat Al-Hamra" means "The Red Fortress." The most important buildings were constructed during the 14th century under Jusuf I and Mohammed V. During this period, magnificent buildings must have been built around the castle ruin of Alcazaba, including administrative and residential buildings, barracks and mosques, schools and baths, along with cemeteries and gardens. The court of the Myrtles, with the adjoining Ambassadors' Hall in the Comares Tower and the magnificent court of the Lions, is still preserved. It is surrounded by the living quarters for the harem, pavilions, ornate columns and baths, and hemmed by a colonnade. At the centre is the imposing Lion's Fountain. The walls are all richly decorated with colourful ornamentation, the base mouldings are faced with bright faience mosaics and the rooms are vaulted with stalactite work. Beginning in 1526, Carlos V had a two-storey Renaissance palace built on the northeastern part of the grounds, which opened onto a circular inner courtyard. The palace was, however, never completed.

Washington Irving's Tales of the Alhambra, published in 1832, contributed to the rediscovery and conservation in the 19th century of one of the foremost monuments of Islamic palace architecture.

Istanbul (Turkey): Süleyman's Mosque (Süleymaniye Mosque)

1550 – 1557, Sinan

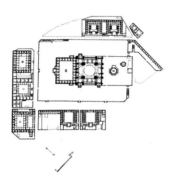

left:
The Süleymaniye Mosque, situated above the Bosporus and the Golden Horn, is the symbol of Istanbul. The main dome, which is supported by retaining walls, has two half-domes as abutments. The walls on the other two sides beneath the dome are in the form of gently pointed arches, and are pierced by rows of windows.

Süleyman the Magnificent had his mosque erected by his court architect Sinan on a commanding position over the golden horn. This was the same spot where the Byzantine Capitol and later the old Seraglio, destroyed by fire in 1541, had once stood. The Sultan envisaged a building on the same scale and with the same ground plan as the Hagio Sophia. Presumably the Sultan, who was at the zenith of his power, wished to dare comparison with Emperor Justinian I, and even to outdo him in terms of size and splendour. Consequently, the mosque that Sinan erected for Süleyman is one of the most important works of Turkish architecture, with the largest dome until that time in the Islamic world. This construction also saw the end, however, of Sinan's involvement with Byzantine architecture. In his subsequent architecture, he ceased to employ such combinations of domes and semidomes, in which the semi-domes have the same radius as the main dome. Although the Süleymaniye Mosque is in most respects slightly smaller than the Hagia Sophia, the dimensions of the two constructions are similar. The Sultan's mosque is 108 metres (354 ft.) long and 73 metres (240 ft.) wide. The central dome, whose apex is 54 metres (177 ft.) high, is supported along its longitudinal axis by two hemispheres. Instead of the vertical and linear juxtapositions of spatial forms that dominate the Hagia Sophia, the architecture of the Süleymaniye Mosque is marked by a constant play between spherical and flat surfaces, between semidomes and the enclosing walls. Additionally, the pure semicircular arches of Byzantine architecture are replaced in Sinan's building by flat pointed arches.

Although the Süleymaniye Mosque evinces many similarities to the plan of the Hagia Sophia, Sinan devised his own, quite unique architectural solutions. He personally regarded the construction as his qualifying work as a "journeyman" – the earlier construction of the Shehzade Mosque (1542-1548) being the work of his "apprenticeship." His "masterwork", the Mosque of Selim II in Edirne (1568-1574), led him in completely new directions.

Isfahan (Iraq): The Royal or Imam Mosque
1612 - 1638, Ali Akbar Isfahni

left:
The mosque, constructed under Shah Abbas I, followed older Persian models in its layout. As with these, a central courtyard is surrounded by columned halls, with a prayer niche at the centre of each of them. The largest of these iwans can be found at the entrance of the domed prayer hall, which is completely covered on the outside with faiences.

Isfahan, the Royal City of Iran, is a flourishing oasis in the middle of a salt desert. In keeping with the image of paradise set down in the Koran, Shah Abbas I resolved at the end of the 16th century to transform Isfahan into a modern city, which would be borne on the two pillars of commerce and a life of piety. This combination of the secular and the spiritual can be most clearly seen at the Royal Square Maidan-e-Shah, where the mosque faces the bazaar. The so-called Blue Mosque is of typically Persian design. It differs from both the Arabian ground plan of a large hall with colonnades, as well as from the Turkish form, which derives from the domed churches of Byzantium. Rising up around a large central court-yard are four façades with colonnades, and set in the middle of each is an iwan, a niche surmounted by a semidome. These four iwans are meant to symbolize the four springs of paradise. The most important and typically largest iwan is located at the entrance to the large prayer hall, which is vaulted by cupolas. Since the rear wall of a mosque (qibla) must also be directed towards Mecca, the otherwise totally symmetrical building lies here at an angle of 45 degrees to its surroundings. For this reason the mosque is connected to the Maidan by a fairly untypical entrance. The true highpoint of the building is constituted by the ceramic tile work and the finely grained ceramic mosaics, which cover every square inch of the exposed walls. The ground colour is blue gently tinged with green, a colour highly typical of Persian Safavid art. It is set off to particular effect in the tiled faiences of the large dome in the prayer hall.

The artistic use of wall tiles gives the construction its characteristic appearance and makes it stand out from the neighbouring buildings, with their mostly unadorned brick walls. The splendour of these bright, radiant colours transforms the mosque into something that the strict geometry of its shapes would never alone have managed: a kind of fantasy product from the Thousand and One Nights.

Agra (India): Taj Mahal
1630 – 1653

left:
The mausoleum of the Taj Mahal lies just opposite the main gate. In between, there is a garden divided by cross-shaped watercourses. The geometric park dates back to Persian influences. The double dome also derives from the architecture of Persia: the inner dome is not even half as tall as the 74 metre (243 ft.) high building.

Shah Jehan erected an immense mausoleum for his favourite wife, Mumtaz Mahal, close to the city of Agra on the banks of the River Jumma: the Taj Mahal. Located on a wide plane, the central building clad in fine, radiant white marble greets the beholder as a structure of incomparable splendour. Although stylistically it is an amalgam of Indian Moghul architecture, Timurid mausoleums and Persian Safavid decorative elements, it is regarded as a unique testimony to Islamic architecture in India. The Taj Mahal is square in plan with chamfered corners. The main dome above the central hall rests on a tambour that is flanked by four octagonal towers, each bearing a smaller pavilion with a cupola. The enormous onion-shaped dome, whose true dimensions can only be seen from outside, had a diameter of 28 metres (92 ft.) and is 65 metres (213 ft.) tall. Opening out on each side are tall, vaulted naves with richly ornamented façades, so-called iwans. The main body of the building is outlined by a square, plinth-like enclosure whose four corners bear slender minarets. These have, however, no more than a compositional function: they lend emphasis to the central domed building. The building takes up only a small part of the park-like grounds. The overall complex is entered through a portal of red sandstone, which contrasts strongly with the white marble of the mausoleum.

The Shah planned a mausoleum for himself in black stone – as a counterpart set on the opposite side of the river. The two mausoleums were to be linked by a silver bridge. After being deposed in 1658 by his son, he was no longer able to realize this plan. On his death in 1666 he was laid to rest beside his favourite wife. Consequently, his cenotaph is the sole asymmetrical element of the Taj Mahal.

Central Asian and Far Eastern Cultures

Central Asian and Far Eastern Cultures

The architecture produced by the countries in Asia is reflected today in a number of monuments in India, Tibet, Burma (Myanmar), Cambodia, Indonesia, China, Korea and Japan, and can hardly be dealt with collectively. There is no real cohesiveness or common identity. This can be attributed not so much to the sort of regional differences, that are also common elsewhere, as to the religious discrepancies that are revealed in the confrontation of the three major Eastern religions, Buddhism, Hinduism, and Shintoism. In the sacred architecture of Buddhism the stupa is the simplest form of cultic monument. The building was originally made of earth and wood and was intended to store relics. Later the hemispherical or bell-shaped building with a round floor plan began to be used as a burial mound for people of importance. The transformation from a building used solely for cult purposes to one with a variety of uses was then only a question of time and occured rather quickly. Over the course of time this massive hemispherical mound of earth, that was already sometimes faced with stone, was fitted with a mast that rose higher and higher, and on which a growing number of "umbrellas" were spanned, one above the other. The oldest examples date back to between the 5th and the 3rd centuries BC. Their proliferation kept step both geographically and chronologically with Buddhism. Initially it was found all over the Southeast Asian mainland, then in Sri Lanka and Java, and in China and Korea. Consequently notable regional variations evolved, for example a form in Java similar to a pyramid. The most important stupa in Buddhism is the Shwe Dagon Pagoda in Rangoon (Yangôn), the capital of Burma, which was begun in 1372. Another variation of the stupa is the classically formed and proportioned pagoda. It quickly became formally independent and experienced about the same level of proliferation as the original form. It is a vertically orientated, multi-level building, generally with a quadratic or polygonal floor plan. These structures reach great heights, as did the stupa, however they had fancifully formed roofs, sweeping upward at the corners of each level, that had been borrowed from the saddle-shaped hip roof used in traditional Chinese hall buildings. In addition to the buildings devoted exclusively to religious cults, one finds, mainly in the formerly inaccessible Buddhist mountain regions of Asia, buildings that simultaneously served a number of purposes, for example the Potala Palace in Lhasa – a combined palace, fortress and monastery.

Unlike Buddhism, Hinduism is not associated with a religious founder and reveals polytheistic traits. It also only succeeded only successful at a relatively late date – starting in the 12th century – spreading over the Indian subcontinent and the neighbouring regions. Its temples are prime examples of symbolic architecture. Therefore, they do not at first seem like buildings, but rather like enormous sculptural forms. They always rise up from a podium that can be approached over a stairway and thus symbolizing the holy mountain Meru. Hindu temples are usually decorated with great fantasy and differ markedly from the comparatively simple Buddhist stupas. The Shintô religion is predominant, above all, in Japan where it dates back to pre-history and thus stood under the influence of shamanism. Religious practice includes praying to the spirits of nature and the forefathers, the so-called kami. They are honoured in shrines that are at the centre of what are considered holy sectors. The latter are enclosed behind wooden fences abscured from sight. The entrance to these light wooden structures is generally through a red wooden door. Because of the ritual washings associated with worship such shrines are almost always found near running water. The oldest intact Shintô shrine is the so-called Ise Shrine on the Island of Honshu. Shintô shrines date back as far as the 2nd century. Inaccessible to the public, they are destroyed every 20 years and erected on an alternative site. This traditional process of renewal (shikinen sengu) has been practiced since 690. Hence, the present-day Ise shrine is the most recent reconstruction. In this manner, architectural tradition is passed on completely from generation to generation. This makes Shintô shrines unique in that even the new buildings can be looked upon as archaeological sites. Since the 6th century, with the infiltration of Chinese culture, different Buddhist architectural forms have also developed in Japan. Particularly multi-level pagodas and halls with hip, tent and saddle roofs, sweeping upward at the corners, became a widespread form of the light construction already typical of countries. The Imperial Palace in Kyôto is a prime example. It was reconstructed time and again according to old drawings, the last time was in 1854. Inspiration even came from Europe until 1700. For example, the Japanese learned the principles of building fortresses from the Portuguese. After that, the forms became set, and standard measurements were introduced for all buildings.

The Great Wall of China
1368 – 1644

A gigantic bulwark: the enormus wall extends from the gulf of Liaotung to the province of Kansu and the Sinkiang desert in the west. Over an incredible 5,000 kilometres (3,125 miles), of which 2,450 kilometres (1531 miles) over mountain and valley are still preserved today, . It was built by the first emperor of China, Chin Shi Huangdi, around 220 BC in order to resist the invading Huns. Although the first separate wall structures had already been established in the time of Zhanguo by individual local monarchs, the new emperor wanted to secure the entire distance of his northern border and therefore ordered the joining of the separate ramparts into one continuous barrier. However, the Great Wall was not yet this. The structure which bears this name today, was only built more than a thousand years later during the time of the Ming dynasty. Originally established on a stone base and filled with compacted earth, the merlon-reinforced brick building was only effective against individual mounted troops, but was unable to withstand organized nomadic armies. Barbarian hordes that managed to breach the wall even formed their own dynasties in China in the 13th and 17th centuries. Ironically it was one of these dynasties that finally protected the borders of China, namely the Qing who ruled from 1644 to 1911. Under their power the big wall slowly went to ruin. Sections of about 100 kilometres (62.5 miles) have survived to this day and gradually been restored. They are 4 to 6 metres (13 to 20 ft.) wide and between 3 and 8 meters (10 to 26 ft.) high. The Great Wall is not only a monument to human creative power, but also a testimony to the fear and a memorial to its victims. Several hundred thousand workers were forced to build it under constraint from an entire army. The building was conducted at a murderous tempo and demanded a high toll in human life.

Wall emplacements have played a significant roll in the history of the human race right up till modern times, especially for the demarcation and military protection of political and cultural spheres of influence. One need only think of Hadrian's wall and the Limes of the Romans or the "protective walls" of the Cold War during the last century.

Beijing (Republic of China): Forbidden City
1406 – 1420

left:
The walled imperial city's impressive appearance, surrounded by a moat, is based primarily on its harmonious whole. Individually, the buildings mostly have more modest measurements. The wooden architecture takes second place to the colour design, which contributes enormously to the unified picture of the Forbidden City.

After the Mongols were forced out of China in the 14th century, Peking (Beijing) was transformed from 1421 into the permanent capital of the Chinese empire under the Ming dynasty. The city, which was largely re-established over earlier constructions, developed into a harmonious entity with a clear, uniform design. In its medieval town planning experiences, Chinese architecture found a classic expression. The main complex was the monumental emperor's palace – the so-called "Forbidden City". The whole design of Peking was more or less reflected in its clear structure. However, its monumental appearance did not initially stem from the dimensions of all those buildings. Mostly it only comprised small, similar, one-storey main wooden buildings and gates, that had lain on the central axis, on stepped terraces of white stone, at a higher level to the stone-paved squares. A crucial role was played by the extension of the proportions of all spacious squares and the expressiveness of the repetitive rhythms and colours. The aesthetic effect of the Forbidden City consisted mainly in the succession of spacious places that led up to the main buildings. The main pavilion, "hall of highest harmony", embodies the peculiarities of the Ming dynasty palace architecture most characteristically: the considered fusion of a white-marbled relief base with multi-coloured columns and golden-yellow, glazed roof tiles.

With the Forbidden City, the Chinese emperors had built themselves a prison. Isolated from the outside world, they increasingly clung despotically to outdated traditions and prevented the opening of the empire to trade and progress. Finally, they became so cocooned in the palace that they lost all sense of reality, and then their power.

Beijing (Republic of China): Marble Ship Summer Palace,

1893

On the banks of the Kunming lake, northwest of the formerly forbidden city lies the famous summer palace, country seat of a whole series of Chinese rulers. The first was emperor Qianlong of the Qing dynasty. Palace and park embody the "Chinese dream of paradise on earth". High hills concealed paths and placid waters. Here on a plain of 3 square kilometres (1.2 square miles) one encounters elements of nature usually only to be found scattered over enormous landscapes. On the west bank of the artificial lake lies a large stone boat that appears alien in these surroundings. Officially it is referred to as the "boat of purity and peace". However, the people call it the marble ship. Originally built in 1755, its composition closely followed Chinese architectural construction. It fell a victim to the flames of the Opium Wars in 1860 when the whole park, which at that time was still called "garden of the clear waves", was doomed to be burned down and sacked by invading troops of the English and French armies. Cixi, the de facto ruler of China, had it rebuilt in 1893 according to a Western model. The boat is 36 metres (40 yds.) long with a massive stone hull. The two-storey marble pavilion in the form of a paddle steamer is laid out with flower-adorned clay brick; the windows are composed of multi-coloured glass.

From every floor the scenery on the bank can be observed through specially erected mirrors. The summer palace was the last imperial garden to be built in China. As permanent domicile of the emperor's wife, Cixi, it was more a centre of feudal hegemony and diplomatic intrigue than a pleasure garden. It was here that the plans were also conceived to end all reform movements such as the so-called Boxer Rebellion.

The reconstruction of the summer garden purportedly cost about 50 million dollars. It was financed with money actually intended for the modernization of the Chinese fleet. Only in 1911 under Pu Yi, the last emperor, did the public gain the right of entry to the palace and garden by paying a fee.

Sanchi (India): Stupa
1st Century BC

left:
Rising up below the remains of a Buddhist place of worship and cloister complex, set on the hill, is Stupa I, which was erected under Emperor Ashoka. This 17 metre (56 ft.) tall, stone-clad earth mound is surrounded by a stone wall with four gates, which are decorated by reliefs depicting legendary scenes from the life of the Buddha. Somewhat simpler in design are Stupa II, built at the same time, and Stupa III, which was built some 100 years before.

At the foot of the Vindhya mountains, on a hill near the small village of Sanchi, stands the oldest stupa of India. In Buddhism they symbolize the holy tree of life and enlightenment. After Buddha's death, the Maurya emperor Ashoka discovered Buddhism for himself and helped bring it to a bloom period in India. Its peacefulness and tolerance impressed him so that he oversaw the establishment of stupas all over the countryside, to store Buddha's ashes as relics. According to the legend, he later opened the stupas to divide Buddha's remains again. In this way, 84,000 large and small stupas were built, each with ash remains of Buddha. The big stupa of Sanchi was established on request of the empress as a special monument. It has a diameter of 36 metres (40 yds.), is 17 metres (19 yds.) high and its four points of access are directed towards the cardinal points. As a centre of a monk's establishment. monasteries and temples surrounded it. When Islam conquered India in the 13th century, the last monks of Sanchi had already left a long time ago and everything was already overgrown by jungle. In this way the Buddhist sanctuaries of Sanchi escaped destruction. Only in 1818 did British army units rediscover the monastery complex that was still in good condition, but crowds of amateur archaeologists and treasure hunters almost destroyed in a few years what the jungle had preserved for centuries. In order to protect the stupas, the Indian government had all the buildings covered in brickwork. Its planned restoration only began around 1900. The three stupas that stand to this day on the Sanchi hill appeared over a period of approximately 200 years. The largest of them is today considered to be the ideal type. It is a massive, windowless reliquary and fulfills an exclusively symbolic function.

Stupas are places of quiet meditation. As a form of grave they extend back to Buddha himself. It is said that after his death, eight of the most powerful monarchs argued over his ashes. As a compromise a division was arranged and over every relic a Stupa was built. However, nothing remains of these eight sanctuaries built from unbaked clay bricks.

Bhubaneshvar (India): Temple of Mukteshvara
9th Century

left:
The temple of Mukteshvara is the most important preserved building of the Hindu temple and pilgrimage site Bhubaneswar. The tower narrows the higher up you go, and is divided vertically by projecting strips, which continue until the coping. The broad grooves between the accurately cut sandstone blocks function as a horizontal counterbalance.

In Bhubaneshvar, the capital of the province of Orissa, 7.000 temples supposedly once stood around the holy sea. Some hundred sanctuaries dating between the 8th and 13th centuries have survived – many only as ruins, however. In the temples of Bhubaneshvar the development of the north-Indian type can best be studied: more than 30 sanctuaries illustrate every step of a constant formal refinement and differentiation. With its classic proportions and canon of forms of its sculptures, the Mukteshvara temple belongs stylistically to the transitional phase between the early and late development group of temple buildings. The lower temple still stands clearly in the archaic tradition: for example, the lion figures which project from the space of the middle-tower height of later buildings are absent, as is the case with the double lions which carry the crown. In contrast to this stands the fine horizontal stratification of the ascending, tapering tower with deep valleys beside a pentagonal vertical structure of projections. All projections extend to the crown, in contrast to later developments. In the walls flanked by stepped, forward leaning alcoves of the square hall are large, honeycomb stone windows. The roof, like the tower construction, is divided into several horizontal layers and has a pyramid-shaped outline. The tem-

ple stands within enclosed walls. In front of the entrance to the congregation room,is built a stone gate with round arch. As building material for the temple, a light sandstone was firstly used from the quarries only a few kilometers away at Udayagiri. The foundations and the enclosure walls are from coarse, dark red laterite that was crushed directly at the place.

In accordance with the Indian proverb: "the real arch does not rest," the Sthapatis, or priest's architects, composed the round arches of the gate not from radial cut stones, but piled them up horizontally. In any event, the round arch is a rarity in Hindu architecture.

Somnathpur (India): Temple of Keshava
13th Century, Janaka Acarya

Under the reign of the Hoysala kings a unique architectural style developed in the later Chalukya empire: the so-called Vesara style – stylistically a mixture of Dravida and Nagara style. The Keshava temple forms the highpoint of this style movement and has best conserved its architectural trait. Moreover, the temple is unique in many respects. The temple possesses three sanctuaries which were consecrated to Vishnu in different incarnations, and which lead off from a column hall: Vishnu appears as a Janardana, a Krishna and a Keshava which is revered as its most important aspect in the middle cella. The whole temple structure is developed from circles and squares.

These basic forms originating from Asia Minor probably reached via Persia and the North-Indian Buddhist empires into the world of forms of Hinduism. So the projections in the outer walls of the three sanctuaries resemble a multi-sided star in its design, formed from twisted squares. The column hall that unites the sanctuaries extends east into a portico. The whole structure is mounted on a platform, which surrounds the whole temple and repeats the outside projections. The perimeter walls are provided with secondary shrines and a cross-shaped gate construction. Three star-shaped main shrines have identical tower constructions which taper off towards the

above:
Three towers, at the sides and at the rear, are grouped around the centre of the Keshava Temple. They are on star-shaped bases equipped with an equally jagged outline. This refined complex forms the last highpoint of the development of medieval architecture in India.

top, and whose vertical structure continues up to the spires. In this respect the temple resembles the North-Indian Shikharas. The South-Indian element of the horizontal layering is found in the strong horizontal profiles of all construction units. The development of this special temple architectural style was brought to an end at the beginning of the 14th century by the Islamic invasion.

The temple was built from the light soapstone that is found in the surroundings of Somnathpur. It can be easily cut, chiseled or worked when freshly broken. The material allows exact detailed sculpture treatments with the possibility of deep undercutting. In the air it hardens and develops a black sheen.

Madurai (India): Gopuras
17th Century

left:
The South Indian place of pilgrimage, Madurai, became in the 17th century the site of an important temple city. At its centre is the square-plan twin temple of Meenakshi and Sundaresvara, whose surrounding walls are dominated by the 60 metre (197 ft.) high gate towers. These gopuras, with their rich relief ornamentation and magnificent paintwork, cast the shrine proper in their shadow.

Madurai, situated at the very south of the Indian subcontinent, is one of the biggest and most striking temple cities of the country and ranks as one of the oldest cities of the world. Its establishment was already mentioned in the Puranas, the legends from prehistoric time, and dates back to a sanctuary from the year 1600 BC. However, its current form essentially dates from the 17th century. The temple of Minakshi and Sundaresvara, in the centre of the city, is a regular structure of almost square layout. Three perimeter walls, so-called prakramas, extend the actual sanctuaries towards the outside. The much larger extended courts lend the temple an appearance of a walled – in fortress. The outstanding architectural feature of the walls are the tower gates, the Gopuras, through which one approaches the shrines step by step – incidentally, non-Hindus are only permitted access into the exterior court. With increasing distance from the cella, the towers become much bigger and finally dominate the whole structure. The actual inner, sanctuary is thereby placed in the shade and more or less removed from view. The temple city of Madurai possesses nine Gopuras, which are up to 60 metres high. The exterior four were built under Tirumala Nayaka between 1625 and 1660. The Gopuras are rectangular by design and have a central opening with wooden doors. Above that point rise peaked towers of varying size. Like the walls and the superstructure of the sanctuary, they are divided into several floors of repetitive stylistic features. On the spires the characteristic compass roofs are featured. The Gopuras are richly adorned: from every storey sculptures glitter from painted stucco and brick.

In the middle of the last century the temple structure of Madurai was restored. The question arose as to whether the Gopuras should be painted in its fabled bright colours. The answer was decided by a popular vote. The unambiguous vote was yes!

Lhasa (Tibet, China): Potala Palace
1600 – 1700

left:
The present-day appearance of the Dalai Lama's fortress-like palace, built high up on a mountain, is the result of a number of different building phases. The compound, which dates back to at least the 7th century, was decisively altered and extended in the 15th to 17th centuries. One of these additions was the 13-storey Red Palace, built after 1682, which towers over the rest of the buildings.

The sacred and the profane worlds in two palaces: the 400 metres (1,312 ft.) long and 13-storey tall building consists of the White Palace (approx. 1645 – 1690) and the Red Palace, which was first constructed after the death of the 5th Dalai Lama in 1682. The White Palace formerly housed the state authorities, the monks' dormitories and the Dalai Lama's living quarters. It encloses the Red Palace, which contains relics and the tombs of saints. The palace is reached via a series of gates and courtyards that were used for the religious celebrations that marked the events of the Buddhist calendar. The large eastern courtyard measures all of 16,000 square metres (172,226 sq. ft.). A raised platform divides the secular from the sacred area. All of the rooms and halls are decorated with a splendour and variety that would scarcely be guessed at on seeing the severe outer walls and simple façades. The walls and beams have been opulently painted. In many cases this ornamentation originates from Chinese and Indian forms. Apart from the murals, the rooms are decorated with silk tapestries, thangkas and mandalas, as well as cloth coverings on the columns. The architectural elements inside the building are largely derived from China, although the beams and consoles have been adorned in a style that must be regarded as a Tibetan reinterpretation of Chinese forms. Similarly, the building's exterior architecture also combines Chinese and Tibetan elements. The curved hipped or pitched roofs on the main halls are Chinese in style, while the ornately gilded turrets on the shrines and halls have been decorated in the Tibetan manner.

Work commenced on the enormous palace under the reign of the 5th Dalai Lama. It is a combination of temple, residential building and symbol of power. Like the majority of Tibetan buildings, its ground plan is asymmetrical. The four-storey complexes, which differ from one another in colour, rise some 200 metres (656 ft.) above the mountain slope. With the Chinese occupation of Tibet, the 14th Dalai Lama was forced to take flight from Potala Palace in March 1959. He now lives in exile in India.

Ise (Japan): Shintô Shrines
1st Century, 5th Century

Japan is a country of wonderful contradictions. While Tôkyô presents itself as a super – modern metropolis, other areas can be found in which traditional elements persist to this day. The fact that it is not always the real historical substance, but rather the traditional image, that continues to exist, is impressively proved by the shrines of Ise, the most important Shintô religious sites. Once the original religion of Japan, Shintô was later modified by Buddhism. The shrines of Ise, however, date back to the pre-Buddhist period: the innner shrine, containing the octagonal mirror which represents the goddess Amaterasu, has existed since the time of Christ, the outer shrine was created some 500 years later and within a few miles' distance. Since the late 7th century both of the shrines have been torn down every 20 years and re-built in absolutely the same form, using new materials, on an adjacent site – the last time was in 1993. This has allowed the method and the form of its construction to be passed down to us without change. The Naiku Shrine, in which the sun goddess Amaterasu is honoured, can be found in Ise around 100 kilometres from Nagoya on the Pacific Ocean bay of the same name. The shrine itself can be entered by priests only. It is built on stilts of cypress and elm, the roof is thatched and there is a gallery around the exterior of the one-storey building. It reflects the earliest form of construction in Japan and its clean lines still fascinate architects today. A stairway provides access to the platform on which the shrine is set. Every element is determined by the logic of wooden construction. The long rafters ('chigi') that point up to the sky and the round wooden logs ('katsuogi') that straddle the ridge of the roof originally served to stabilize the structure, but in the meantime they have become decorative elements in their own right. The shrine's Shinôtist design, called 'shinmei-zukuri', has become a typical form of Shintô construction and therefore may not be reproduced outside of Ise.

The main shrine in the Naiku district of Ise is dedicated to the sun goddess Amaterasu – an ancient descendant of the Japanese Imperial Family. The type of Shintô shrine found in Ise presumably developed from the local form of imperial palace architecture. Clay models, found during archaeological excavations, support this theory.

Kyoto (Japan): Kiyomizu-dera Temple
1633

left:
A temple was said to have stood here long before the city was founded. Asian monasteries take note of the form of their surroundings, thanks to the way they allocate functions to individual buildings. This is in contrast to monasteries in the West, with their rigid form of rooms arranged around the cloister.

Unlike other famous temples, Kiyomizu-dera does not belong to any particular sect, but appears rather to be common property. For over 1,000 years, pilgrims have climbed the hill in order to pray to the wooden statue of the 11-headed Kannon-, an incarnation of Buddha as the embodiment of mercy, and to drink from the sacred fountain: kiyomizu means "pure water." The shrine is located on a mountain and faces away from the city. It is reached through a temple suburb with gateways, a bell tower and a three-tier pagoda. The two-storey main gate to the west of the site is flanked on both sides by the figures of temple guards, so-called Kongo Rikishi. From here a path leads to the outer shrine and then back to the entrance. The increase in the location's holiness is clearly demonstrated by the long path, with its gates and twists in various directions. The forecourt of the main temple is in the form of a platform above a cliff. The veranda, which is built 50 metres (164 ft.) above the ground on a tall wooden substructure like a stilt house, is a marvel of Japanese carpentry. Thanks to this overhang, the countryside that it faces is transformed into a three-dimensional still life, for the direction in which the pilgrims pray and look is at right angles to the direction in which they walk. The present buildings date from 1633, and go back to the founding of the temple in 805. They are characteristic of the Momoyama Period, which lasted from 1568 to 1615. This brought to a conclusion a particular kind of person in Japanese culture – one who was essentially formed by the atmosphere of palaces and cloisters. The 17th century already marked the beginnings of an urban culture.

Kyôto (Japan)
The Stone Garden of the Ryôan-ji Temple
ca. 1499

The stone garden of the Ryôan-ji Temple, which is located northwest of Kyôto, is considered one of the most impressive and simultaneously one of the most enigmatic artefacts of Japanese culture. As early as 1873, a local scholar admitted that he was unable to fathom the garden. Kyôto, which was still called Heiankyô in the 19th century, was the seat of the Japanese emperor for 794 years, until 1868 when Tôkyô became the capital city. It is the only major city in the country with a population numbering in the millions that was completely spared destruction in the Second World War, and it is therefore the real seat of Japanese tradition. In keeping with Chinese ideals, streets laid out in a grid at right angles still determine the pattern of settlement which originally measured approximately five by five kilometres. Most of the temples are to be found to the north and west, on the slopes of the hills surrounding the valley in which the city is located. The grounds of the Ryôan-ji Temple would not be considered one of the most important sights in the city if not for the Zen garden supposedly attributed to Sôami, the famous painter and garden planner who died in 1525. Fifteen large stones are distributed in groups of 5, 2, 3, 2, and 3 over an area measuring 30 by 10 metres. They rise like moss-covered islands in a sea of accurately raked white stones. The rectangular garden area is surrounded at the back by an earthen wall and on the temple's side by a wooden terrace from which visitors can view the ensemble. There is, however, no position from which one can see all of the stones at once. As a strictly formal garden intended for meditation, it can neither be entered nor does it lend itself readily to interpretation, even when one is aware of the fact that the individual elements stand for mountains, water and islands and therefore depict an entire cosmos en miniature.

Zen Buddhism reached Japan at the end of the 12th century and initially found adherents among the local warlords who then ruled the country. The most important cultural artefacts are what were to become the meditating gardens, of which many are located near Kyôto, and which manifest the immaterial essence of Zen Buddhism in their abstract form and encourage individual contemplation.

Himeji (Honshu, Japan): Palace
1601 – 1609

left:
The largest and most impressive of the nine fortress complexes that have been preserved to this day in Japan, the palace was decisively reconstructed and expanded in the early 17th century. One of these additions was the five-storey main tower at the centre of the complex. Its silhouette, determined by the lines of the surrounding roofs, is reminiscent of pagoda architecture.

Due to its snow-white towers and walls which rise like a bird floating in the sky behind the enormous stone walls, the Japanese also name it "Palace of the White Heron": the palace of Himeji is the most characteristic and impressive of twelve remaining Samurai castles in Japan. Like all other buildings, this also reverts to an earlier fortress from the fourteenth century based on construction principles that were brought to the country by the Portuguese. The impressive castles appeared, however, only after the inner turmoil ceased. Himeji offers one of the best examples of a defensive establishment. A labyrinth of outposts, passages and entrances to confuse the enemy. More than ten gates of different construction had to be crossed in order to reach the main tower in the inner citadel. The feudal lords used them while under siege or for military exercises. Once the five-storey tower accommodated the armoury. For defensive purposes it was equipped with portholes and slits through which aggressors could be repelled with stones or boiling oil. Samurai castles are famous for their elegantly concave curved walls that were also intended to frustrate their surmounting by invaders. The empty basement of the main tower is built from stone; the wooden building on top is covered with heavy layers of brilliantly white plaster-work as a fire retardant. Today there is a museum in the palace with objects to illustrate life in the castle; e.g. Samurai weapons and armour.

The first Samurai castles were used exclusively for purposes of war and were thus built mostly on hills. However, after the end of their defensive function they continued to exist as a certain typological form with all their stylistic peculiarities. They were also later established in unprotected valleys, still with thick walls and towers, sometimes also with moats. In this form they were soon developed into administrative, trade and cultural centres.

Kyôto (Japan): Katsura Villa
1615 – 1663

"Pure unadorned architecture ... the fulfilment of modern desire ... so beautiful one could cry," such were the notes made by the German architect Bruno Taut when he first visited the Katsura Villa after his emigration to Japan in 1933. Present day visitors still find the gardens to the southwest of Kyôto, with their pavilions, tea-houses and residences grouped around a winding pond, to be the perfect union of art and nature. With its variety ranging from gentle landscapes on the water's edge to an arrangement of stones, the park represents the whole world on a small scale. In addition, there is the clean and elegant building style that Taut perceived as "absolutely

modern". Indeed, the construction of the palace at Katsura followed criteria that were often enthusiastically espoused by modern architects in the 20th century – at the same time the traditional Japanese house found its most ideal form here. The manner in which the villa was constructed can be clearly recognized because of its exposed wooden frame. The separation of the rooms by sliding walls and doors allows for a maximum of flexibility in the floor plan as well as for optimal ventilation. It also makes it possible to open the interior of the building to nature. The builders achieved a decorative effect simply through the materials they used: unfinished wood, ochre

above:
The villa from the Edo period rises above a ground plan that is stepped and very right-angled.
All rooms are linked together with sliding doors and are also opened to the garden. The
modern architecture of the early 20th century found a model in these villas, both in terms of
their simple strictness, without symmetrical dictates, and their flexible use of space.

coloured plaster, and rice paper doors. For a long time
the Katsura complex was considered to be the work of
the famous Japanese garden planner Kobori Enshû. Now
it is clear that two of the garden's commissioners were
also intensely involved in its design: Prince Toshihito,
who began the building around 1615, and his son,
Toshitada, under whom it was completed in 1663.
Compared with the fortresses built by the new Tokugawa
rulers with the intention of manifesting their power, the
Katsura Villa demonstrates a culture of highest courtly
refinement.

"Harmony, respect and purity in perfect balance
lead to silence," such is the description of the
Japanese tea-ceremony provided by one of its
masters, Sen no Rikyû, in the 16th century. Special
little houses were built for this practice of spiritual
cleansing; in the park of the Katsura Villa alone
there are four tea-houses. Traditionally, one entered
the tea-house bowing at the waist through an extremely low door; the interior rooms intended for
the meditative ceremony itself are small and simple,
but exhibit harmonious proportions.

Java (Indonesia): Borobudur
8th – 9th Century

left:
The seven-stepped pyramid-like monument was built between 780 and 850 AD above a mandala-formed ground plan 118 metres (387 ft.) in diameter. Four roughly square levels and three round ones form the substructure for the central stupa. It is surrounded by 72 stupas, containing seated Buddha figures, ordered concentrically and partially opened in an artistic manner.

The Borobudur in central Java, close to the city of Yogakarta, is considered to be the biggest Buddhist monument outside of India. Possibly between 780 and 850 AD, during the Sailendra dynasty, the Stupa Borobudur had its origins. At that time different cultural and religious movements, particularly from India influenced Java. During the 19th century it was rediscovered and finally restored during the 20th century at great expenditure, and today this site belongs to the world cultural heritage. Borobudur cannot be called a temple in the real sense, because it does not possess interiors. In reality it is a stepped pyramid aligned in four directions extending over nine terraces. From the 123 metres (135 yds.) square base that comprises 36 divisions, axially arranged steep steps lead up to the head stupa. The east steps represent the central access point. The cosmic spheres, khamadhatu (sphere of desire), rupadhatu (sphere of form) and arupadhatu (sphere of formlessness) divide the construction body into three sections and symbolize the way of knowledge to redemption. A 2.5 kilometre (1.6 miles) long band of relief's reflecting scenes from the life of Buddha accompanies the journey of the pilgrim to Arupadhatu. 72 stupas, which are latticed, pierced bell-shaped stones containing figures of the meditating Buddha, accompany the decorative reliefs to illustrate the contrast of body and spirit. The pilgrimage ends in the eight metres (26 ft.) high head stupa in the interior of which rests a Buddha figure, strangely unfinished.

According to the legend, it was Buddha himself who created the form of the stupa. He took his garment and folded it up into a type of hill on which he placed an upturned begging bowl topped with a small stick. This is how the subdivision into three spheres supposedly came about.

Java (Indonesia): Prambanan
10th Century

left:
In its lower layers, this step pyramid is built of quadratic terraces. That is followed by three further terrace steps with a round ground plan. Their small stupas prepare the main stupa, albeit without the crown it originally had.

To the south of the Merapi volcano (Central Java), surrounded by paddy fields, lies the biggest Shivaistic temple arrangement of Indonesia, the Prambanan. It was started in the eighth century and completed approximately in 915. The construction falls under the epoch of the syncretism. This can be ascribed to its close proximity to Borobudur and the same time period. Evidently both buildings were worked on at the same time for Shiva's as well as for Buddha's supporters. The complex is built on a right-angled base consisting of eight temples. These were surrounded by 156 shrines, most of which have been destroyed. The symbolism of the arrangement is based on Hindu belief according to which a highest divinity exists which adopts three embodiments on earth as trimurti: as a Brahma, Vishnu or Shiva. The main temple, Lara Jonggrang, is consecrated to Shiva and is the best preserved. Here, as a clear analogy to Borobudur, the vertical tri-section also serves as a symbol of the cosmos. The temple depicts four cellae of which the main chamber is adorned with rich ornamentation. A three metres (10 ft.) high statue of Shiva stands guard at the rear wall. To the south of the building lies the Brahma temple, to the north the Vishnu. Both possessed one cella and have been substantially destroyed. Confronting these three sanctuaries were the temples of the mystic riding animals of the Trimurti of which only one still exists. On the side of the terrace were two small temples which probably served as a treasury.

In reality the main temple does not lie in the intersection of the terrace's diagonals. During restoration works, an urn with grave accoutrements was discovered in the intersection (under a statue). The building is believed to be a tomb for kings and monarchs.

Angkor (Cambodia): Angkor Vat
12th century AD

The city of Angkor was founded around 889 AD as the capital of the Khmer Empire. It was characterized from the very start by extreme artifice, and was planned to the finest constructional detail. In 1431, Angkor was conquered by the Thai and then gradually abandoned. Away from all of the modern trade routes, the area was reclaimed by the tropical rain forest. It was only rediscovered in 1860, by the Frenchman Henri Mouhot, who was mapping the area for the French Indo-Chinese government.

A masterpiece of classic Khmer architecture is Angkor Vat, to the south of the city centre. This funerary temple was built under King Suryavarm II with the intention of besto-

wing him with immortality, and simultaneously as a shrine to the Vishnu cult. The construction is set on a rectangle that was originally surrounded by a 200 metres (656 ft.) wide artificial moat. The central building was built symmetrically on stepped platforms that rise up to the 65 metres (213 ft.) tall central tower. The four corner towers are linked on each step in concentric rings by long covered galleries with rectangular columns. A broad causeway leads through a monumental gate to the entrance.

The building materials consisted of wood, bricks, and above all sandstone. Despite their competence in perspective and construction, the Khmer master builders lacked

above:
The great Angkor Vat Temple, which is the centre of a large city complex, is not only the largest but also the most beautiful of all the temples built on the Indo-Chinese peninsula. The four corner towers of the central building, which is set symmetrically on stepped platforms, are grouped around the main tower, which measures 65 metres (213 ft.).

sufficient experience with stone. They simply treated it as they did their customary building material – wood – and thus fitted it with joints and wedges. The visual effect was excellent, but the results for the construction were fatal: because even the simplest connecting elements were missing or wrongly attached, the walls were bound sooner or later to collapse.

Angkor Vat is a self-contained fantasy world that boasts a riot of sculpted decorations and carvings. Particularly outstanding is the intricate, interwoven figurative frieze over 500 metres (1,640 ft.) long, which runs around the inside of the gallery of the central sanctuary. The name Angkor Vat came into being when it was transformed into a Buddhist temple, and approximately means: "The Royal City that was transformed into a Buddhist temple."

Angkor Thom (Cambodia): Bayon Temple
13th Century

left:
This Buddhist temple, built around 1200, is the last important example of Khmer architecture. The central shrine that rises up 42 metres (138 ft.) is surrounded by eight auxiliary chapels in a radial arrangement. The most poignant feature of the temple are the towers of faces. Each has four enormous faces directed toward each of the four directions on the compass. They depict King Jayavarman VII as Buddha.

The most original and highly expressive buildings ever created by the Khmer: even though their execution leaves much to be desired – in contrast to Angkor Vat, the architecture of the Angkor Thom is virtually of a baroque fullness. The building of Angkor Thom was begun under king Jayavarman VII around 1200. The city forms a square with a side elevation of 3 kilometres (2 miles) surrounded by a 100 metres (110 yds.) wide moat. The architecture of the city reaches its climax in Bayon that simultaneously forms the centre. It stands in great contrast to the clearly arranged and near-professionalism of Angkor Vat. Its original building plan was constantly supplemented and amended during the course of construction. This led to a very multi-layered, complicated structure, rich in forms, which no longer had anything in common with the classic Khmer epoch characterized by clear geometrical forms, but was nonetheless a magnificent and unique creation. Originally planned as a flat-roofed temple, Bayon has finally become a temple mountain whose central tower rises 42 metres (46 yds.) high. This round temple, following the Mandala of Buddhism, is a very complex construction and consists of a central chapel with eight radially arranged adjacent chapels as well as an anteroom and cella. Its five adjacent towers reveal altogether 216 bright gigantic faces of King Jayavarman VII sunk in meditation as a Buddha. The borders of architecture are transgressed with them and the distinction becomes blurred between building and sculpture and is even dispensed with.

Angkor Thom is a gigantic chaos of stone with an overwhelming diversity of form: Imposing corner towers and triple Gopuram extend over its perimeter and to the altogether sixteen face-adorned towers are added still more in simpler forms which collectively form something resembling a forest.

Rangoon (Burma): Shwe Dagon-Pagode
14th Century

left:
The Shwe Dagon Pagoda is the most-admired religious building in Burma. It was only constructed in its present form in 1564. The building is gilded on the outside, 115 metres (377 ft.) high, and rises above two terraces directionally aligned. A covered walk with praying halls, small votive stupas, and numerous Buddha figures leads around the pagoda.

The stupa Shwe Dagon in Rangoon is an unusual monument of Buddhist sacred architecture and was mentioned for the first time in the 14th century. In the ensuing time, which was characterized by family disputes, the Shwe Dagon underwent several structural changes. In the middle of the 15th century it was gilded on the orders of queen Shinsawbu. It was rebuilt after an earthquake in the sixteenth century and finally received its present form in 1768 under king Hsinbyushin. Surrounded by 64 small and 4 bigger stupas, the bell stupa – which was inspired by the Indian language of forms – is the core of the sanctuary. Starting from a square, 6.4 metres (21 ft.) high base, it tapers off immediately to adopt a concave line. Three terraces lead to the "round band zone" from where, finally, the bell zone arises. At the top it connects with the zone of the wound turban, the "lotus zone" with symbolic ornamentation, the "banana bud" and, finally, the screen that is a type of crown with seven floors, which tapers towards the top. These are adorned with small bells and banyan leaves (Buddha allegedly found his inspiration under a banyan or fig tree). Above the "weathervane" is the "diamond bud" at a height of 99.4 metres (109 yds.) which is decorated with precious stone to form the crowning conclusion. In spite of the numerous zones and square as opposed to bell-shaped base, the monument has a harmonious overall effect. The master builders achieved the optical impression of a round building by gradating the corners. The proportions and the magnificent exhibits serve to make the whole composition of Shwe Dagon the most famous stupa in Burma.

Due to its religious importance, the Shwe Dagon also attained national importance: When the British occupied the stupa hill for strategic reasons during the colonial era in the 19th century, it became the focal point of resistance.

Seoul (Korea): Ch'angdokkung Palace
1405 – 1412 /17th century

left:
The highpoint of Ch`ang-dokkung Palace is the "secret garden", with its stone and wooden bridges, pavilions and other small buildings, it is the quintessence of a landscape garden.

The Ch'angdokkung Palace is one of the most impressive monuments in Korea. It was used for the greater part of the Yi dynasty (1392 – 1910) as the main palace, although it was never planned as such. The third king of the T'aejong Dynasty (rule: 1400 – 1418) had it built as a secondary palace after moving the capital in 1404 from Songdo back to Hanyang (Seoul). During the Japanese occupation from 1592 to 1598, this palace was destroyed alongside the main palace (Kyongbokkung). Unlike the latter, Ch'angdokkung was rebuilt between 1607 and 1610. During the revolt of King Injo (rule: 1623 – 1647), the complex was again destroyed by fire and rebuilt in 1647. While a main palace would have required strict symmetry, this was not necessary for the "Palace of Illustrious Virtue." This is the reason why a complex could develop in which 20 or more individual, different-sized buildings nestle around the uneven landscape at their midst. The palace area is reached by the oldest stone bridge in Seoul, the Geumcheon-gyo bridge, whose sculptures show bestiaries intended to ward off evil, and then through the Great Gate, which was completed seven years after the actual palace grounds. The numerous halls and pavilions each served different purposes in the court protocol and daily course of events.

Only the small audience chamber Soniongjon was roofed with bluish-green tiles, which were reserved solely for the king. The highpoint is the "secret garden," the Huwon, which occupies by far the largest part of the 405,000 square metres (4,359,461 sq. ft.) palace grounds. With its stone and wooden bridges, pavilions and other small buildings, it is the quintessence of a landscape garden.

Scarcely anything has been changed in the site since the occupation of Korea by the Japanese in 1910. Consequently, it gives a picture of royal life at the dawn of the 20th century, complete with a vintage car standing in a garage converted from a hall.

Mesoamerica and the Cultures of the Andes

Mesoamerica and the Cultures of the Andes

The term Mesoamerica refers to the inhabited part of Central America of the pre-Columbian period. It stretches from present-day Mexico to Belize, and on to Honduras and El Salvador. Numerous peoples populated the area, including the Aztecs, Toltecs, Totonacs and Maya. The periods of advanced Mesoamerican civilizations are the "pre-classical period"(2000 BC to 300 AD), the "classical period" (300 – 900 AD), and the "post-classical period" (900 – 1520). Each of these three periods is further divided into early, middle and late phases. Despite all the differences between the various peoples and periods, the similarities in the buildings can be attributed to mutually shared cultural factors: the kinship of the religious systems, the Neolithic stage technology and the late introduction of metalworking. The pyramid is the most important kind of building in Pre-Columbian Mesoamerica. It differs both in form and function from the Egyptian variety: truncated pyramids were set in several steps one on top of the another, and the top platform bore a temple or altar (nowadays generally missing). Unlike in Ancient Egypt, the pyramids rarely served as tombs, but instead were the "abodes of the gods," and consequently representations of the mountain conceived of as heaven. Characteristic of the pyramids is that a new building was added to the top on the regularly occurring dates for world renewal, as set down in the ceremonial calendar. Closely connected with them was the sacred ball game pelote, for which sacred ball courts – rectangular, often lower-set fields – were specially laid out. The uniformity of Mesoamerican architecture is revealed not only in the kinds of buildings and their functions. The recurring forms of their arrangement (geographical alignment) and certain building techniques (cut stone with lime stucco, etc.) are also clearly recognizable. The pre-Columbian building complexes that have been preserved were centres of worship or administration, surrounded by residential buildings. Apart from the Mesoamerican civilizations, South America was also home to the Andes cultures of the Incas. The culture of the Incas is split into four periods, each with four horizons. At the end of the "pre-ceramic period" (2500 – 1900 BC), the first large building for ritual and social representation was built on the Peruvian coast. The first irrigation systems date back to the "initial period" (1900 – 1200 BC). At the middle of the "early horizon" (1200-300 BC) came the cultures of the Chavin, who are named after their centre in North Peru. The "early intermediate period"

(300 BC – 600 AD) witnessed the development of various regional styles of art and craft skills. The "middle horizon" (600 – 1000) spread out from the basin of Lake Titicaca. In the "late intermediate period" (1000 – 1476), buildings made of unfired mud bricks were built along the coasts. Around 1300 the Incas founded the capital of Cuzco, and extended their dominion over other peoples. They reached their apogee during the "late horizon" (1476 – 1532), when they constructed monumental stone buildings, particularly in the highlands.The rectangular stone house was the basic model for their temples and palaces, which were mostly planned and built in connection with fortifications and residential areas. The Incas linked their towns by means of a network of roads. Characteristic of Inca architecture is the use of large stone ashlars, which were fitted together without mortar. The façades are interspersed by trapezoid doors and windows. They laid out terraces for agriculture in the steep Andes valleys.

Teotihuacán (Mexico): Sun Pyramid
3rd Century

The classical cultures of Mesoamerica developed during the first centuries AD. In the broad, high-lying valleys, which seemed to be made for sedentary farming, Teotihuacán developed into the largest centre of this civilization, and today remains the epitome of a glorious past. The ruins of the extensive pyramid site are situated some 50 kilometres (31 miles) northeast of Mexico City. Nothing is known of the erstwhile inhabitants, for even the Aztecs had no more than memories of the former metropolis. It may be assumed that the centre of Teotihuacán already existed by 300 BC as a small place of pilgrimage. The first-known buildings date from the

period around 100 BC. The city reached its heyday around 500, when it had some 150,000 inhabitants. The sacred area of Teotihuacán, which is a little less than five square kilometres (1.9 square miles) in size, is the setting for the giant Sun Pyramid. With a height of 65 metres (213 ft.) and a length of 220 metres (722 ft.) at its base, it is the largest pyramid to be erected in one period in Mesoamerica. It was built of one million cubic metres (approx. 35 million cubic ft.) of adobe brick. The overall form is created by five increasingly small, truncated pyramids placed one on top of the other. To the west is a large frontal structure consisting of several terraces

above:
The pyramid of the sun, built in the 3rd century, was probably the largest building of the city development. It is 200 square metres (2153 sq. ft.) at the base, 64 metres (210 ft.) high, and was aligned along a ceremonial street. The building was constructed with air-dried tiles and consists of five receding pyramid steps. A temple originally crowning the pyramid has not been preserved.

and a stairway. Nothing remains of the temple, which originally must have been located on the upper platform. The main façade of the pyramid faced the point where the sun descends on the day it passes its zenith. All of the other ceremonial buildings, as well as the Avenue of the Dead, are pointed in the same direction. Originally the friezes and plinths of the buildings were adorned with continual reliefs depicting feathered serpents and heads of the rain god Tlaloc.

The city received its present name Teotihuacán from the Aztecs. It means "Place of those who have become gods," and expresses the conviction that the existent world came into being in Teotihuacán. With the appearance of the Toltecs at the beginning of the 9th century, the classic city of Teotihuacán was destroyed.

El Tajín, Veracruz (Mexico): Pyramid of Niches
7th Century

El Tajín, or "Lightning Bolt," was the name given by the Totonacs to their capital, which is situated some 10 kilometres (6.2 miles) southeast of Poza Rica, close to the central Gulf Coast. This classic civilization flowered between 100 and 900 AD, and underwent a renaissance from the 11th century, before the city was deserted in the 13th century. Today parts of the site are overgrown by dense tropical vegetation. The actual centre of El Tajín lies between two rivers. The pyramids and platforms are grouped around open spaces. The best-preserved construction among the ruins on the 95 hectare (approx. 220 acres) site is the 25 metre (82 ft.) tall, seven-stepped niche pyramid from the 7th century. It is built on a more or less square base. The upper platform is set above six terraced steps and bears a flat temple, which was dedicated to the god of lightning and whirlwinds. Particularly remarkable about this pyramid is its method of construction: its outer walls were formed from layered slabs of sedimentary rock. The vertical, upper parts of the landings are adorned with square niches. A cornice consisting of a stone plate marks the tops of the niches. Presumably an additional niche formed the temple on the apex. The motif also appears elsewhere: five projections each with three niches divide up the length of the central stairway. The total of 365 niches is probably intended to symbolize the days of the year. Nothing remains of the pyramid's original frescoes, which were executed in many colours. Like many other pre-Columbian edifices, El Tajín is a calendar building.

The Mexican Gulf Coast is still not yet popular with tourists. El Tajín, the most often visited by travellers is hidden away here in the jungle. Only a small part has been excavated. Apart from the Niche Pyramid, it is also famous for its reliefs showing the sacred ball game.

Uxmal (Mexico): Palace of the Governor

A centre for ceremonies and the administrative hub of the surrounding towns: Uxmal, situated about 80 kilometres (50 miles) south of Mérida, is built largely in the style of the Puuc (land of the low hill ranges) from the late classic Maya Period. According to legend, a dwarf whom his witch-mother hatched from an egg created it in just one night. The Puuc style distinguishes itself by its smooth walls, which were fashioned by the technique of veneer masonry (encasing rough wall fillings with finely cut squares of limestone). The walls were decorated with friezes, which were separated by a cornice from the otherwise plain wall surface. Uxmal reached its peak between 800 and 1000 AD, and for

reasons unknown was abandoned around 1150. Standing at the entrance to the site is the oval-plan Pyramid of the Magician. On a terrace to the south of this is the 96 metres (315 ft.) long, 12 metres (39 ft.) wide, and eight metres (26 ft.) tall Palace of the Governor. It was built between the 10th and 11th centuries, and consists of a central tract 55 metres (180 ft.) long and two wings measuring 15 metres (49 ft.), which are connected by means of vaults. Set before the central building is a monumental stairway. Eleven entrances in the building's plinth lead to chambers. The palace's smooth walls are decorated by an almost four metres (13 ft.) wide relief frieze, consisting of geometrical patterns

above:
The most impressive building of the ceremonial centre of the Maya is the Governor's Palace lying on a huge platform. This shows an over 3.5 metre (11 ft.) high mosaic frieze above an undivided wall opened up with rectangular spaces. Its figurative and geometric depictions are composed of 20,000 individual stones.

and figures made of some 20,000 mosaic elements. Beside the palace is a small temple with a cornice of sculpted turtles. Also of note are the so-called "Nunnery Quadrangle" and the "Dovecot," whose name is derived from its toothed roof construction.

In the Mayan language Uxmal means "thrice built," and was only first excavated in 1930. The sometimes richly ornamented relief friezes are seen at their best in the evening light, when the feathered serpents seem especially lifelike.

North Yucatan (Mexico)
Chichén Itzá Observatory
10th Century

left:

The 27 metres (89 ft.) high Caracol (snail) is the oldest building of the ceremonial centre, founded by the Maya in the 5th century. The round tower is named after the interior spiral staircase. It was erected above a two-level terrace, whose upper platform was reached via open stairs, which were set against each other. The upper storey of the tower is badly damaged, but the ordering of the windows in accordance with astronomic criteria allows us to conclude that it was used as an observatory.

Chichén Itzá ("At the fountain of Itzá") was founded in the 5th century by the Maya as a place of worship for their rain god. Around 1000 the Toltec tribe of the Itzá migrated from the highlands of Central Mexico and conquered the Maya. The following two centuries saw the construction of enormous buildings. Chichén Itzá had already been partly abandoned by its inhabitants as the Spaniards reached the location in 1546. For many centuries the site, located 120 kilometres (75 miles) east of Mérida, remained forgotten, before being rediscovered in 1841 by British archaeologists. Only some 25 of the hundreds of buildings that are buried under the jungle have been uncovered and in some cases restored. The oldest building of Chichén Itzá, from the time of the Toltecs, is the 28 metres (92 ft.) tall Caracol ("snail"), a circular tower on a two-stepped terrace on the south side of the area. Inside is a narrow spiral ramp, which gives the tower its name. The building has a diameter of 18 metres (59 ft.) at its base, and tapers to 14 metres (46 ft.) diameter at the top, having an overall height of 11 metres (36 ft.). The roof bears the remnants of a small circular building. Seven narrow, rectangular openings in the heavily damaged upper storey are directed to points of astronomical importance – the Caracol was used as an observatory. At the centre of Chichén Itzá is the 30 metres (98 ft.) tall step-pyramid of Kukulcán. 365 steps lead up to its upper platform, symbolizing the days of the year.

The stone serpents' heads at the northern portal of the Kukulcán Pyramid ("Feathered Snake") produce an impressive play of shadows by both day and night. With the changing position of the sun, the heads become almost lifelike. Bodies appear to slowly wind their way down the steps – like the descent of the god Kukulcán.

Machu Picchu (Peru): Fortress City
around 1450 AD

Machu Picchu lies 112 kilometres (70 miles) away from Cuzco, 2,450 metres (8,038 ft.) above sea-level on a high saddle in the Andes. On three sides of the town the land drops some 500 metres (1,640 ft.) to the Rio Urubamba. The 15th-century site served as a border fort, and was connected to the outside world by one single path. For over four centuries the city was unknown to the Western World, before its "discovery" in 1911 by Hiram Bingham. In 1983, Machu Picchu was placed on the UNESCO World Heritage list. The Inca town is approximately 900 metres (2,953 ft.) long and 500 metres (1,640 ft.) wide. Spread along spacious terraces are three main complexes of 216 buildings, palaces and temples: the upper town or royal quarter, the sacred district and the lower town. The three-stepped rectangular Intipampa Plaza separates the upper and lower towns. The area can be reached by over 100 flights of stairs. Standing in the royal or palace quarter of Hana is the famous semi-circular military tower. Not far from this are the palace of the princess and the royal palace. Behind the palace quarter is the sacred district with the Intihuantana, a solar observatory carved from the rock. To the east of the district is the "Temple of Three Windows." Facing the upper town is the lower town, Hurin, with residential, prison and storage areas. The narrow residential areas optimally exploit the space on the terraces. Machu Picchu is surrounded by hanging gardens.

The Incas were the strongest power in South America. In the mid-15th century, during what is termed the "Late Horizon," they created monumental stone constructions: polygonal blocks of rock were placed together without mortar, so that the joints fitted to the millimetre. Presumably the Incas found these in natural quarries and first transported the roughly hewn rocks and then cut their surfaces at the construction site to produce an exact fit.

Pre-Roman,
Roman and
Gothic Architecture

Pre-Roman, Roman, and Gothic Architecture

Pre-Roman

While in Byzantium architecture progressed further, in the West Roman territory it initially stagnated. Mainly smaller, very simple buildings were erected. Only the new techniques for constructing monasteries are noteworthy. These originated with the Benedictine Order (est. in 529), with the buildings arranged around the cloister. A new architecture was only developed with the Carolingian Renaissance. When the Roman Empire was realigned politically under Charles the Great, early central Christian buildings (Palatinate Chapel, Aachen) basilicas (Seligan), and antique decorative schemes (Lorscher Gate Hall) emerged. Large crypts (Saint-Germain, Auxerre) and Westworks (Corvey) belong to the innovations of this time. The Ottonians built monumental buildings derived from this architecture, many with double choir arrangements and some already with Romanesque block capitals (Hildesheim). In addition, crossing (Gernrode) and division of the exterior building arrangement (Saint-Pantaleon, Cologne) were already in place.

Roman

In the Upper Rhine, Normandy, and Burgundy a much more pronounced systematization and division of interiors became evident at the turn of the millennium. The vault bay as a repetitive, limited space (Speyer I, Durham) became predominant prior to the development of the High Romanesque style. Furthermore, choir galleries with radial chapels (Tournus) and large hall crypts made an appearance in the early Romanesque era. At the end of the 11th century, the arch became a central theme (Speyer II). In Normandy (Caen) double tower façades and ribbed vaults illustrate two formulas that would determine the arch's subsequent development. An independent, structural component oriented to Antiquity is found in the buildings of the Proto Renaissance in Florence (baptistery). When the Gothic style made its appearance in France, the Romanesque idiom in Germany became increasingly excessive. However, with the Hirsauer reform monasteries (Alpirsbach) a tendency towards simplification was discernable.

Gothic

The Gothic manifested itself on the Ile-de-France as Normandian and Burgundian Romanesque. The choir of Saint-Denis can be considered a point of departure, but it took many more buildings (including the Nôtre Dame in Paris) to lead to the High Gothic style of Chartres and Reims. Compared to the decorative opulence of the late Romanesque, the early and classic Gothic can be viewed as a logical, sober style. In Rayonnant (from 1270) and Flamboyant (from 1370), the interest in decoration became increasingly important, with the tracery being the central decorative motif in a building style that increasingly used glass (Sainte-Chapelle, Paris). A reduced form of the Gothic dominates the architecture of the Cistercians (Eberbach), who played an important role in the expansion of Gothic with their cloister affiliations. In England, meanwhile, Gothic forms were already established by the end of the 12th century and developed their own particular styles (Salisbury), while in Germany the opus franzegenum manifested itself more slowly. Gothic buildings in pure form can only be found after 1230 (Cologne), and individual developments appeared only at the end of the 13th century (Freiburg). In northern Europe a distinct form of brick Gothic appeared (Lübeck, Marienburg). In the Late Gothic period, when building activity came to a standstill in France during the Hundred Years War, the style progressed in the empire territories (Prague) with the Gothic halled church as a distinct form of construction (Swabia, Gmünd). The style repertoire was also adopted in secular buildings (Castel del Monte, Karlstein), and new building requirements came to the fore in the Late Gothic (civic buildings, warehouses, town halls, hospitals).

Aachen (Germany): The Palatine Chapel
790 – 805, Odo von Metz

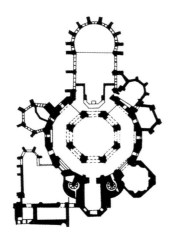

left:
The simply arranged apse of the Pfalzkapelle of Charles the Great was replaced under Charles IV by a high-Gothic glasshouse, whose walls are almost entirely covered in glass surfaces between the flying buttresses. The architectural godfather for this was Sainte-Chapelle in Paris, built more than 100 years beforehand under Louis.

After having spent the first year of his reign almost continuously underway, Charlemagne had Odo von Metz build a palatinate (imperial residence) for him in Aachen in 790. The Palatine chapel, as a symbolic structure and as the seat of imperial power, was intended to be the architectural highlight of this conglomeration of diverse buildings. The layout of this central-plan church, which was completed in 805, is inspired by Justinian architecture, examples of which – Hagios Sergios and Bakchos in Constantinople and, above all, San Vitale in Ravenna – can be seen as direct models. Like Ravenna, the octagonal central room is vaulted and surrounded by a cross-vaulted ambulatory which, however, is built over two storeys in Aachen. It opens up into the central room through round-arched arcades, which do not, as was the case with its early Byzantine predecessor, sweep out into the de-ambulatory. The different levels of the domed space and the ambulatories is also reflected in the exterior, the west side of which is accentuated by a tower and high portal niche. The rectangular Carolingian choir was replaced in the 14th century by a High Gothic one modelled after Sainte-Chapelle. Originally the emperor looked down on the once modestly proportioned choir from the opposite gallery on which his throne stood. Charlemagne's Palatine Chapel soon took a prominent position in European architecture, a fact underlined by the large number of similar structures that followed, one such example worth mentioning is the abbey church in Ottmarsheim (ca. 1030).

The word platinate, derived from the Latin word "palatium", refers to a walled and imposing residence of a sovereign. As well as Aachen, there were a number of other important palatinates in the Carolingian period: Ingelheim, Frankfurt am Main, Worms and Nijmwegen. Among the palatinates of the Ottonian, Salian and Staufer periods, the following were noteworthy: Magdeburg, Quedlinburg, Gelnhausen, Nuremberg and Wimpfen.

Michaelisplatz

Hildesheim (Germany): St Michael
1010 – 1033, Bishop Bernward

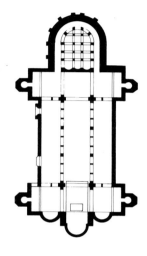

left:
The basilica, which was built between 1010 and 1033, shows from the outside an assemblage of unarticulated structures that seem to produce an additive effect.
Square crossing towers mark the point of intersection of the nave and the two transepts, thus emphasizing the double choir so typical of early mediaeval architecture. Their bipolarity is further emphasized by the polygonal stair towers with their rounded tops, which stand before the front side of the transepts.

Among the very few examples of Ottonian architecture that have been preserved, St Michael in Hildesheim is, along with St Cyriakus in Gernnrode, undoubtedly one of the most outstanding buildings of the age. The monastery to which the church belonged had been financed by Bishop Bernward of Hildesheim, in 996. As Otto III's chancellor and mentor he enjoyed a prominent position in Empress Theophanu's court. The church, which was begun in 1010, would ultimately serve as a final resting place for Bernward (whom his biographer characterized as a man "of great learning, experienced in the art and science of bronze casting and in every aspect of architecture"). The church is built as a basilica with a nave and two aisles. Its longitudinal axis is framed by two poles of equal architectural and religious importance. The fact that with these transepts structures of equal status intersect the nave is expressed by the wide arches at their crossings that are of the same height as the rest of the church. The pilasters and columns in the nave, that alternate according to the Saxonian system, determine the rhythm of the interior and indicate that the series of bays typical of Romanesque architecture was in the offing. Hence, the quadratic pilasters in the central nave define three squares, the modules of which are reflected again in the crossing and the arms of the transepts. Other elements found here, the hall-like crypt and the block capital, were destined to be emulated in the architecture of the 11th and 12th centuries.

Bishop Bernward, a universal scholar, commissioned works of art – in the form of the Bernward Column and the bronze doors – that are still some of the most important examples of Ottonian sculpture and medieval bronze work. They reflect, along with illuminated manuscripts and smaller pieces of artwork, the style that came to be called "Bernwardian," after its patron, one of the most important schools of Ottonian art.

Caen (France): Sainte-Trinité
ca. 1060/65 – 1120

left:
The western façade of S. Trinité is one of the oldest preserved double tower façade of European architecture. It thus marks the start of the development of the front sides of early and high Gothic cathedrals in France and England. Powerful buttresses subdivide the main body into three zones, which continue on the outside as two powerful towers divided by blind arcades.

William the Conqueror and his wife, Mathilde, donated two abbey churches during the middle of the 11th century: the convent of Sainte-Trinité as well as the monk's abbey of Saint-Étienne. Both Romanesque monasteries were built possibly around 1060/65. Through them the architecture of Normandy reached its highest climax. Two towers dominate the west façade of Saint-Trinité – a widespread stylistic element of the Romanesque basilicas of Western and Northern Europe. The nave, built around 1075/85, consists of a main vessel and two aisles. Through the single nave transept, the layout of the church resembles a Latin cross. In the convent the main apse was enclosed by the side choirs. Earlier there was a split-level choir that was higher than the nave on account of the crypt. On the ground floor of the long choir the false arcade is still recognizable on the wall. These false arches are also to be found in the apse. Above it are windows of a simple design, and above these up till about 1100/10 was a barrel vault that was later dismantled. This flange arch can still be recognized. The nave of Saint-Trinité, unlike Sainte-Étienne, has no lofts, but a false triforium. From Burgundy new ideas arose concerning the construction of vaults and supports. This came about during the reconstruction of the nave at Saint-Étienne around 1120/25 by means of a six-sectioned ribbed vault. The cross ribs did not yet serve a weight-bearing function but probably a decorative one.

Also in England, where William the Conqueror became king (1066) following the battle of Hastings, attempts were made in the construction of ribbed vaults. The cathedral of Durham (1093 – 1130) possesses a six-sectioned ribbed vault. This achievement was an important milestone on the journey to Gothic architecture.

Tournus (France): Saint-Philibert Abbey
11th Century

left:

The sanctuary of St. Philibert is dominated by a monumental crossing tower. The choir bay and the apse are surrounded by an ambulatory set within the row of inner lateral aisles. Already adjoining the ambulatory, but not yet in the form of a closed ring, are the radial chapels that were to become a customary feature of the Gothic era. "Opus reticulatum" (rhomboid pattern masonry) on the high choir and fluted pilasters (upper storey of the tower, 12th century) allow the influence of Antiquity in Burgundy to be seen.

The façade of the former abbey church Saint-Philibert in Tournus is plain. Narrow openings project from the brickwork that consists of small, irregular stones: the methods used were favoured by the early Romanesque churches of southern France. The influence of Carolingian architecture is still easily discernible here. More impressive is the church's interior which was completed around 1066: imposingly built round pillars extend upwards from the central nave. They provide evidence that the master builders of Tournus must have given thought to the nature of the vault. They also came under the influence of the order reforms which emanated from the Burgundian Cluny around 1000. Originally the nave of the abbey was flat-roofed. After it was damaged at the beginning of the 11th century, the monks set about reconstructing it again around 1020/30. Another reconstruction followed in 1050. The sudden collapse of the barrel vault required further structural measures, possibly around 1070/80. A special solution was devised: a central nave curved by diagonal barrels in combination with cross-ridged, arched aisles. Consequently, the former abbey of Saint-Philibert belongs to the first churches whose triple nave was completely curved.

Saint-Philibert merges Carolingian and Romanesque structures; this is especially well illustrated in the choir gallery. From the nave the way leads over the crossing into the choir which is surrounded by a gallery. The apse adopts this semicircular form, but its three unconnected rectangular, radial chapels still date from the simple and severe pre-Romanesque times. The crypt is located beneath the whole complex of the choir, gallery and chapels.

Florence (Italy): Baptistery
ca. 1060 – 1150

left:
The baptistery is arranged octagonal, like the early Christian models. On the exterior buildings, there is that blind division borrowing from Antique models, which Brunelleschi and Alberti still believed to be from the old Roman Empire: Corinthian capitals, fluted pilaster, and aedicule framing of the window.

The Baptistery in Florence, once the centre of religious and cultural life in the city, took on its present form during the course of the 11th and 12th centuries. Various theories on how it came to be built on the site draw parallels to structures that played a central role in the latter days of ancient Rome. The stylistic vernacular of such structures was often quoted in early Christian baptisteries. The octagonal floor plan, the apsidal annex on the west side and the pyramid roof give a characteristic shape to the baptistery, which was originally set on a platform. This platform has been concealed since the surrounding streets were raised. The ornamentation of the façade with its white and green marble revetments (Marmo di Carrara and Marmo di Prato) can be found again at the Basilica di S. Minato al Monte and indicates that Florentine architecture continued to be orientated towards the traditions of ancient Rome. While the two-tone incrustations create an impression of the sort of plasticity found in classical architecture, they also negate its weight and consistency, serving only to delineate the individual segments and as decoration. The use of this classical technique is an example of the unique Tuscan form of Romanesque architecture described as Proto-Renaissance. At the same time it provided a preview of how façades would be arranged during the Renaissance. Panels of marble are again the essential element in the interior of the baptismal church, which is crowned by a large Byzantine-style mosaic that covers the entire ceiling of the dome.

The doors of the Baptistery by Lorenzo Ghiberti should also be noted. The first one was created after a competition held in 1401. "The Gates of Paradise," Ghiberti's most important work, was created by the artist between 1425 and 1452. It depicts scenes from the Old and New Testaments.

Speyer (Germany): Cathedral

1025 – 1106, Conrad II, Benno von Osnabrück, Otto von Bamberg

left:
Different elements struc-
ture the massive and
powerfully towering east
part of Speyer Cathedral.
There are simple round-
arch friezes between the
lesenes at the gable of
the choir and at the
upper stories of both
wing towers. However,
with the apse, which
arose after 1082, there is
a colossal blind arcade,
crowned by a dwarf
gallery.

In order to create a fitting tomb for the Salier dynasty, Kaiser Konrad had an early medieval church in Speyer replaced by a bishop's church in 1025. Its enormous dimensions, for the period in which it was built, were meant to architecturally document the imperial dynasty's claim to sovereignty. By the time it was finally consecrated, in 1061, a pilaster basilica with a nave and two aisles was created in which the long nave to the east opened up into a wide transept. A semi-circular choir continued on from its semi-truncated crossing. It was, in turn, flanked by angular towers. A monumental crypt hall extended under the entire eastern section. This was an innovation of similar importance in this period as were the dwarf galleries on the exterior of the embedded portal of the massive western section. Around 20 years after the completion of the early Romanesque building (Speyer I) Heinrich IV began its reconstruction (Speyer II) The plan adopted foresaw vaulting over all of the spaces and a heightening of the crossing by means of a cupola. The previously geometric patterns of the building's ornamentation was now replaced by more antique motifs. The greater monumentality is just as much an indication of the transition to High Romanesque as was the rhythm introduced by the cross-vaulting and the alternation of the wall patterns.

The cross-in-square plan refers to a layout that was common above all during the German Romanesque period. The nearly quadratic yoke of the nave is complimented by two quadratic transept yokes. An early form resulted from the vaulting later added on the central nave in Speyer and the consequent combination of what were originally pairs of rectangular yokes.

Alpirsbach (Germany): Monastery
1095 – 1125

left:
Work began on the church in 1095. It is probably the most impressive example of a successor building to St. Peter and Paul in Hirsau. As with all representatives of the Hirsau school of construction, an east wing in the form of a Benedictine choir is attached to a flat covered nave arranged as column basilica. The external building, altered into Gothic, is dominated by the flanking tower above the northern secondary choir.

The monastic church of Alpirsbach in the Black Forest belongs to one of the numerous monasteries which appeared at the end of 11th century amidst the background of reforms of the Benedictine Order, and its well preserved state makes it an excellent example of its epoch. Its establishment in 1095 falls within the time frame of the so-called Investiture Controversy. Under massive disputes, the emperor and pope argued not only about the right to occupy sacral offices, but also over the question of power. An important impulse for the execution of Alpirsbach came from the Hirsauer School of construction. The monastery of Hirsau, centre of the Benedictine Order, came under the influence of the reforms that were instituted after 1000 in France by the Burgundian monastery of Cluny. According to the rules of Benedict, the monks led a life of asceticism and meditation. Their architecture was severe and monumental: Flat-roofed church naves devoid of any painting or sculpture, with extremely steep rooms. The current monastic church was built approximately between 1125 and 1133. The first nave vault bay in front of the discarded crossing is prominent due to the side aisles, which reveal a barrel curvature, while the rest is flat-roofed. Due to this, the "chorus" which was east orientated was separated from the "chorus minor". Additional division took place by means of a choir barrier that no longer exists. Despite many alterations, the cloister in the centre of the cloister walk remains intact.

That Alpirsbach can look back on a long tradition as a monastery town is reflected in the community's coat of arms. Guests of the monastery complex can receive helpful assistance from the monastery museum, the information centre and the city's historical museum.

Durham (England): St Cuthbert
begun 1093

left:
The cathedral lies at the highest point in Durham above the River Wear. Its windows are contracted pair-wise, something only visible from outside. With six-part vaults this only makes sense above two bays each. However, in the nave now there are simple cross-rib vaults above just one bay. Does this mean that a curvature was planned from the very beginning?

The first Romanesque churches were erected in England in the pre-Norman period; however a more intensive building period only began after the Norman Conquest. Even before the Battle of Hastings (1066), the new rulers commissioned the first abbey. Traces of influence from Normandy can be found in the Norman architecture that followed, but it was more decorative than the Romanesque architecture on the Continent. In 1093 Bishop Carilef commissioned the construction of St Cuthbert. Large arcades with high, wide columns determine the impression made by the interior. Above it there is a gallery and the celestory with a walkway typical of Norman architecture (also in France). The middle nave is covered by a quadri-partite ribbed vault. The question as to which parts of the frontal elevation of the wall, as well as the vaulting, are original has been the subject of great controversy among art historians: ribbed vaulting, that was to become a determining element in the development of Gothic style, was created either here or in Caen, and that during the Romanesque period. Presumably it was only introduced in Durham later, or the plans for the completion of the nave were changed during the building process, around 1130. In this conjunction the upper storeys were adapted to fit the central nave, whereby its decoration was also changed. The opulent decoration of the interior also seems to indicate that the vaulting can be dated to around the middle of the 12th century, hence it would have been built shortly after the vaulting in Caen.

In contrast to barrel vaulting – and cross-vaulting is a form of barrel vaulting in which the vaults intersect – ribbed vaulting does not distribute the load over the entire wall of the high nave, but discharges it only at certain points in that the boss distributes the thrust to the ribs and these, in turn, distribute it to the walls. At these points reinforcements are needed, but the wall in between can be thinner. The earlier ribbed vaults, however, had more of a decorative than a static function.

Eberbach (Germany): Monastery
from about 1147

left:
The transept of the abbey church was built between 1178 and 1187 using proportions based on the crossing square. Its lack of any ornamental or figurative sculptures shows the typical severity of Cistercian architecture. This formal restraint also corresponds to the clear construction of the twin-sectioned wall. The transverse arches of the groin vault rest on vertical supports before the walls, which are bevelled off at the height of the impost in the arcade region so that they almost seem to be suspended from the vault.

The monastery complex of Eberbach belongs to the most important medieval monastery buildings of Europe and is, apart from Maulbronn, Germany's best-preserved Cistercian abbey. On account of its position in a wooded valley of the Rheingau, the monks were able to practise wine making and trade from its establishment in the 11th century right up to its dissolution in 1803. The abbey was established in 1135, during a period that was characterized by reform movements within the monasteries. To resist against a more profan order, they reverted back to the rule of the holy Benedict: "Ora et labora". The Cistercians adhered to them severely, and strictly adopted these ideals in their architecture. The basilica, an impressive example in the romantic style and barely changed architecture, clearly illustrates this with its unadorned walls, massive pillars and simple round-arched arcades. The church (built approximately between 1147 – 1186) formed the centre of the structure. The cloister building was connected directly behind it. The monastery path separated the area of the monks from the monastery of the lay brothers. The so-called Konversenbau (lay brothers' building) is in actual fact a very good example of Cistercian architecture. The hospital was established a short distance from the monastery. The high triple nave hospital ward remains unaltered and transports the guests back to the Middle Ages. Finally, an encircling wall encloses everything: it is 1100 metres (1200 yds.) in length, 5 metres (5.5 yds.) high and completely preserved to this day.

Since the filming of the novel "The Name of the Rose" by Umberto Eco as well as many other shoots, Eberbach has become synonymous with the typical medieval monastery complex. Eberbach also gained popularity through its century's old tradition of wine making. Today cultural events, wine auctions and tasting are held in the entirely redeveloped rooms.

Andria (Italy): Castel del Monte
1240 – 1250, Frederick II

While the architecture of the Middle Ages was dominated, above all, by church buildings, there were also a number of fascinating secular structures. Frederick II of Sicily, the last great Staufer to hold both the titles of king and later, emperor, had a network of secular buildings erected in Italy. One of the most interesting is the Castel del Monte in the Southern Italian region of Apulia. Almost 20 kilometres from the nearest city, it is idyllically located on a hill. The construction of the Castel del Monte was begun in 1240, and by the time Frederick II died, in 1250, it was completed. The monumental, perfectly octagonal building is surrounded in turn by eight octagonal peel towers. These are equipped with stairs, and some of them even have baths and toilets. The only decoration is around the portals. The crusaders learned the use of squared-stone masonry, as it is found here, from the wall surrounding the city of Constantinople. In the building's architecture one finds parallels to the building style of the Cistercians, while the floor plan is similar to an Umayyad palace, the water system is constructed according to Arabic models, and the sparingly used sculptural ornamentation is Gothic. Castel del Monte bears witness to the wide range of influences that came to play on Classical architecture during the Middle Ages. Southern Italian eclecticism bears witness to the many contacts with other cultures.

When viewing the building, one is led to assume that there must have been a fortress there during the age of chivalry. But this is far from true. The building, with its peel made of cyclopean masonry, was a pleasure and hunting castle. One of the highpoints of the raucus festivities held there was probably the wedding of the Staufer son Manfred, later king of Sicily, to Beatrice of Savoy. Later the building was put to a number of different uses, ranging from a prison to a fortress, before it was taken over by the Italian government in 1876.

Paris (France): The Choir of Saint-Denis
1140 – 1144, Abbot Suger

left:
The western building (1130/1135, tower until 1148) of Saint Denis was heavily worked over in the 19th century, but it still reveals Suger's fundamental approach. The vocabulary of the choir was already used here, albeit not so stringently and at times quite clumsily, as for instance between the rounded and pointed arches. The circular windows, which originally had no tracery, are the predecessors of the rose windows that came later.

As a sign that he wanted to be buried on the spot where the church was later built, Dionysius, the first Bishop of Paris who was decapitated in the 3rd century, is supposed to have carried his head there. In the 5th century a building was erected in the form of a Necropolis, in 775 a new church followed and in 832 the crypt was extended by adding a Lady chapel with a nave and two aisles. In the Carolingian period St Denis was a basilica with a nave and two aisles, a transept and an apsidiole. In roughly 1130 Abbot Suger, who acted as Louis VII's regent while the latter was on the Second Crusade in 1147, began the reconstruction of St Denis, starting with the façade. This part of the building was finished in 1140 and is still thoroughly Romanesque: heavy, closed and decorative with a choir. Suger however wanted to create a building that was much lighter than anything that had been built before, since he saw light as a symbol of divinity. The presbytery is separated from the ambulatory and the radial chapels by columns. Between the chapels one finds pilasters on the outer building that serve as pylons for the celestory and allow the close succession of windows on the ground floor. Pointed arches, cross-ribbed vaulting and piers – all established vocabulary – find their way

into a logical, constructive system that facilitates the systematic construction of the building and permeation of the walls. The French kings were entombed in the choir at St Denis and Gothic architecture is seen to have its origins here. Suger had already entertained plans to replace the Carolingian nave, but no measures were undertaken until the 13th century. At that point Suger's choir was also found to have sustained damage and had to be renewed, with the exception of the ambulatory and the chapels.

With the employment of piers, shafts and ribs on the interior, and flying buttresses on the outside, a form of skeleton construction was developed in the Gothic period that made it possible to substitute more and more of the wall with glass. It was, however, still not possible to calculate the load distribution, so it was a case of trial and error, which sometimes led to collapses.

Paris (France): Notre-Dame
begun 1163, Maurice de Sully

left:
The Royal Gallery above the region of the portal is now occupied by figures that Violett le Duc added after the originals were destroyed during the French Revolution. In 1977, the original 21 heads were discovered during restoration work, and are now – still partly with their original paint – on view at the Musée Cluny in Paris.

The Cathedral of Notre-Dame is an example of late early Gothic architecture. Measuring 35 metres (115 ft.) up to the roof, it was one and a half times as tall as all of the previous big building projects of the day to do justice to the expectations of what was then the largest city in the world. In 1182 the choir and the crossing were completed and from 1180 the buttressing of the nave was constructed. The latter would ultimately allow Notre-Dame to be built without galleries. Inside it is possible to distinguish between two master-builders. The first (responsible for the choir and the eastern transept) used clustered shafts and left quite a bit of wall standing. The second (western transept and the nave) used pilaster strips and en-délit shafts in the style of Laon. In the 19th century Viollet-le-Duc reconstructed the original vertical elevation in the area of the crossing: over the arcades and the galleries there are spaces with tracery windows and small transoms. Around 1225 the celestory windows were enlarged after the fashion in Reims. The extension of the transepts was begun in 1258. An inscription names Jean de Chelles as the architect of these new façades. The southern façade was completed by Pierre de Montreuil. The centrifugal tracery gave Rayonant Style (from about 1230 onward) its name.

When viewed from the interior, the rosette window utilises the space under the vaulting. From outside it seems out of proportion as its casement encroaches on the base of the tower (Notre Dame in Laon). The aisle windows seem too small and only when two aisles were added in Paris (after 1208) was a more balanced distribution achieved. The corners of the towers (each on a different nave) extend downward by reinforcing the front of the wall to create three wide strips of nearly the same size. The royal gallery and the moulding on empty spaces on the walls provide horizontal structure with the rose window in the middle.

Chartres (France): Cathedral of Notre-Dame
1194 – 1220

Chartres has been in possession of one of the Virgin Mary's veils since 876, and it still attracts many pilgrims to the Cathedral. After the relic was said to have effected a number of miracles (for example driving out the Normans in 911), people began to believe that a garment that had come into contact with the shrine in which the relic was kept, could protect mothers and babies during childbirth. The Cathedral of Notre-Dame at Chartres is one of the key structures in French High Gothic. It is a basilica with a nave and two aisles, two additional aisles in the choir, a nave and two aisles in the transept, as well as a double ambulatory and radial chapels. The vertical elevation of the nave can be divided into three zones. The transepts were only built in 1230 and it was not consecrated until 1260. The Carolingian church of Notre-Dame, was destroyed in a fire in 1020. When the new church was built, the remains of the aisles which had withstood the fire were used for the crypt. In the middle of the 12th century the church was renovated, but the building was destroyed by another fire in 1194. Only the façade, with the oldest intact jamb figures in Europe, remains from this phase. Since Mary's veil miraculously survived these fires, a flood of donations for a new church poured in. The system of flying buttresses used in the new building, with arched buttresses providing support from above the side roofs rather than having tower buttresses set underneath, made it possible to refrain from building a gallery to distribute the load of the vaults. It was possible to structure the interior vertical elevation in three zones for the first time (arcade, triforium, celestory). A number of innovative features such as three levels, flying buttresses, group windows (which later gave way to tracery), combined piers (instead of a system of columns and arches) and quadrapartite vaulting were all brought together in Chartres and then became the fundamental forms of High Gothic, which was initiated here.

The master-builder, unknown today, left his mark on the floor of the cathedral at the centre of the labyrinth. Labyrinths were often used as signatures, and the names of a number of builders could be found in an order that depended on the work they had done. This labyrinth is modelled on Minos Daedalus Labyrinth in Knossos.

Salisbury (England): Cathedral
1220 – 1266, Richard Farleigh

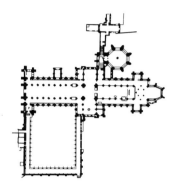

left:
The nave of the cathedral illustrates the differences to contemporary French cathedral Gothic. Its upper reaches are clearly reduced, in contrast to the verticalization there. Also, the storeys are arranged as horizontally continuous bands with respectively independent structures instead of the continuous pattern running continuously from the floor to the vault there. The deep pattern dominates.

Salisbury Cathedral is considered the most uniform structure built in Early English style, the early form of English Gothic. Typical of this style is the decisively cubic structure of the building's parts: the first transept is rectangular and intersects the building in the middle, a second, smaller but also rectangular one intersects the choir. The ambulatory is squared off and penetrated by the rectangular retrochoir. The flying buttresses of French cathedrals are not found here, or only in a reduced form under the roofs. Since the English structures never reached the heights of their French counterparts, and the walls in England were also never permeated to the same extent, but rather tended to remain solid, such a sophisticated system of load distribution was not necessary. The interior of the building also has little to do with French-style buildings and vertical structuring (instead of great heights) dominate the building. Like the first Gothic cathedral in England, Canterbury, Salisbury exhibits the typically southern English en-délit shafts which contrast in colour to the rest of the piers. On the whole, Salisbury Cathedral is quite simple. This reduction serves to highlight details like the use of eight shafts and a wider spectrum of forms in the choir, while in the nave each arcade pier has

only four. Typical of English Gothic is the resolute use of Gothic decorative forms. The 123 metres (ca. 400 ft.) central tower was erected in the 14th century in Decorated Style.

English cathedrals have capital houses attached to the cloisters. In contrast to the capital rooms on the Continent, these were separate buildings. In Salisbury (second half of the 13th century) this house was enlarged and then had an octagonal floor plan in Decorated Style, with the spandrels meeting at the middle pier forming a large star. The walls almost entirely consist of glass windows.

Paris (France): Sainte-Chapelle
after 1239 – 1248

Sainte-Chapelle was once a part of the royal palace in Paris. It was first an important private chapel, a new task for builders, and was intended to provide a fitting location for the most important French relic, Christ's Crown of Thorns. Louis IX had purchased the Crown of Thorns from the emperor in Constantinople in 1239, and Pope Innocence IV proclaimed that this meant that Christ himself crowned the kings of France. The construction seems to have been directed by Robert de Luzarches, who also built the Cathedral of Amiens, or perhaps by Thomas de Cormont. Forms similar to those used in Amiens were employed (particularly in the choir chapels): in the couronement of the tracery at the end of the choir one finds a group of three reclining trefoils and the exterior decorative gables penetrate the parapet on which the roof is set. The upper chapel is, in contrast to the lower one, flooded with light. The low buttresses on the exterior are concealed behind the clustered shafts. There are sculptures of the apostles on these which led to the upper chapel being seen as a sort of shrine turned upside down. The slender construction could only be stabilized by means of metal ring anchors fastened around the building. Sainte-Chapelle provides us with an indication of how colourful cathedral buildings must have been, since the original interior has been reconstructed using what remained. The construction above the shrine (a reconstruction) was erected around 1260.

Relics were extremely prized in the Middle Ages. 100,000 livres were paid for the shrine for the Crown of Thorns while the construction of the building cost only 40,000. The Crown of Thorns alone cost 135,000 livres. Relics were not just memorabilia. It was assumed that a saint's characteristics were conveyed by his remains and his clothing and that these relics could pass these characteristics on to the faithful, or even continue to perform miracles (or miracle healings).

left:
The Paris chapel of state relics marks the start of a tradition of small Gothic churches, whose walls almost completely dissolve in glass. Here, a new style impulse originates from the surroundings of the Royal Family, as with the emergence of Gothic beforehand.

Reims (France): Notre-Dame
begun 1211

left:
The pier columns of the tower of Notre-Dame in Reims are covered – according to the model of Amiens – in the region of the portal by the wide-extending jambs of the funnel-shaped portals. The tall triangular gables cover the wall beneath the rose section, where in Paris the Royal Gallery is located. With the glazing of the tympanum, the representations that would normally be placed there had to find space on other parts of the façade.

The cornerstone for the Cathedral in Reims was laid on 6 May, 1211. The liturgical choir (including the last three yokes of the nave) was reported to have been first used in 1241. As the church in which coronations were held (using oil from the "Sainte Ampoule," which is supposed to have been brought from heaven by a dove), Reims stood in direct competition with Saint-Denis, the church regularly attended by the royal family and in which they were entombed. According to legend, the archbishop of Reims is supposed to have set fire to the previously existing structure in 1210 in order to finally have a more lavish church than his suffragans. Sculptures found during excavation of the old choir, which was torn down, exhibit no evidence of fire. Hence it can be assumed that the old church could have been renovated. Indeed, its towers stood in the way for quite some time. Soon after construction was begun, financing became a problem that had to be solved by the sale of dispensations, yet the construction of the building continued on into the 15th century (the upper level of the tower by Jehan de Dijon was completed in 1475. The labyrinth, which was destroyed in 1779, provided information on four architects who worked on the construction of the naves: Jean d'Orbais, Jean le Loup, Gaucher de

Reims and Bernard de Soisson. In Reims, the system of High Gothic, which had been developed in Chartres, was perfected A notable example are window groups found in Chartres become tracery in Reims. Previously there had been two separate vertical windows and a round window. Here they are combined as one. Only stone mullions separate the individual forms. These windows became popular all over Europe.

The statuary in Reims, originally over 2,300 figures, also found wide emulation: the Naumburg Masters, the creators of the Bamberger Reiter and the Vierge doré in Amiens, must have trained here. The smiles of the "Reims Angels" are characteristic. The Annunciation scene reveals a proximity to the antiquity not previous found.

Prague (Czech Republic): St Vitus Cathedral
begun 1344, Matthias von Arras (until 1352), Peter Parler et al.

left:
In 1344, work started on Wenceslas Cathedral in Prague. However, it was not until the end of the 19th century that the double tower façade was constructed by the Cathedral master builder Joseph Mocker in neo-Gothic forms. Like Cologne Cathedral in Germany, the building's completion became an expression of newly awakened national self-confidence.

St Vitus takes a special position both in history and in architecture. For one, the building documents the growing importance of Prague, which advanced under Charles IV to the political and cultural centre of the Holy Roman Empire. For another, the cathedral – particularly the eastern section designed by Peter Parler – is considered a key work of late Gothic architecture. The designation of Prague as an archbishopric in 1344 necessitated the construction of a cathedral. The cornerstone was laid the same year in the presence of King John of Luxembourg. However, the initiative for this ambitious project can be attributed to his son, the future Emperor Charles IV. He engaged Matthias von Arras as the first master-builder of the cathedral. The latter began to build the choir in the style of southern French cathedrals. Only after Peter Parler was called in, in 1356, was there a fundamental change in the stylistic vernacular – which had been High Gothic up until that point. Hence, he introduced a dynamic in the architecture of the upper regions of the cathedral that was thoroughly innovative, and which established St. Vitus reputation as one of the initial works of Late Gothic. In addition to the completion of the choir, Peter Parler also designed the southern side of the church, which faces the city. He created emphasis here by including a tower, the Wenceslaus Chapel and a vestibule set in front of the transept's portal. Work on the cathedral, that was carried on by his sons, Wenzel and Johann, got bogged down in the 15th century, so that the nave and the double tower façade could only be completed at the beginning of the 20th century.

Peter Parler's portrait busts on the triforium can be considered an important contribution to Gothic portrait sculpture. His own portrait bust, which appears between the busts of the emperor and the archbishops, documents a self-confident artist who has already risen above the anonymity of the early age, one who came from the same family of master-builders destined to make a lasting mark on 14th century German architecture.

Malbork (Poland): Marien Castle

1274 – 1398, Nikolaus Fellenstein et al.

Marien Castle (now Malbork), once headquarters of the German Order, is one of the largest castle complexes in Europe with important symbolic value. Around 1274 the knights of the order had begun to build a strongly reinforced castle according to an extended rectanglular plan close to the bank of the Nogat. It was named after their patron. The central buildings were finished in 1280 but the whole structure was only completed in 1398. The greater part of Marienburg was erected on an artificially created hill. The oldest section of the complex is the main castle in which chapel, dormitorium, chapter hall, prison and archives were accommodated. Around 1300 it had already

grown to an enclosed four- winged complex. During the 14th century the complex presented itself as a gigantic building site. The central castle with the knight's hall and hospital as well as the castle church, Saint Mary, were established. The grand master's palace is the most magnificent building of the castle complex and was probably built during the term of office of grand master Conrad Zöllner von Rotenstein. The exterior appears fortified with its heavy walls, watch-towers and merlon fortifications. On closer scrutiny a completely different aspect reveals itself. The attributes of high-class represen-tation are in the foreground. The walls are divided

above:
Marienburg was built between 1274 and 1398 on the banks of the River Nogat as the headquarters of the Teutonic Order. Its turreted enclosure wall and crenellations give the instant impression of a well-fortified castle. A second look reveals, however, the way the building chiefly conveys power and status, not least by its finely composed façades interspersed by large windows, and its magnificently appointed chambers.

plastically with large window introdos and fine pillar arrangements. The most important interiors are lavishly decorated, and the star vaults are supported by a single granite pillar; a climax in vault construction. After its destruction in 1945 and a fire in 1959, it was gradually restored.

Marienburg is the largest European military establishment built from brick in the Middle Ages and is additionally one of the most important secular Gothic buildings. On the foundation stone in the inner court of the high castle is inscribed in Latin: "Milan was built from marble, Ofen (Buda) from stone and Marienburg from mud".

Bohemia (Czech Republic): Karlstejn Castle
1348 – 1370

left:

Castle Karlstein, which was built in 1348 as the residence of Charles IV. and as the repository of the Insignia of the Holy Roman Empire, is one of the most impressive secular buildings of European Gothic architecture. The combination of a fortified castle and prestigious imperial palace can also be seen in the exterior, with the so-called High Tower that looms majestically above it. Located inside the tower is the magnificently appointed Chapel of the Holy Cross, the most important room of the castle.

Karlstejn is one of the most impressive Gothic castle buildings in Europe. Its founder was Charles I, Bohemian king from 1346 (and also as Charles IV from 1355 as Roman emperor). The castle served as a defence as well as a place of refuge and for the safekeeping of the imperial relics. Its construction occurred during a time of war and epidemic; in 1348 the "black plague" broke out in Europe. Karlstejn was erected 20 kilometres (12 miles) southwest of Prague on a 72-metre (80 yds.) high lime rock above the river of Berounka. The well-preserved castle layout is divided into a fore and main castle. Over a drawbridge one enters the forecourt, then through a gate into the courtyard of the actual castle. A two metres (6.6 ft.) thick stone wall divides the fore and inner castle. Inside, the three-storey emperor's palace first presents itself. These were the living quarters for the emperor, the empress and their courtiers. The chapel of St. Nicholas belonged to the palace as well as a representation hall with wall paintings of the "Luxembourg family tree" (today almost completely reconstructed). Opposite the emperor's palace is the Marian tower with the Church of Our Lady and St Catherine's Chapel. The high tower dominates the castle layout and its "Chapel of the Holy Cross" forms the real core of the castle. In this richly adorned, well preserved room the valuable crown jewels were stored. The Gothic ribbed vault is decorated with stucco and is gilded. The wall lining of semi-precious stones are patterned in the form of ornamental crosses. These incrustations were also to be found in the imperial private chapel.

During the middle of the 14th century various different cultural groups worked in Bohemia. In architecture it was the French examples that were most noticeable (Charles was educated at the French court), while the magnificent and colourful organization of the interiors remind one of Byzantine works.

Renaissance, Baroque and Rococo

Renaissance, Baroque and Rococo

The early modern period in Europe began with the Renaissance, which had in turn emerged from Humanism. What was new at the beginning of the 15th century was a rational, scientific mode of thought that ultimately helped to overcome feudal domination, the church's intellectual monopoly and, with that, the "Dark Ages." Simultaneously the hierarchical social structure, of which the emperor and the pope were the figureheads, disintegrated and gave way to a multifaceted process in which Humanism, the Renaissance, pragmatic politics, early capitalism and the Reformation converged in the creation of a new socio-political situation. Italy played a leading role in the culture in this age. In Tuscany, individual artists were, supported by other élites (wealthy aristocrats, humanists and territorial princes) to develop a new stylistic vernacular for the building projects at hand. The study of antiquities, and the attempt to revive them, provided the basis for a completely new architecture in which buildings had clear forms, fine surfaces and structuring elements reminiscent of the Classical Age. A building's form and its method of construction no longer needed to be in accord with each other. In the solid structures of the Renaissance, supporting masonry and the elements used to structure the façade could now diverge. The latter could be freely designed as a sort of "dressing," whereby the orders of columns, window forms, moulding and ornaments became dominant elements. Leon Battista Alberti formulated the theoretical basis for Renaissance architecture, the main characteristic of which he saw in symmetry and in a balanced system of proportions extending over the entire building and each of its parts. The buildings that were created, particularly Brunelleschi's Ospedale degli Innocenti, demonstrate in exemplary manner the elegant, but also the principally formalistic, concept of architecture. Harmony and proportion determined the High Renaissance style that represented a further development upon the principles established during the early Renaissance in Florence. It was propagated particularly by Bramante, after 1500, and was characterized by a monumentality that was orientated on the Roman imperial period. Seeking more plasticity and dynamism, Michelangelo refrained from using singular and balanced forms for detail, and turned towards fluid and expressive modelling in order to achieve a dramatically heightened overall effect. Following his lead, many architects in the 16th century began to adopt the free and subjective attitude toward the combination of forms that was to characterize Mannerism. As Baroque begins to develop, individual forms, surfaces and building masses are engaged into processes of movement, the power and resoluteness of which are able to dominate large spaces and whole series of spaces. As architecture becomes more dynamic, it starts with the floor plan, and goes on in the High and Late Baroque period to effect the vertical plane and finally encompasses every individual aspect of architecture. The unity of architecture, painting, sculpture and ornamentation is what distinguished the late Baroque period, which reached its zenith in 18th century Rococo, an ornamental late phase of French Baroque. Originally it was purely a style of ornamentations then it began to converge with architecture in the spatial forms introduced by Borromini and Guarini. During the course of the Renaissance there was again a shift in the focus of power to the favour of the territorial princes and absolutist rulers. In Rome, the city's function as a territorial residence in a church state was combined with its function as the centre of the Catholic church. Having fallen into disrepair, Rome was supposed to be put in order again by means of an ambitious building programme. Here, as in Paris, one started with a city of small particularistic sections and moved on to more open systems. In the absolutistic spatial order of the Baroque period, the barriers between architecture, garden design and landscape planning, as autonomous fields, are dissolved; everything is seen as part of a single unit which was in turn subjected to dominant continuous axes.

Florence (Italy): Ospedale degli Innocenti
begun in 1419, Filippo Brunelleschi

left:
The loggia of the orphanage opens up to the Piazza Santissima Annunziata via a quiet succession of Corinthian columns, whose distance is exactly equal to their height. Small tondi are fixed between the round arches and the beams they stand on. It was not until 1487 that they were filled with the glazed terracotta relief of babies created by Andrea della Robbia.

The Ospedale degli Innocenti is, without question, one of the most important symbols of 15th century humanist culture in Florence. The construction of the building, which was commissioned by the Arte della Setaî, was begun in 1419 on the basis of a plan drawn up by Filippo Brunelleschi. It represents a concrete architectonic answer to a pressing social need. After opening its doors in 1445 it served to house, heal and educate foundlings and can, therefore, be seen within the context of a series of major public building projects undertaken for the benefit of the Republic of Florence. Although its design echoes building forms dating back to the Middle Ages, the symmetry of the floor plan, with its regular pattern of rooms grouped around courtyards, was an innovation. Just as innovative was the treatment of the traditional colonnade that, for the first time extended along the entire front of the façade representing a connecting element between built-up and open space. The orphanage, one of Brunelleschi's first building projects, reflects the most important characteristics of both his work and of Italian Renaissance architecture in general and is recognised by the reduction of individual building elements, their perfect, harmonic proportions, the systematic order and clearly calculated geometric orchestration of the building's various parts. The span of the reinforcing arches corresponds precisely with the Tuscan-Corinthian columns and the depth of the colonnades. The simple construction composed of squares and semi-circles is emphasized by the contrast between the stuccoed surfaces and the supporting elements made of grey sandstone.

The façade was completed using blue and white ceramic tiles manufactured by Andrea della Robbia in 1487. Eight circular terra-cotta elements depicting foundlings are each displayed in a different pendentive.

Florence (Italy): The Dome of the Cathedral, 1418 – 1472, Filippo Brunelleschi

In 1368 the decision was made to add an eastern section to the Florence Cathedral. It, in turn, was to be crowned by a huge dome. It may have been overconfidence, that made the plan for such an enormous roof seem feasible; but by 1410, when the drum, measuring up to 45 metres (147 ft.) in width was completed, it was gradually realized that a hole of this size could not be vaulted. A competition was held in 1418 from which Brunelleschi would emerge in 1421 as the "Goveranatore della Cupola Maggiore." He proposed a "climbing framework" that would be supported by the dome itself as an alternative to using supports rising up from the ground. In order to distribute the thrust, he expanded the drum by four exedra – semicircular niches. The dome has a thicker inner and a thinner outer shell which support each other reciprocally and is built of layered individual octagonal rings. In another competition in 1434, Brunnelleschi again submitted plans for the lantern on top of the dome. This was completed after his death. The golden cross by Verrocchio was erected in 1472.

left:
From the outside it can clearly be seen that the so-called dome is actually a "medieval" monastery vault. Such a vault consists of individual domes, which collide together with ridges, in contrast to the dome, which is half a ball. Here, the ridges are underneath the domes on the outside.

The rest of the dome is a masterpiece of Gothic architecture. The sculptor and architect Arnolfo di Cambio was commissioned in 1296 with its construction but only a few parts of the nave and the façade were finished before he died in 1302 Sculptures are to be seen in the Cathedral Museum. Work resumed in 1331 and in 1334 Giotto, the then master-builder of the cathedral began the Campanile and Francesco Talenti completed it and continued the work on the nave according to new plans. The eastern annex was built according to a model created by "eight masters and painters." The present-day Neo-Gothic façade was completed in the 19th century.

Florence (Italy): Palazzo Rucellai
1446 – 1470, Leon Battista Alberti

left:
With the succession of the three classic orders, Alberti falls back on both Antique motifs, as in the three-part entablature or the opus reticulatum of the foundation zone. However, he transfers the plastic construction of Ancient Roman buildings in a primarily graphic context. In this way, the flat pilaster withdraws completely into the wall level.

Leon Battista Alberti's plans for the construction of the Palazzo Recellai date from 1446. However, the first phase of building was not begun until 1455, under the direction of Bernardo Rossellino. The intention was to connect a number of existing buildings by means of a façade with eight or nine window axes. Even at the end of the second building phase, which lasted from 1465 to 1470, this was still incomplete. The design for the Palazzo Rucellai represents the first time that the great theorist of Renaissance architecture used a superposed order of pilasters in order to structure an entire façade. In doing so, he relied on the stylistic principles of classical art that he had derived from the ruins of the Roman Empire, when writing his "Ten Books on Architecture" as a re-examination of Vitruvius's treatise. The wall of the Palazzo Rucellai is made of smooth squared-block masonry with strata at differing heights and divided into equal parts by flat pilasters. On the ground floor a portal field takes its place in between two closed fields, each marked by high square windows. The dome-shaped windows on the two upper floors correspond in their proportions to the fields defined by the pilasters. The architraves installed at the height of the transoms is intended to emphasize the harmony. Rusticated stone arches outline the dome-shaped windows and increase in the portal axes, barely noticeably, by one layer in height, giving the façade a rhythm of its own. Alberti was opposed to heavy, rusticated architecture. His architecture, which strove for harmony and correspondence between all of the building elements, seems new and spacious.

The Loggia Rucellai and the Cappella Rucellai which were part of the palace complex were also designed by Alberti. The Tempietto del Santo Sepolcro is in the Cappella Rucellai. The Florence Baptistery was his inspiration.

Rome (Italy): San Pietro in Montorio (Tempietto)
1502, Donato Bramante

left:
Despite the extremely low size, Bramante successfully bestows the Tempietto with monumental character. It results above all from the clear arrangement of the architecture, which is characterized by Antique motifs. The round core building is vaulted with a dome and surrounded by a peristyle, whose Doric columns support a three-part entablature and a balustrade.

The small circular temple, with columns in Doric order, radiates a majestic sense of dignity. It seems less like a structure enclosing inner space and more like a sculptural work of art. It is the first important building in the High Renaissance and breathes the true spirit of antiquity. Originally the temple was supposed to be surrounded by a circle of columns that were never erected. It seems almost of little consequence that the building is actually a double chapel with a crypt below and a cella above, both of which are connected through an opening. What is important is the reduction, the search for an archetype, as was typical for the architect Bramante. Donato Bramante was an architect, an engineer, a painter and a poet. He translated ancient architecture, with a monumentality all of his own, into a Christian architecture that won him papal commissions to design buildings for the Vatican and Saint Peter's. Giorgio Vasari, the great biographer and chronicler of his day, was quite taken by Bramante's terribilità, the awe-inspiring nature of his works. But no other building was as important for Bramante's reputation as the little temple located on the spot on which St Peter is said to have been crucified. Bramante created a work that not only used antique forms, it also seemed to infuse the architectural ideals of antiquity with new life.

In 1499 the French drove Milan's artists to Rome and Renaissance buildings were erected. Antonio da Sangallo the younger, Raphael, Baldassare Peruzzi and Giulio Romano were trained in Donato Bramante's workshop. They took his style to other regions of Italy.

Mantua (Italy): Palazzo del Te
1525 – 1531, Giulio Romano

The Palazzo del Te was named after the island on which it was built. The Isola del Te was surrounded by a canal, that flowed along the medieval city wall of Mantua to the south, as well as by a number of lakes. Work on the palace began at the end of 1525. It was designed by the Architect Giulio Romano, and commissioned by Federigo Gonzaga. Romano's plans aimed at the construction of a pleasure palace that would architecturally underline Gonzaga's social standing, and into which the remaining walls of former stables were also to be integrated. The progression of rooms from the atrium, the square building structure, centred around an inner

courtyard, to the loggia and out to the gardens reminds one of the principles according to which the domus antica was laid out. Romano used columns in Doric order with triglyphic friezes which attest to an antiquarian orientation. Other clearly classical elements included the round arches and columns that make up the loggias as well as the wall elements defined by pilaster strips. In the façade, the clearly decorative combination of varying and sometimes contrasting elements like cyclopean masonry, deeply recessed niches and windows, as well as an almost whimsically staggered arrangement of triglyphs, all serve to create a plastic relief on the wall and blend

above:
The garden façade of the east wing was altered substantially in 1774. Its increased monumentality makes it different from the other sections of the Palazzo. This is based among other things on the strictly structured central portal, whose three round arch arcades each rest on groups of four columns. The Palladian motif created in this way also continues in a modified form at the sides.

with the interior decoration in an expression of Mannerist influence. This is underlined by the integration of a natural element into the architecture in the form of an expansive garden.

The singular and unmistakable ambition of Giulio Romano to realize this total work of art came from the skills and experience he had acquired while working for Raphael in Rome. In Mantua he then demonstrated a maturity of his own, supplying the countless drawings for the interior decoration of frescoes, friezes, fireplaces and carvings, and monitoring its execution.

Renaissance, Baroque and Rococo   211

Florence (Italy): The New Sacristy of San Lorenzo Medici Chapel

ca. 1529, Michelangelo

left:
Michelangelo built the New Sacristy as a burial chapel for the Medici. Its basic layout follows that of the Old Sacristy, built around a century earlier by Brunelleschi. However, his rather restrained wall arrangement becomes more plastic and dynamic with Michelangelo. The primary contributory factor here was the close succession of fluted pilasters and marble aedicules.

Michelangelo began to draw up the architectural plans for the new sacristy at San Lorenzo in 1514. But the construction of tombs for the Medici family was delayed, when the rulers were driven out of the city, and it was only completed after Michelangelo had left Florence for Rome, never to return again. When viewing the plan it becomes obvious that it was meant to pay homage to Brunelleschi. Michelangelo designed a square floor plan, a small apsidal annex and a half dome. Even with this first architectural project he broke many of the rules considered valid up until that point. Instead of a few clearly ordered elements with simple proportions, there is a densely compressed combination of motifs. Balance turns into tension, while these forces that are not in balance, but rather directed against each other, are in effect on the inside as well as the outside of the building. This is clearly demonstrated by the stark contrasts between the pronounced decorations and recesses. A row of elegant windows that becomes narrower toward the top, emphasizes the upward movement that is continued in the coffered dome and finally leads into the lantern. The symbolic value of this movement on the vertical axis can hardly be overlooked. The high degree of segmentation on the walls, created by pilasters which define narrow fields, also creates an impression of energy and dynamism, particularly around the deeply recessed wall niches.

In building the New Sacristy, Michelangelo diverts from the path of objectively valid traditional rules of order – derived from antiquity – and paves the way for the artistic forces that would later express themselves in Mannerism. Michelangelo's comprehensive approach can be recognized in the combination of architecture and sculpture. The allegorical figures and the tombs become a part of the spatial orchestration.

Moscow (Russia): Basilius Cathedral
1555 – 1600, Barma and Posnik

left:
With its numerous, differently constructed domes, the Cathedral of Saint Wassili is one of the most original creations of Russian architecture. The design of the exterior is already very richly varied, but this is emphasized still further by its wealth of colours. However, both the patterned onion domes and the polychrome painting were added later.

On Moscow's Red Square, in front of the Kremlin walls stands the Basilius Cathedral situated on a high pedestal base in order to level the slope towards the Moskwa river. Ten buildings, with inter-connected passages, form a decorative church ensemble. The main church is surrounded by eight independent chapels, each with its own characteristic steeple and onion dome. The cathedral, a column church crowned by a tent-like structure, practically marks the completion of this architectural type. The layout is based on a central church with apse, surrounded by polygonal main and secondary chapels. The domes were originally in the form of a helmet, but were later replaced by multi-faceted ribbed and onion domes. However, their origin is still uncertain in the context of Christian architecture. They probably date back to Byzantine and Islamic influences since the building combines Western and Eastern stylistic elements. Romanesque arcades, Gothic peaked arches and Renaissance motifs, together with Moorish battlements and Islamic domes result in a highly exotic cultural mixture. Originally the colour of the church exterior was dominated by the red of the brickwork, with details of white limestone. Only in the 17th century was it adorned with multi-coloured decoration. The focus of the cathedral lies in its exterior adornment. All areas are decorated, and this dominates in the form of pillars, lesene, rosettes, and likewise over the architectural elements. Conversely, the interior of the church is designed in a somewhat understated manner.

The Basilius cathedral, considere the climax of Moscow architecture in the 16th century, was erected in 1588 by Ivan IV (Ivan the Terrible) to honour the 1552 conquest of the Tatar Khanate of Kazan on the Volga and the liberation from Tatar dominion. The building was named after Vassili Blashenny, who was revered by the people as "God's jester". He is buried in one of the north-east section chapels.

Vicenza (Italy): Villa La Rotonda
from 1567, Andrea Palladio

left:
As the embodiment of Palladio's ideas of the ideal of architecture, Villa Rotonda near Vicenza has a completely symmetrical central structure, with one six-columned portico set on each side. With this villa, the architect, who trained in the architecture of Antiquity and the High Renaissance, transposed for the first time a motif to a residential building that previously had been the preserve of sacred buildings.

In Palladio's buildings humanist ideas and those derived by Alberti from Classical-Vitruvian tradition are combined with his own studies on symmetry and proportional harmony. He made use of existing topographical conditions without subordinating himself to them; indeed, he employed them in order to frame his architecture. Hence, it is on the top of a hill on the outskirts of Vicenza that he located the Villa La Rotonda for Prelate Almerico. The building, with its quadratic floor plan, came to dominate its surroundings. Seeking an expression of the absolute truth in mathematics, Palladio developed his system of ideal architecture, according to an axially symmetric and centralized scheme. Every side of the villa has a portico with a temple front and a stairway leading up to it. Inside, the central building contains a rotunda that is crowned by a cupola. These architectural elements, borrowed from ecclesiastical architecture, become, when used in the construction of private dwellings, symbols of spiritual and intellectual superiority and an expression of the builder's image of himself and his station. Palladio's villas are made, for the most part, of masonry and plaster. The window openings are cut into the smooth surfaces of the façades without any structuring ornamentation, seeming to express a renunciation of sculptural effects. Simple and perfect forms – the square, the circle, the cube and the sphere – are the recurrent theme and a fundamental principle the Renaissance, the gradual increase in the height of the building's elements leading up to the central dome, is evidence of a Baroque tendency towards more vertical inclination which was already making itself felt.

With the international spread of Palladianism in the centuries that followed, the Villa Rotonda was often copied in a variety of settings, sizes, and styles.

Rome (Italy), Il Gesù

1568 – 1584, Giacomo Barozzi da Vignola, Giacomo della Porta

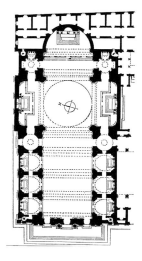

left:
The façade was erected by Giacomo della Porta following Vignola's death. It became the model for numerous Jesuit churches. In addition to the two-story construction, they also adopted the lateral volutes and the crowning triangular gable. It is true that structuring using pilaster and lesenes already had numerous predecessors in the Renaissance, but the sculptural concentration in the centre of the building gave momentum to Baroque façade design.

Vignola began the construction of the mother church of the Jesuit Order in 1568 after receiving the commission by Cardinal Alessandro Farnese. He designed a cruciform structure in which the barrel-vaulted pilaster church, in which the nave is located, ends in transepts that are barely extended and behind which there is a semi-circular apse at the eastern end of the church. Illuminated by the windows in the dome's drum, the crossing is featured as the brightest area in the church, becoming the optical focal point of the interior. By combining a longitudinal-plan building together with a centralized eastern orientation, a type of building was created that was destined to provide impulses for Roman Baroque, as well as for architecture north of the Alps in the 17th and 18th centuries. The façade that was erected according to plans drawn up by Giacomo della Porta, between 1573 and 1577, had a similar initial effect. Its two storey structure crowned by a gable became the obligatory style for the façades of Roman sacred buildings during the Early and High Baroque periods. The sculptural accentuation of the middle axis introduced a dynamic into this stylistic vocabulary, taken over from the Renaissance, and ended up being intensified in many of the buildings that followed.

The Order of Jesuits, which was founded by Ignatius of Loyola in 1539, soon advanced to one of the main proponents of the Counter-reformation. Architecture also entered the service of Re-Catholicization by striving to combine with sculpture and painting for a total work of art in order to make the church and its beliefs address the senses. It is therefore not surprising that the mother church of this order was the initial Baroque church.

Rome (Italy): St Peter's Cathedral and St Peter's Square the Colonnades

1506 – 1667, Bramante, Raphael, Giuliano da Sangallo, Baldassare Peruzzi, Antonio da Sangallo the Older, Michelangelo, Giacomo Vignoly, Giacomo della Porta, Domenico Fontana and Carlo Maderno

left:
The colonnades Bernini constructed in 1655–1667 guide the view to the 113 metre (371 ft.) wide façade of St. Peter's. Maderno structured its main storey using a colossal pilaster order, which forms a sculptural gable at the centre of the building. The benediction gallery is also there above the main portal. It is from here that the Pope bestows his blessing "urbi et orbi" on major holidays.

Julius II laid the cornerstone for this project which intended the rebuilding of an early Christian basilica in order to create a new cathedral. This enormous project was financed, in no small measure, through the sale of dispensations. Hence, the construction of the sacred centre of Christianity was destined to contribute to its division. The first designs were submitted by Bramante, but only the crossing area was completed before he died. His successors made only minimal progress, hence it was up to Michelangelo who was commissioned by Paul III in 1546, to further the work. He made decisive changes in the work that had been done by his predecessors, including having parts that had already been completed removed. By the time he died in 1564, construction on St Peter's had only reached the level of the dome's drum. The dome itself was completed by his successors in 1593, with only slight changes to his plan. The cupola rises up over a 16 windowed drum on four enormous pentagonal columns (24 metres or 79 ft. each in diameter). On the exterior it is accentuated by 16 pairs of columns that appear between the windows that are shaped like aedicules. The lasting effect of the combination of central and longitudinal-plan architecture, practiced for the first time in Il Gesù, was destined to take hold in St Peter's, which was originally planned as a central-plan church. Hence, Paul V. had a nave in the form of a pilaster church added on to the east side. It has a two story narthex with a benediction loggia. St Peter's Square was given its present form between 1657 and 1666 with the colonnades created by Bernini.

The singular importance of St Peter's is illustrated by its enormous dimensions. The overwhelming size of the church is illustrated by the fact that Borromini's church, San Carlo alle Quattro Fontane, could fit easily into one of the crossing columns and that the capitals in the nave are the size of a van.

Heidelberg (Germany), Friedrichsbau
Heidelberg Castle
1601 – 1607, Johannes Schoch

left:
When designing the Friedrichsbau, Johannes Schoch oriented himself on the Ottheinrichsbau, which had already been started in 1556. From this he borrowed the uniform and symmetrical façade arrangement, the succession of the classic orders, the aedicule framing of the windows, and the niche statues. The building that was realized at the start of the 17th century was already outdated stylistically. An impression of excessive luxury dominates, despite the fact that the flamboyant decoration was withdrawn.

The Heidelberg castle was constructed over a period of 300 years, thereby excluding the possibility of a uniform architectural style from the start. The biggest bloom period occurred during the Renaissance, but its owners also desisted from giving a uniform architectural style to the structure. Like a solitaire, the Otto Heinrich building is a self-realization programme of its owner– builder of the same name, and lights up its late-medieval surroundings. The elector Frederick IV also added his own palace, the so-called Friedrichsbau to the ensemble. It was to a certain extent an opposition plan to the approximately 30 years previously established Otto Heinrich building which was formed nearly entirely according to models from antiquity and illustrated with figures from the Old Testament and the gods of the ancient world. In the Friedrichsbau, the pilasters that were on top of each other but of different designs, adopted the vertical order again. The lower floor with the chapel is strongly stressed, but the three higher floors show the same dimensions with the window openings tapering off towards the top. The facade strictly follows the architectural theory of that time which recommended different column arrangements for different purposes: Tuscan for the castle chapel on the ground floor, Doric for the living quarters of the elector, Ionic for the electress and Corinthian for the "ladies rooms". The front façade is adorned with sixteen highly individual principality pictures, a stone gallery of ancestral portraits which extends from Charles the Great up to the last owner builder. The sculptor Sebastian Götz of Chur built it. The building is a typical example of the mannerist style.

The Heidelberg castle was deliberately destroyed between 1689 and 1693 by the troops of French king Louis XIV. in the Palatinate War of Succession. Only the ruins remained. The first successful reconstruction attempts were made at the end of the nineteenth century, when Friedrichsbau was restored under Karl Schäfer. Since then the upper floor interiors were created independently in the historicism style of the Renaissance.

Rathaus Augsburg (D)

1615–1620 (Innenausbau bis 1624), Elias Holl

links:
Die Hauptfassade des 1615–1620 durch Elias Holl errichteten Augsburger Rathauses spiegelt die Disposition des Innenraumes wieder. So werden die wichtigsten Räume durch einen kaum hervortretenden Mittelrisalit akzentuiert, der ausschließlich durch große Fenster mit variierender Ädikularahmung gegliedert wird. Dieser setzt sich als imposanter Giebel auch oberhalb der Dachbalustrade fort, die den oberen Abschluss der flankierenden Bauteile kennzeichnet.

Nachdem das Rathaus 1944 bei einem Luftangriff schwer getroffen worden und fast vollständig ausgebrannt war, wurden der Goldene Saal sowie ein Fürstenzimmer 1980–1984 zum 2000-jährigen Stadtjubiläum Augsburgs denkmalgerecht saniert. Die Wiederherstellung der originalen grau-violetten Farbgebung der Fassade stieß zunächst auf erbitterte Ablehnung. Es dauerte drei Generationen, bis sich die Architektur der italienischen Renaissance im übrigen Europa ausbreitete. Dabei wurden zunächst vor allem die dekorativen Elemente übernommen. Vor diesem Hintergrund ist das vom damaligen Stadtbaumeister Elias Holl errichtete Augsburger Rathaus von Bedeutung: Es gilt als wichtigster Profanbau der Renaissance nördlich der Alpen. Orientiert an florentinischen und venezianischen Vorbildern, der Piazza della Signoria und dem Palazzo Ducale, reflektiert es das Selbstbewusstsein der damaligen freien Reichsstadt Augsburg, die mit den Finanz- und Machtzentren ihrer Zeit konkurrierte. An der symmetrisch schlichten, zum Rathausplatz von einem Mittelrisalit geprägten Fassade ist die innere Organisation des Baus deutlich ablesbar: Im Erdgeschoss und ersten Obergeschoss des Mitteltrakts liegen die beiden dreischiffigen Hallen des Unteren und Oberen Fletzes mit

den Amtsstuben der Steuer-, Gerichts- und Bauherren, darüber der dreigeschossige, mit prächtigen Malereien im Stil des Manierismus, Goldtäfelungen und einer Kassettendecke geschmückte Goldene Saal. In den Eckräumen des Erdgeschosses waren die Wachen und Gerätschaften untergebracht; die beiden Zwiebeltürme beherbergten das Stadtarchiv. Den Goldenen Saal umgaben vier Fürstenzimmer. Diese und der Saal selbst waren vor allem für zukünftige Reichstage gedacht. Doch dazu kam es nicht mehr: der Dreißigjährige Krieg brach aus.

Das Augsburger Rathaus ist der letzte Bau der deutschen Renaissance, bevor mit dem Dreißigjährigen Krieg jegliche Bautätigkeit zum Erliegen kam. Die Baumaßnahme selbst war zudem Teil eines groß angelegten Arbeitsbeschaffungsprogramms für die Not leidenden Handwerker der Stadt.

Banqueting House, London (GB)

1619–1622, Inigo Jones

Das Banqueting House ist eines der bedeutendsten Werke der gesamten englischen Baugeschichte. Mit ihm fand die italienische Renaissance eine relativ späte Aufnahme in England. Architekt Jones, der bereits drei Jahre zuvor das Queens House in Greenwich als Sommerresidenz für die Gemahlin König Jakobs I. begonnen hatte, markierte damit den Beginn eines neuen architektonischen Zeitalters auf der Insel. Das Banqueting House gilt als das erste und zugleich wichtigste Bauwerk des englischen Palladianismus. Jones, bis dahin lediglich als Schöpfer spektakulärer Festspieldekorationen hervorgetreten, hatte den klassischen Baustil Palladios und dessen grundlegendes Werk während zweier Studienaufenthalte in Italien studiert. Sein nun völlig neuartiger Baustil fand im noch von der Gotik dominierten England aber vorerst kaum Nachahmung. Im Palastareal von Whitehall blieb Banqueting House deshalb stets ein Fremdkörper. Vielleicht hat es so auch dessen Zerstörung während des Brandes von 1698 unbeschadet überstanden. Der kubische Baukörper strahlt klassische Strenge und monumentale Würde aus. Die Fassade des zweistöckigen Gebäudes wird durch Säulen und Pilaster gegliedert, im Untergeschoss in ionischer und im Obergeschoss in korinthischer Ord-

nung. Die drei mittleren Fensterachsen sind durch Säulen betont, die nur leicht stärker als die Pilaster hervortreten. Ein Girlandenfries betont die Zone über den oberen Fenstern und eine luftige Balustrade bildet den Abschluss des Gebäudes. Insgesamt wird die Komposition durch Symmetrie, Klarheit und die harmonische Durchdringung der plastischen Elemente bestimmt. Um die gestalterische Harmonie der Hauptansichtsseiten nicht zu beeinträchtigen, wurde das Eingangsportal an die Seite des Bauwerks gelegt. Das Gebäude enthält einen einzigen großen zweigeschossigen Festsaal mit umlaufender Galerie, den ein Deckengemälde von Rubens schmückt.

Die Geschichte des Hauses ist eng an die Regentschaft der Stuarts geknüpft. Jakob I. erteilte 1619 den Bauauftrag und sein Sohn Karl I. trat am 30. Januar 1649 aus einem der Fenster auf das davor errichtete Schafott zu seiner Hinrichtung.

S. Andrea al Quirinale, Rom (I)
1658–1671, Gian Lorenzo Bernini

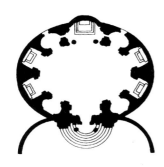

links:
Zwischen seitlichen Gartenmauern, die halbrund aus der Flucht der Straße zurückspringen, tritt die als monumentale Ädikula gestaltete Fassade plastisch hervor. Als Vorwegnahme des im Grundriss ovalen Innenraums erhebt sich über einer halbrunden Freitreppe ein Säulenportikus. Dieser wird von einem gesprengten Giebel bekrönt, zwischen dessen Voluten sich das Wappen der Papstfamilie fast freiplastisch abhebt.

Obwohl in ihren Abmessungen vergleichsweise bescheiden, ist die Kirche ein Hauptwerk des römischen Barock. Wie die nur wenige Meter entfernte Kirche S. Carlo alle Quattro Fontane seines persönlichen und künstlerischen Widersachers Francesco Borromini steht auch Berninis Bau exemplarisch für die Dynamisierungstendenzen des Hoch- und Spätbarocks. Bernini schuf den architekturgeschichtlich bedeutenden Bau als Kirche des jesuitischen Noviziathauses im Auftrag des Kardinals Camillo Pamphilj, einem Neffen Innozenz' X. 1870–1946 diente sie als Hofkapelle des italienischen Königshauses. Eine originelle baukünstlerische Lösung bildet insbesondere die Gestaltung der der Straße zugewandten Außenseite, mit ihrem für diese Phase der Barockarchitektur so typischen Gegeneinander konkaver und konvexer Formen. Zwischen seitlichen, halbrund einspringenden Gartenmauern tritt die streng gegliederte, tempelartige Fassade plastisch hervor. Sie wird von einem halbrund vortretenden Portikus über einer breit angelegten Freitreppe dominiert, der auf das bekrönende Wappen hin komponiert ist. Die gerundeten Fassadenelemente leiten zur Gestaltung des Innenraums über, der, dem hochbarocken Raumgefühl folgend, über dem Grundriss eines quer gelegten Ovals errichtet wurde. Dieser Zentralraum wird durch acht Seitenkapellen über ovalem beziehungsweise rechteckigem Grundriss erweitert. Eine kassettierte Kuppel schließt den reich mit Marmor und Stuck ausgestatteten Innenraum nach oben ab.

Der bereits in der Architektur früherer Epochen verbreitete und in der Renaissance als idealer Bautypus propagierte Zentralbau wurde im Hochbarock den epochentypischen Dynamisierungstendenzen unterworfen. Diese schlugen sich auch in der Wahl ovaler oder überaus komplizierter Grundrisslösungen nieder.

ALEXANDRO VII PONT MAX
OB AEDEM SAPIENTIAE
TOTO AMBITV PERFECTAM
ET BIBLIOTHECA
HORTOQVE MEDICO INSTRVCTAM
SACRI CONSISTORII ADVOCATI
POSS MDCLX

S. Ivo della Sapienza, Rom (I)

1643–1648, Francesco Borromini

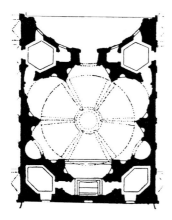

links:
Borromini fügte die Kirche S. Ivo meisterhaft in den bereits gegen Ende des 16. Jahrhunderts erbauten Innenhof der Universität ein. Den zweigeschossigen Aufbau der seitlichen Loggien führte er als Blendgliederung über die segmentbogig einschwingende Fassade fort. Deren dorische und ionische Pilaster werden durch die korinthischen Pilaster des kleeblattförmigen Kuppeltambours zu einer Abfolge der drei klassischen Säulenordnungen komplettiert.

Mit S. Ivo della Sapienza schuf Borromini einen der originellsten Sakralbauten des römischen Barock. Mit seiner dynamischen Formensprache steht der Bau ebenso beispielhaft für die Gestaltungsprinzipien des Hochbarock wie für das Gegeneinandersetzen konkaver und konvexer Elemente. Die ehemalige Universitätskirche ist in den für Papst Sixtus V. Ende des 16. Jahrhunderts von Giacomo della Porta errichteten Palast der Sapientia (Weisheit) eingeschlossen, der bis 1935 als Sitz der römischen Universität diente. In diesen bestehenden Komplex fügte Borromini dann seinen Kirchenbau ein, dessen konkav geschwungene Fassade den eindrucksvollen zweigeschossigen Arkadenhof nach Osten hin abschließt, indem sie seine bauliche Struktur aufgreift. Mit einer einschwingenden Fassade kontrastiert Borromini die konvexe Form seiner im unteren Teil kleeblattförmig ummantelten Kuppel, die nach oben hin in einer spiralförmigen Spitze endet und somit in ihrem emblematischen Charakter auf antike und mittelalterliche Vorbilder verweist. Den Innenraum gestaltete Borromini über einem Grundriss, der durch zwei sich überlagernde gleichseitige Dreiecke gebildet wird, die an ihren Spitzen nischenartig abgeschlossen werden. Die Kuppel nimmt mit ihren konkaven, von jeweils einem Fenster durchlichteten Teilflächen diese Raumstruktur wieder auf. Die Stukkaturen des Innenraums mit ihren heraldischen Motiven beschränken sich in ihrer Farbgebung auf Weiß und Gold.

Zu den wichtigsten Gestaltungsprinzipien des Hoch- und Spätbarock gehört die Verschleifung einzelner Teilräume zu komplizierten Grund- und Aufrissgebilden, wie etwa der aus der Durchdringung von Dreiecken entstehenden Figur, die Borrominis Bau zugrunde liegt und den Innenraum bis in die Kuppelzone bestimmt.

Schloss Vaux-le-Vicomte, Melun (F)

1657–1661, Louis Le Vau

links:
Im Zentrum des 1657–1661 durch Louis Le Vau errichteten Landschlosses befindet sich ein über zwei Geschosse reichender Salon. Dessen ovale Form ist am überkuppelten Mittelpavillon der Gartenfassade ablesbar. Dieses einzige gerundete Element des Außenbaus wird jedoch keinesfalls betont, sondern durch einen zweigeschossigen Blendportikus in die von einer flächigen Gliederung geprägte Fassadengestaltung mit einbezogen.

1657 erhielt Louis Le Vau von Nicolas Fouquet, dem Finanzminister Ludwigs XIV., den Auftrag zur Errichtung des unweit von Paris gelegenen Landschlosses Vaux-le-Vicomte. Die finanziellen Mittel erlaubten die Errichtung des Rohbaus binnen eines Jahres. Die von Charles Lebrun geschaffene prachtvolle Ausgestaltung der Innenräume wurde ebenso bis 1661 vollendet wie die Anlage der ausgedehnten Schlossgärten. Die Freude des Auftraggebers an seinem Besitz währte nur kurz, wurde er doch noch im selben Jahr inhaftiert. Le Vau gestaltete das Schloss als eine einflügelige Anlage über kompliziertem Grundriss. Ein an den Ecken mit Pavillons besetzter rechteckiger Baukörper schwingt in der Mitte seiner Hofseite konkav ein, um im Zentrum dieses Mauerrücksprungs einen das Vestibül aufnehmenden Risalit auszubilden. Dieser rechteckige Eingangsraum öffnet sich zu einem über zwei Geschosse reichenden ovalen Salon, der sich am Außenbau der Gartenseite als überkuppelter Mittelpavillon artikuliert. In der plattenförmigen Schichtung der einzelnen Gliederungselemente unterscheidet sich die Fassadengestaltung Le Vaus erheblich von der plastischen Außengliederung des kaum älteren Schlosses Maisons, das sein Rivale François Mansart 1642–1656 errichtet hatte. Den dort kontinuierlich umlaufenden Pilasterstellungen setzt Le Vau das Nebeneinander kleiner und kolossaler Ordnungen entgegen, das den einzelnen Teilen des Gesamtbaukörpers eine gewisse Eigenständigkeit verleiht.

Ein integraler Bestandteil barocker Schlossbaukunst war die Gestaltung der umliegenden Landschaft. Mit André Le Nôtre gestaltete der bedeutendste Landschaftsarchitekt seiner Zeit die Gärten von Vaux-le-Vicomte als dreigeteilte Anlage aus Broderieparterre, Bosketts und natürlich belassenem Wald.

Schloss Versailles (F)

**1661–1710, Philibert Le Roy, Louis le Vau, Jules Hardouin-Mansart
Robert de Cotte, André Le Nôtre, Jacques-Ange Gabriel**

Als größte und prächtigste Schlossanlage der Welt stellt Versailles gleichsam das architektonische Denkmal des Absolutismus dar, der seinen Höhepunkt unter dem Sonnenkönig Ludwig XIV. erreichte. Er war es auch, der die bereits 1623 als Jagdschloss Ludwigs XIII. begonnene und wenig später durch Philibert Le Roy erweiterte Anlage zu einer repräsentativen Residenz von riesigen Ausmaßen erweitern ließ. Im Jahr 1668 erhielt Louis Le Vau den Auftrag für die Ummantelung der bereits bestehenden Bauten. Mit der endgültigen Verlegung des zuvor im Louvre befindlichen Wohn- und Amtsitzes im Jahre 1677 begann der entscheidende Ausbau durch Jules

Hardouin-Mansart. Von den durch ihn errichteten Bauteilen zeigt vor allem die Gartenfront jene von monumentaler Grundhaltung geprägte Formensprache des für die Staatskunst unter Ludwig XIV. charakteristischen Classicisme. Von den in Zusammenarbeit mit dem Maler Charles Lebrun entstandenen Innenräumen verdienen vor allem der Spiegelsaal und die Schlosskapelle besondere Beachtung. André Le Nôtre gestaltete die Parkanlagen zu einem Höhepunkt barocker Gartenarchitektur. Die unter Ludwig XV., durch Jacques-Ange Gabriel errichteten Bauten markieren bereits den Übergang zum Klassizismus.

oben:

1677 begann Hardouin-Mansart mit dem Ausbau des bereits für Ludwig XIII. erbauten Jagdschlosses zu einer riesigen Residenz. Hierbei schloss er zunächst die in der Mitte des Gartenflügels verbliebene Terrasse durch die 73 m lange Spiegelgalerie, wobei er sich an der älteren Fassadengliederung Le Vaus orientierte. Diesen Wandaufbau übernahm er auch bei der Gestaltung der Gartenfassaden des Süd- und des Nordflügels. Diese Front ist – neben Perraults Ostfassade des Louvre – der Inbegriff der Profanarchitektur des Classicisme.

Im Gegensatz zu Deutschland und Italien vermochte sich die dynamisierte und räumlich komplexe Formensprache des Barock in Frankreich kaum auszubreiten. Vielmehr bildete sich mit dem „Classicisme" eine an Andrea Palladio orientierte Architektur he-raus, die durch formale Strenge und fast monotone Gliederungen charakterisiert wird. Als Protagonisten dieser vor allem durch die 1672 gegründete „Académie Royale de l' Architecture" propagierten Stieltendenz gelten neben Hardouin-Mansart auch Louis Le Vau, Claude Perrault und Francois Blondel.

Dôme des Invalides, Paris (F)

1679–1690, Jules Hardouin-Mansart

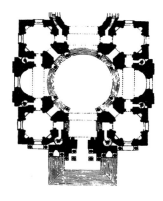

links:

An der Fassade des Invalidendoms fasste Hardouin-Mansart einen quadratischen Baublock mit einem hohen Kuppelaufbau zu einer einheitlichen Schauseite zusammen. Die rhythmisch verteilten, sich zur Mitte hin verdichtenden Säulen des Portikus korrespondieren mit den von Doppelsäulen besetzten Streben des Tambours. Die Kuppel orientiert sich an der Peterskirche in Rom, ist aber durch die zusätzliche Attikazone unter der steil geführten Kuppelschale und die von einem spitzen Obelisken bekrönte Laterne deutlich vertikalisiert.

Bereits unter Heinrich IV. und dessen Minister Richelieu gab es in Paris Einrichtungen zur Versorgung und Pflege von im Krieg versehrten Soldaten. Als solche gab Ludwig XIV. 1670 das Hôtel des Invalides in Auftrag. Dazu gehörte auch die Église de Soldats, an deren Chor Hardouin-Mansart 1677–1690 den Invalidendom anbaute. Zunächst als Grablege des Sonnenkönigs vorgesehen, wurde 1861 der Porphyrsarkophag Napoleon Bonapartes in die durch Louis Visconti geöffnete Raummitte gestellt. Der Grundriss des Invalidendoms zeigt einen Zentralbau in Form eines Quadrats, dem ein gleicharmiges Kreuz einbeschrieben wird, dessen ovale Arme in eine Rotunde münden. In den Ecken befinden sich elliptische, durch Nischen erweiterte Kapellen. Am Außenbau markiert ein zweigeschossiger Portikus, dessen Säulen sich zur Mitte hin verdichten, die optische Verbindung zwischen dem kubischen Baublock und der Kuppel. Das dieser zu Grunde gelegte Vorbild der römischen Peterskirche erfährt durch die zwischen Tambour und Kuppelschale eingefügte Attikazone und die mittels eines Rings von der Kuppel abgesetzte Laterne eine starke Vertikalisierung, die in dem abschließenden Obelisken gipfelt. In ihrem betonten Höhenzug und der Dynamisierung der Gesamtkomposition übertrifft die Kuppel des Invalidendoms jene der etwas älteren Kirchen Église de la Sorbonne und Val-de-Grâce.

Wie zahlreiche Sakralbauten des Barock erfährt auch der Invalidendom eine Akzentuierung durch eine zentrale Kuppel. Die plastische Gliederung ihres Außenbaus greift auf das in immer wieder neuen Variationen nachgeahmte Vorbild der von Michelangelo entworfenen Kuppel des Petersdoms zurück.

St. Paul's Kathedrale, London (GB)

1675–1710, Sir Christopher Wren

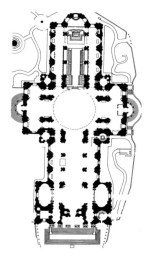

links:
Mit ihrer am zweige-
schossigen
Säulenportikus verdichte-
ten Pilastergliederung,
dem reliefierten
Tympanon des
Hauptgiebels oder den
Fensterädikulen zeigt
sich die klassizistische
Grundhaltung der an
Andrea Palladio orientier-
ten Bauten Wrens.
Daneben finden sich mit
den an Bauten
Borrominis erinnernden
Turmhelmen oder den
scheinperspektivischen
Fensternischen des
Untergeschosses auch
Elemente des italieni-
schen Barock.

Unter Cromwells Herrschaft geschän-
det und als Pferdestall missbraucht,
wurde die alte St. Paulskirche während
des großen Londoner Brandes 1666
vollständig zerstört. Mit dem Wieder-
aufbau wurde 1668 Christopher Wren
beauftragt. Sein ursprünglicher Entwurf, das so genannte Great Model,
beruhte auf einem griechischen Kreuz
und verzichtete auf Mittel- und
Seitenschiffe. Die traditionalistische
kirchliche Kommission lehnte diesen
Vorschlag allerdings ab. Akzeptiert
wurde schließlich das „Warrant
Design": Es sah eine trichterförmige
Kuppel mit pagodenähnlicher Turm-
spitze über einem langgestreckten
basilikalen Bau klassischen Stils vor
und berücksichtigte auch Wrens
Vorliebe für eine Barockkirche, die von
einer erhöhten Mittelrotunde dominiert
wird. Die grandiose barocke Kuppel
von St. Paul's ist innen wie außen die
auffälligste architektonische Leistung.
Sie vereint alle Gestaltungselemente
des Bauwerks und ordnet sie ihrer
Masse unter. Durch den Kompromiss
zwischen dem geforderten basilikalen
Langhaus und Wrens Idee eines
Zentralbaus rückt sie zur Mitte des
Langbaus hin. In ihrer technischen
Finesse konkurriert sie mit denen der
Peterskirche in Rom und des Doms in
Florenz. Trotz der barocken Elemente
gilt die Kathedrale als das bedeutendste Bauwerk des englischen Klassizismus. Das ringsum zweigeschossige
Äußere lässt ihren traditionellen basilikalen Aufbau nicht erkennen. Die über
eine breite Freitreppe zugängliche
Westfront wird von einem Portikus mit
paarweise angeordneten korinthischen
Säulen und Tympanon gebildet, der mit
seinen antiken Zügen die Kuppel und
die gemäßigt barocken Türme konter-
kariert. Alle Bauteile der Kathedrale
sind stilistisch klar voneinander
getrennt und blockhaft zusammen-
gesetzt. Das gibt dem Bau einen sach-
lichen Charakter, der sich dem
Klassizismus palladianischer Prägung
annähert.

Infolge der unüblichen flächendek-
kenden Bauweise dauerte es 21
Jahre, bis der erste Gottesdienst im
Chor abgehalten werden konnte. Zu
diesem Zeitpunkt war mit dem Bau
der Kuppel noch nicht einmal
begonnen worden. Dennoch war St.
Paul's die erste Kathedrale, die
noch zu Lebzeiten ihres Architekten
vollendet wurde.

Madrid (Spain): Hospicio de San Fernando
1722 – 1723, Pedro de Ribera

left:
The most important architect of the Spanish late baroque probably created his most famous work with the main portal of the Hospicio de San Fernando (1722–1723). On this occasion, the architecture of the altarlike frame is overgrown with ornate and imaginatively designed decoration. The gable is plastic and coluorful in its outline, seemingly unattached to the ledge of the roof behind it.

Established as a private initiative in 1668, the hospital already enjoyed the pleasure of royal patronage, but only under Philipp V, for whom Pedro de Ribera had designed a representative building with the outstanding feature being a lavishly adorned main portal. Riberas' neoclassical critics viewed it as a design lacking in breeding and taste, believing him to be a suitable candidate for the madhouse. This so-called "madness" he shared successfully, however, with contemporaries like the Churriguera brothers or Narcisco Tomé. The Hospicio de San Fernando is an extended two-storey building whose central axis adopts a faced portal frame. It contains several pilasters decorated with capitals at the top. As a conclusion, it forms an open round gable that rises above the height of the building – in keeping with the Spanish late Gothic. The architectural structure becomes over-burdened by heavy decorations whose imaginative ornamentation is even three dimensional in places. This oldfashioned faced portal framing is a characteristic of Riberas' buildings. With its acquisition by the city of Madrid in 1924, the building was spared from demolition. Until 1926 it was carefully restored and has served since then as a "Museo Municipal". From the first big exhibition, "Antiguo Madrid", it has had an extensive influence: It sharpened the consciousness of the public for the urban and monumental nursing problems of the city and so helped to prevent some "sins".

In the 17th century the unadorned architectural style had spread throughout Spain and was known as "Desornamentado". From 1690 the brothers José, Joaquin and Alberto Churriguera, a dynasty of decorators / sculptors / architects who covered their buildings extensively with excessive decorations, opposed this "Habsburg architecture". To their company were later added the "mad" Ribera, Tomé and Andres Garcia de Quinones.

Vienna (Austria): Upper Belvedere
1720 – 1723, Johann Lukas von Hildebrandt

Belvedere is the High Baroque summer castle of prince Eugene of Savoy. He served the Austrians as a field marshall and was victorious in the war against the Turks. The castle grounds contain two palaces: lower Belvedere as a residence and upper Belvedere as representative building. A park with water features and cascades on rising terraces connects them. The dominating position on the raised terrain is held by upper Belvedere, which is fascinating because of its pavilion-like structure with the height gradation of the hip roof and the illusion of the fading silhouette. It is a single, extended building with four domed octagonal corner

pavilions. The high rectangular windows of the two-storey wings have stone frames. The south side possesses a projecting triple-axis gate structure with round arched portals. Sphinxes keep watch on the drive-way ramps. In addition to the richly decorated façade, the section of the upper roof contains mythological stone figures on pedestals and balustrades. Today the interiors are considerably altered as a result of war damage and its use as a museum. The original interior was mainly the work of Claude Le Fort du Plessy and the plasterer Santino Bussi. The entrance hall, originally open to the park, collapsed in 1732. In the reconstruction that took

above:
The Upper Belvedere was built in 1721–1723 and was virtually staged in its scenic surroundings. Lukas von Hildebrandt laid it out as an ensemble of individual building units, which are staggered towards the central pavilion. The result was a stage-like effect, giving the castle one of the most impressive silhouettes of Baroque secular architecture.

place, four atlases support the vault. The park connecting the palaces was constructed completely according to the wishes of the owner. The terraces were divided into three sections, each portraying different themes: the lower section depicted the effects of the elements; the middle section formed Parnassus, and the high terrace with the castle was intended to depict the heavens. The present outlay shows this concept only in a rudimentary fashion. In the formal sense, the garden was a synthesis of Italian mannerist and French Baroque gardening art.

Prince Eugene of Savoy (1663 – 1736) was not only the most able general of his time, but is also recognized as a visionary politician and large benefactor of the arts and science. With Belvedere, he established one of the most interesting and important Baroque castle grounds of Europe.

Oxfordshire (U.K.): Blenheim Palace
1705 – 1724, Sir John Vanbrugh

left:
Blenheim Palace was arranged as a huge construction surrounding a rectangular court of honour. The exterior exhibits a lively silhouette, above all on the courtyard façades, which are underlined by the crowns of the corner towers, which appear to be sculptured. Their form is aligned towards the crowning of Elizabethan houses, forming a counterpoint to a form repertoire which otherwise follows the English Palladian tradition.

Blenheim Palace was a present from the Queen and the Parliament to the English General John Churchill, first Duke of Marlborough. On 13th August 1704 he was victorious in the Danube valley in the battle of Blindheim (near Höchstädt, Bavaria, Germany) over troops of the French Marshal Tallard. The success was celebrated as a victory of English parliamentarianism over French absolutism. The castle was intended to have a national character and relate the fame of its general. No person was more suitable to execute this idea than John Vanbrugh, the man of theatrical gestures, scenic effects and heterogeneous architectural forms. To this day architectural critics and art historians find it difficult to accurately classify his building, which resembles a theatre backdrop. Baroque façades are interchanged with medieval fortress towers, Doric columns with Corinthian arrangements. Voltaire thought Blenheim to be nothing but a solid assemblage of stones without charm and taste. Like many others, he also did not understand the dramatic creativity of Vanbrugh that spans the big gap between order and liveliness on the one hand, and tradition and non-conformism on the other. The inside of the castle has decorative and figurative stage settings which portray a walk through the history of the battles of Marlborough. During his lifetime a salon was completed which was also known as the hall of peace. It was done in a little English trompe- l'œil. The park of this largest private house in Great Britain is a creation of the renowned English landscape architect Lancelot "Capability" Brown, and represents a technical masterpiece. He had masses of earth moved in order to create an impressive lake area. Because every duke strove to immortalize himself there, little is left of the original.

Sir John Vanbrugh (1664 – 1726) only turned to architecture late in life. He began his career as a soldier, spy and author of comedies. His love for the stage is clearly reflected in the histrionics of his buildings. With Blenheim Palace he created the last big building of the English Baroque which lasted only a short period.

Vienna (Austria): Karlskirche
1716 – 1737, Johann Bernhard Fischer von Erlach

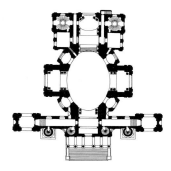

left:
Together with the two pavilions at its sides, the façade of the Karlskirche stands before the actual church as an independent structure. Just a small passage connects the portico – which is as flat as the rest of the façade – with the oval space of the church. The tambour and domes of the church are, on the other hand, equally part of the façade composition. The roof of the dome corresponds to that of the columns, and the roofs of the dome lanterns with those of the pavilions.

In 1713 emperor Charles VI pledged to build a church, only if God would terminate the rampant Black Death in Vienna: the so-called Karlskirche (Charles' Church) was consecrated to the plague revered Charles Borromaeus. The commencement of construction began in 1716 according to the design of Fischer von Erlach`s following a competition against his rival von Hildebrandt. After the death of Johann Bernhard, his son, Joseph Emanuel, completed the building. In 1738 the church was transferred to the "Kreuzherrenorden" (Order of the Knights of the Holy Cross), and in 1783 it became the emperor's parochial church. Lengthways, the church is an oval building with transverse-like extensions and a rectangular chancel. The structure of the façade was developed completely independently of the interior formation: In its centre is located a portico, copied from that of the Pantheon in Rome. The central motif of the complex iconographic façade programme are the two 33 metres (36 yds.) high columns, which are erected in front of it: formally they are similar to the Trajan Column (Rome), beyond that the arrangement in pairs symbolize on the one hand the temple of Solomon as described in the Bible: "and he erected the two columns in front of the hall of the temple" (1 Kings 7; 13 – 22), on the

other hand, the columns of Hercules. These symbolized the end of the known (ancient) world. Thus the architect structurally represents the claim of the Habsburgs: to govern the known world wisely (temple of Salomon) as successors to the Roman Empire (Trajan column).

The temple of Solomon (965 – 926 BC) in Jerusalem is described in the Bible with numerous references to building technique and fittings. Attempts at reconstruction and representations (for example by Giotto) always tend to show a rather contemporary building in each case.

Dresden (Germany): Frauenkirche
1726 – 1739, Georg Bähr

left:
The interior hardly makes itself noticed through the quadratically jacketed exterior building. In this way, the stone dome seeks no reference to the structure of the round sermon hall, whose height it far exceeds. The fact that the massive helm roof has been assigned a primarily urban development function can be seen not least from the fact that the tambour only starts at the height of the peak of the dome in the interior.

By combining a domed central-plan structure with the Evangelical tradition of gallery churches in the Frauenkirche, George Bähr undoubtedly created one of the most important Protestant contributions to Baroque sacred architecture. Inside is a simple semi-dome on eight fragile piers in a radial arrangement. These are so slender because of the differentiated distribution of the vault's thrust. Four galleries were suspended in between causing the church with its round central space, and 3,600 seats, to sometimes be called the Protestant "Preacher's Pipe." The disposition of the interior space is hardly reflected in the quadratic exterior structure and its subtle stylistic vocabulary already reveals the emergence of Classicist influences on the architecture of the late Baroque period. Hence, the steeply inclining outer stone dome does not strive to establish any relationship to the structure beneath it, exceeding its height by far. This is, not least, a function of the drum's being set on a level above the peek of the cupola on the interior, indicating that the primary function of this massive helmet was in conjunction with the city around it. The dome made the Frauenkirche a landmark which helped to give the city of Dresden its characteristic silhouette

In 1945 the Frauenkirche was destroyed in heavy allied bombing. It was left for decades to stand in a ruinous condition as a monument for the victims of the bombing, until a citizen's group took the initiative in 1990, within the framework of the peace movement, to coordinate efforts to reconstruct the church. The first step, which involved the removal of 26,000 metric tons of rubble and stones, was accompanied by architectural archaeological studies which formed the basis of the reconstruction project which will be completed in 2005.

Turin (Italy): Villa Reale di Stupinigi
from 1729, Filippo Juvarra

The Stupinigi Castle was built for the King of Savoy and Piedmont between 1729 and 1733, according to plans by the architect Filippo Juvarra. It was intended to serve the royal family as a domicile during their hunting parties. Juvarra went on to create his architectonic masterpiece. In his plan, he combined the principle of a dominant axis with a system of spaces arranged along an axis that penetrate each other. He was able to realize his plans without compromise on a plane on which there had been no previous building. The layout clearly expresses the desire to integrate the building into the garden, and the park into the landscape. The dominant axis begins at the royal residence in Turin, continues on beyond the city's fortifications, approaches the vicinity of the castle as a wide thoroughfare and, finally, passes by the castle's outbuildings, on the left and the right, ending on a semicircular forecourt. Across from it an archway invites the visitor into a polygonal cour d'honneur. The castle is laid out like a star with a large, central, elliptical hall, from which four wings radiate like a St Andrew's cross. Two of these wings are connected by galleries that also serve to enclose the courtyard. The central room is the intersection and focal point of the many horizontal and diagonal axes that radiate into

Filippo Juvarra started work on his Stupinigi hunting castle near Turin for King Victor Amadeus in 1729. He went on to create his architectonic masterpiece. In an almost set-designer interpretation of architecture, the rising building units are subdivided by pilaster and lesenes in an almost frame-like way and are stepped towards the centre. Together they form, as it were, the apron to the great hall in the centre.

the building's wings, its garden and the road. Beyond the castle there is a large garden rondel with an axes leading once again from the centre to the horizon.

Like many Baroque architects, Juvarra works with a seemingly endless sense of expansion that suspends the borders between architecture, gardens and landscape, and places everything under the command of continuing axes at the intersection of which the building is placed. Mainly Venetian artists under Juvarra's direction completed the interior decoration around 1734.

Staffelstein (Germany)
The Pilgrimage Church Vierzehnheiligen
1743 – 1772, Balthasar Neumann

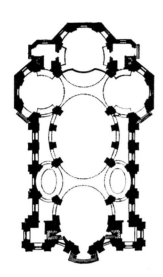

left:

The pilgrimage altar created by Johann Michael Feichtmayr in 1763 forms the spatial and liturgical centre of the Wallfahrtskirche Vierzehnheiligen. The Baldachin and the oval balustrade surrounding it were arranged as an autonomous Rococo ornament, at a somewhat enlarged scale. The composition rises above the figures of the 14 auxiliary saints up to the Christ child, which appears at the top four times.

This church of pilgrimage, visible from a great distance, sits up high on a field overlooking the valley of the Main River. It has belonged to the Cistercian monastery in Langheim since the Middle Ages. Shepherds from the monastery had had repeated visions of the Fourteen Holy Helpers between 1445 and 1446. The first chapel built on the site was destroyed during the Peasants' War. The larger one built in its place was, in turn, replaced by another commissioned by the abbot of Langheim and Prince Bishop Karl von Schönborn. This new church was built between 1743 and 1772 according to plans by Balthasar Neumann. The simple exterior, accentuated only by a monumental double tower façade, forms the shell for one of the most spectacular creations of interior architecture found in the late Baroque period. These outer walls that are dominated by simple right angles harbour a very diversified floor plan composed mainly of elliptic and circular spaces that border, overlap and displace each other. By combining a gallery basilica with a centralized domed building, Neumann develops a fascinating spatial constellation, in which the architectural and the sacral centres are consciously focussed at different points. Hence Johann Michael Feichtmayr's Altar of Mercy is not located at the crossing of the cloverleaf-shaped choir, but rather under the main dome in the nave.

The building's decoration makes an important contribution to the very subtle amalgamation of its individual parts. Hence, the white surfaces of the walls and ceiling are decorated with Feichtmayr's highly animated Rococo plasterwork. The harmony of muted colour is echoed in the columns and pilasters and then intensified in the more robust colours used for the fixtures on the altar. Appiani's illusionist ceiling frescoes transform the building into a total work of art that one experiences sensually. It is a classic example of Baroque architecture combining all of the arts to create a homogenous whole.

Classicism, Romanticism and the 19th Century

Classicism, Romanticism and the 19th Century

With the beginning of the first Industrial Revolution, around 1760, a pronounced change in the living conditions and consciousness of the populations of nascent industrial nations made itself felt. Natural sciences, technical discoveries, modern economic thought and a shift in the dominant power structures characterized the new industrial society, which believed in a modern concept of progress to the extent that every problem seemed as if it could be solved by industry and technology. In the wake of these powerful currents, architecture seemed somehow backward, ambivalent and locked into traditions that had evolved during the Renaissance. The ideals of clarity and balance, held high during the Renaissance, were again of great importance in Classicism, particularly as reflected in the canon of forms passed down from Antiquity. Having evolved as a counter movement to late Baroque and Rococo, and informed by exacting archaeological studies of Roman and, for the first time, Greek Antiquity, Classicism with its Doric-Roman style spread quickly among the European avant-garde. The rationalism of Classicism was reflected in the Ecole d'Architecture, founded by J.F. Blondel in the mid-18th century, as well as in Étienne-Louis Boullée's studies of ideal forms. This was not the first time that basic geometric shapes – squares, circles, cubes, spheres and pyramids – engaged architects' imaginations. However, these forms mainly played a role in studies of ideal forms and the design of public monuments. Ledoux's architecture is exemplary in that it combines geometric rigor and symbolic functionalism with a romantic view of nature. Indeed, this period was marked by an increasing sensibility of the beauty of nature and the picturesque quality of architecture that found its most pronounced expression in both English landscape paintings and English landscape gardens. Paired with the newest archaeological discoveries of the day, this led to a picturesque Romantic Classicism distinguished by exact, imaginative details and harmoniously balanced proportions. In Germany, this was reflected in Schinkel's Neo-Greek designs that, in turn, could be linked to Langhans's and Gilly's Prussian style of early Classicism. The creative dialogue with Antiquity had begun in the early Renaissance and was followed by a period of stylistic pluralism and an eclectic mix of styles marked by continuous struggles between rival schools of Historicism. The lack of generally recognized, objective criteria became clearly obvious in the arbitrary use, modification and combination of elements from the most diverse historical styles. These were adapted to fit into the Historicism of newly emerging, public building projects, whereby the desire for real renewal often did not go beyond formal aesthetics and, hence, seemed to repudiate the very powers that spurned society on to ever greater achievements in science, industry and technology. Modern engineering was one expression of these forces that was ultimately destined to facilitate a renewed correspondence between a building's form and its method of construction, something that had been lost since the Gothic period. Aided by the newly acquired ability to calculate the exact forces at work within a structure, as well as by new building materials, solutions were found for new types of buildings with dimensions that had been hitherto impossible. An expression of this new aesthetic can be seen in the Eiffel Tower, created for the International Exhibition in Paris in 1889. The definition of functionalism formulated by Sullivan in 1896: "form follows function," became not only the starting point for the first Chicago School with their skyscrapers designed primarily with their purpose and their construction methods in mind, but also for architecture in general in the coming century.

Twickenham (Great Britain): Strawberry Hill
1753 – 1776, Horace Walpole

left:
The country house Strawberry Hill consists of individual components placed at a clear distance from each other, which is already discernible in its exterior. In contrast to the later Arts and Crafts, here elements of medieval high architecture are picked up in the tower, chapel, and hall. Different forms of detail clearly distinguish the components from each other.

In 1747 Horace Walpole, the younger son of British Prime Minister Robert Walpole, acquired a hilly ground above the Thames in Twickenham, southwest of London. This picturesque region alongside the river became, a sought-after villa quarter for English societyat the beginning of the 18th century – writers in particular settled here. As a passionate letter writer (his correspondence comprises 48 volumes), Walpole was a chronicler of the society of his time. In addition, he was known as an art collector and published books, including The Castle of Otranto (1765), which established the "Gothic novel" as a mixture of knight's romance and the contemporary English horror genre. The novel is set in a house based on his domicile in Twickenham. Walpole made successive alterations and extensions to the building over a period of two decades. Initially, the existing arrangement was supplemented with a library and dining room, then by an extended gallery and an immense round tower; finally, a large dormitory and another tower were added. The interlocked arrangement in the Gothic style, which nevertheless reveals the comforts of an English country house, is the product of an art enthusiasts' architectural dilettantism. Apart from Walepole himself, the "Committee of Taste," which was founded by friends of the owner, also participated in the planning. The forms largely adhere to the Late Gothic style and some are explicit quotations, though Walpole was not particularly interested in the original context. He converted Gothic grave monuments into fireplaces and applied constructive stone elements copied from stucco purely as decoration. Strawberry Hill, the result of a Walpole whim, is considered the key building of the Gothic Revival.

In England the Gothic tradition never died off completely – even 17th-century architects such as Christopher Wren occasionally made use of Gothic forms. However, a new, romantically fuelled interest in the Middle Ages led to a rediscovery of the Gothic. The home of the architect's colleague in Greenwich, John Vanbrugh (1718/19), is an early example. Characteristic of the architecture of the Gothic Revival was an unabashed utilization of the building elements of this historical style. The aim was to create a fantastic mood rather than correctly apply functional or historical forms.

London (Great Britain): Kenwood House
1764 – 1769, Robert Adam

left:
With the 1764–1773 rebuilding and extension of the country residence of Lord Mansfield, Robert Adam created a building whose monochrome white façades, with their clear, restrained composition, demonstrated a stylistic continuity between the "anti-Baroque" Palladianism of the 17th and early 18th centuries and true Classicism.

Robert Adam began his career with a series of alterations. In England he revamped buildings dating from the beginning of the 18th century that were mainly erected in the neo-Palladian style. Not only his later works such as Seton Castle (1789-91), but even the earlier modifications Adam made on the periphery of London between 1760 and 1770 show the architect's interest for the picturesque in the sovereign changes of the differently proportioned halls. In addition, Adam borrowed elements linked to Antiquity. Occasionally he combined them arbitrarily and applied Classicism in a consciously non-academic way. Kenwood House was also established at the beginning of the 18th century. The earl of Mansfield acquired it around the middle of that century and later allowed Adam to make the changes . Today it can be ranked as a classic example of an English country house of that period. While the bright, radiant building has the later builtstreet between the north London suburbs of Hampstead and Highgate as its northern border, to the south it adjoins the vast park of Hampstead Heath, thereby affording one a distant view of the city of London. Adam raised the main building by one storey and emphasized the entrance façade facing the street by means of a portico. But the best view of the building is afforded from the park, where one can see an elegantly plastered façade with three middle window axes that are stressed by means of a pilaster and tympanum. Analogous to the lower orangery in the west, the architect added a library wing in the east. The understated, refined Classicism of the library hall, which is divided by opposing columns in a central area and two apses, represents one of the climaxes of Robert Adam's work.

With his buildings, Robert Adam explored a new aesthetic which he stressed in the foreword to his book Works in Architecture, published in 1773: "The massive pillar framework, the ornate coffered ceiling, the heavy framework (...) have now exploded universally." Instead of oppressive forms, Adam demanded "movement" to stress the picturesque aspects of a composition. In this way a varied outline is established, "with the appearance of a grouped and contrasted painting and with a multiplicity of light and shade, lending a great deal of spirit and beauty to the composition."

Wörlitz (Germany): Palace

1769- – 1773, Friedrich Wilhelm von Erdmansdorff

left:
The Gothic house by F.W. von Erdmannsdorff and Georg Christoph Hesekiel marks the beginning of German neo-Gothic. Whilst strolling in the landscaped garden, its annex buildings can be seen repeatedly along lanes cut into the structure. Walkers are thus provided with diverse themes for conversation.

In 1764, Prince Leopold III Friedrich Franz of Anhalt-Dessau began laying out a park in the small village of Wörlitz, a few kilometres east of Dessau on the River Elbe. With this, he created the first park in continental Europe to be modelled on the English landscape garden. The focus was turned to picturesque composition, in place of the rational principles that determined the geometrically styled French parks; the atmosphere was to be created by nature, and was intended to evoke a variety of moods. By including pastures, meadows and fields, beauty was combined with practical usage; the park simultaneously became cultivated soil, and developed through the addition of other park areas into the „Garden Kingdom Dessau-Wörlitz." The effect created by this well-preserved park, which right from the start was open to the public, was enhanced by a series of buildings based on the temples of Antiquity, but that in some cases have a mediaeval air or quite exotic features. There is even a cast-iron bridge that is a copy of the Severn Bridge near Coalbrookdale, England, that was completed shortly beforehand. In 1773, the architect Friedrich Wilhelm von Erdmannsdorff began work on the "Gothic House," and with that introduced the Gothic Revival from England; the details are borrowed from Venetian and North German buildings. In the years prior to this, Erdmannsdorff built the palace, which is informed by the English Neo-Palladian style of architecture. A square, white building is set off merely by a portico and four columns. This extremely clear and simple design makes Wörlitz Palace a key work that marked the departure from the Baroque in Germany and the beginning of Classicism. Simultaneously the Prince, who was interested in the ideas of the Enlightenment, distanced himself from the courtly culture that set the tone in Potsdam and Berlin, and which was decidedly French.

The "Grand Tour" during the 18th century took artists to Italy, above all to the sites of Antiquity that had become part of the artistic canon. The journeys that the architect Erdmannsdorff and the Prince of Anhalt-Dessau undertook to Italy as well as England influenced their concept for the park buildings of Wörlitz, which in some cases cite historic models. There was even a miniature Vesuvius on an artificial island that could be made to erupt by pyrotechnic means.

Arc-et-Senans (France)
The Royal Saltworks of Arc-et-Senans
1775 – 1779, Claude-Nicolas Ledoux

Through the good offices of Madame Dubarry, a mistress of Louis XV's, Ledoux became the Commissaire des Salines in 1771, thereby entering royal service as an architect. He evolved from the darling of the ancien régime to one of the most productive proponents of Revolutionary Architecture. His saltworks combine a concept of the ideal city informed by Rousseau's natural philosophy, with both the architecture of social control and early industrial architecture. The new saltworks were supposed to utilize the saltwater not required by the neighbouring Chateau-Salins. It was brought into the saltworks via a system of canals and evaporated in salt-

pans. The firewood required was available in the woods of Chaux, which was an important consideration for the choice of location. Factories were seen in those days as less prestigious buildings, ornamental elements like cyclopean masonry, columns, porticos and architraves were usually reserved for the aristocracy and clerics. Ladoux used these elements in designing both the worker's living quarters and the workshops just as for the gatehouse and the director's villa, a decision that initially displeased Louis XVI. All of the buildings in the saltworks are arranged in a semi-circle, refraining from any sort of theatrical Baroque appeal, the block-like buildings seem

above:
The salt-works of Chaux is the most important monument of Revolution Architecture, apart from the few remaining Paris tollhouses. What is typical here is the rigid form with simultaneous fantasy-filled treatment of the antique repertoire, as can be seen here with the uniform array of triglyphs in the frieze and the bosses on the columns.

like pavilions in a park. The production process and its organization in separate buildings stood in the foreground. A stylised grotto, decorated with stone drops of crystallised salt water, forms the entrance to the salt works. On both sides of the gatehouse – which housed a bakery, a laundry and a prison – there were the workshops and houses for the coopers and smiths, arranged in a semi-circle. The director's villa; with its administrative offices; is centrally located on the opposite end of the "axis of power" that leads to it from the gatehouse. It is flanked by the actual salt-pans, as well as two buildings for the administrative staff.

This ensemble, which has been preserved with the exception of the director's villa, is a World Heritage site. Since its restoration it has been used by the Centre du Futur.

Paris (France): Église de la Madeleine

1806 – 1842, Pierre Alexandre Vignon et al.

left:
The Madeleine has a façade that is 43 metres (141 ft.) across and its columns are over 15 metres (49 ft.) high. The gable relief shows Le pardon Accordé à la Madeleine and was completed in 1833 by Philippe H. Lemaire.

Like many Classicistic churches, the Église de la Madeleine is built in the style of an ancient temple. A cella is concealed behind a peridromos, an ambulatory lined with Corinthian columns, like in the windowless core of an ancient temple. In 1755 J.-A. Gabriel constructed the Place de la Concorde as an intersection between the Tuileries, the Champs-Élysées, Palais Bourbon and a medieval church, that no longer seemed to fit in with its surroundings. Subsequently Contat d'Ivry designed a new domed cruciform church in 1763. Louis XV laid the cornerstone and, starting in 1777, G.M. Couture directed the construction for a short period. A design by Étienne-Louis Boullée was created in the style of the Pantheon in Rome, but was never built. After a new competition, Napoleon Bonaparte decided that the building should be fashioned after the Acropolis in Athens. Vignon was commission to build not a church, but rather a "Heroic Temple of the Army." A building was begun in 1806 that was supposed to match the peristyle that was added to the front of the former Palais Bourbon (then the Assemblée Nationale) in 1803-1807. After the Treaty of Paris (1814) Louis XVIII (Restauration), decided to have the building completed as a church of atonement (for the executed Bourbons), whereupon Vignon modified his plans. Louis-Philippe, the "Citizen King" since 1830, was against this glorification of the dynasty and determined Mary Magdalene as the patron saint. In 1842 Jean-Jacques Marie Huvé completed La Madeleine.

Classicism was faced with the problem that Christian churches, in contrast to heathen temples, had bells and therefore needed belfries. Building one, however, means destroying the symmetry, as can be seen in the buildings by Alexander "Greek" Thompson (for example the United Presbyterian Church in Glasgow, 1865).

Charlottesville (Virginia, U.S.A.)
The University of Virginia
1817 – 1826, Thomas Jefferson

left:
The rotunda stands at the head of the campus. It has such a deep portico that it can already be called a columned hall. The brick building was inspired by the Roman Pantheon. Both its lower storeys are occupied by classrooms and meeting rooms. The library Jefferson assembled can only be found in the domed area.

After his third term in office as president of the United States, Thomas Jefferson founded the University of Virginia (UVa) in 1809. The buildings that he designed for the university were laid out to form what was to become a classic campus: a group of individual buildings on three sides of a green. This concept clearly differed from the building styles of earlier universities, which were based more on monastic or absolutistic building complexes. Jefferson's university was based more on pavilion system of the type used for hospitals in Europe. The library building stands at the top of the green at UVa. Despite the building's rectangular base it clearly wants to be seen as a "Pantheon of Books", with the shallow-domed rotunda (which gives the building its name) and the portico, typical of the period, that dominate the view of the front elevation. Pavilions, connected by low arcades, line the length of the green on either side. Each of these ten buildings stood at the disposal of a professor. The open end of this building arrangement was intended to allow for the construction of further pavilions. It was, however, later closed off. All of the pavilions follow a different order, or draw on a different antique ideal, so that Jefferson created a three-dimensional sketchbook for those architects, who would have to give the new nation its architectural identity.

Jefferson felt that this puristic Federal Style of American Classicism befitted free citizens in the wake of Independence, while at the same time he considered the English Georgian Style too ornate. With the University of Virginia he not only created a new concept in terms of learning, focussing on written knowledge, but he also regrouped the repertoire of Classicism before Historicism was to take centre stage.

Sketchbooks have long played an important role in the history of architecture as collections of architectural drawings and as an essential part of more comprehensive architectural theories. The great architectural theorists of antiquity, for example Vitruvius's "Ten Books on Architecture" (1st century BC)came first. The next on record, date from the late Gothic period. Villard de Honnecourt's manual of a master-mason was written (ca.1225-1235) but it is more of a travelogue. Others were the "finial books" of the end of the 15th century and comprehensive treatises (Alberti) were compiled in the Renaissance. The more concise works were regarded as most important, for example the Serlio's sketchbook short versions, (with the carpenters' architecture for the canals) in Amsterdam.

Berlin (Germany): Altes Museum
1822 – 1830 (reconstruction 1958 – 1966), Karl Friedrich Schinkel

Schinkel's Museum is a very prominent example of Neoclassical architecture. Along with the Glyptothek in Munich, designed by Leo von Klenze, it had a determining influence on museums built thereafter. This impressive building was devastated by fire in 1945 and only reopened in 1966, after extensive restoration. It has been listed by the UNESCO as part of the world's cultural heritage since 1999. It was in 1830 when this first independent building of a museum was opened in Berlin, the capital city of Germany. Its representative location across from the city palace and the monumental style of its façade underline the importance of the building. Interest in

the construction of a museum in Berlin had come in the wake of an exhibition of works that had been confiscated from various castles and palaces in Berlin by Napoleon, and had finally been returned to the city. Karl Friedrich Schinkel and Alois Hirt had submitted the first plans for a museum 30 years earlier, but their solutions were not very well received. Hence it took until 1822 for the project to become topical again. This time Schinkel presented plans for a two-storey building with four wings based thoroughly on the building principles and aesthetics of Classical Antiquity. He created a Neoclassical style that did justice both to tradition and to considerations of

above:
Schinkel conceived an open stairs as a veranda to the City Palace in the centre of the extended façade. The broad façade of the Altes Museum was the model for the corresponding structure of the Neues Museum by Mies van der Rohe.

practicality. A monumental flight of stairs, a colonnade, reminiscent of a Greek stoa and a portico dominate the façade. The heart of the building is, however, the central rotunda with a height of 23 metres (75.5 ft.). The architect modelled this grandiose cupola on the Pantheon in Rome. A circle of 20 Ionic columns impressively frame sculptures of various Deities. This hall extends over two storeys. On the upper level it is surrounded by a gallery. The rotunda serves as an entrance hall, a gathering area and as a popular place for staging events.

Karl Friedrich Schinkel's Old Museum was one of the first purpose-built public museums anywhere. Moreover, it still is one of the most important buildings on the "Museum Island" of the river Spree on which many of Berlin's museums are located; the Old and the New Museum, the National Gallery, the Bode Museum, and the Pergamon Museum.

Washington, District of Columbia (U.S.A.) The Capitol

1793 – 1865, William Thornton, Stephan Hallet, George Hadfield, Benjamin Henry Latrobe, Charles Bulfinch, Thomas Ustick Walter

left:
You can clearly see that the Capitol is a conglomerate building. Thornton built the part of the building to the right of the centre section. Latrobe built its pendant to the left. That was followed by the section from Bulfinch with the once-classicistic dome in the middle. The side wings with their colossal order and neo-Baroque dome are from Walter.

After the Congress of the United States of America decided, during a session in Philadelphia in 1783, to establish a new capital, George Washington bought a piece of land measuring 257 km (10 by 10 miles) at the point where the Anacostia flows into the Potomac River. It was to become the District of Columbia. Starting in 1792, the City of Washington was built on the site, according to plans drawn up by the French architect Pierre L'Enfant. The construction of the Capitol began in 1793. The original plan was by William Thornton, but it was modified by the architects Stephan Hallet, George Hadfield, and Benjamin H. Latrobe. Although it was completed in 1807, Latrobe made further alterations to the floor plan of the Senate, the Supreme Court and the House of Representatives after the building was burnt and plundered by British troops in 1814, and Charles Bulfinch later designed the portico. The wings of the building and, more importantly, the monumental drum dome were only added to the Capitol between 1855 and 1865 under the direction of Thomas U. Walter. It is made of cast iron and establishes a precedent in that it is the first example of the use of aristocratic or insignia in the construction of a democratic institution. In this regard the dome provided an argument for the employment of a similar roof structure on Wallot's Reichstag building in Berlin. The White House and the Capitol, which lie at opposite ends of Pennsylvania Avenue, as well as many other buildings from this period and the wide avenues connecting them make Washington a prime example of an approach to city planning around 1800 that came to be known as "white Classicism," and which was a precursor of the City Beautiful Movement that emerged around 1900.

In the 18th and 19th centuries the École des Beaux-Arts in Paris was the most important institution for training architects. Their award "Grand Prix de Rome," gave students an opportunity to study antiquities in the heart of Italy. Many Americans studied there and were influenced by Neo-Baroque Historicism. This triggered the American City Beautiful Movement first seen as "White City" at the World's Columbia Exposition in Chicago (1893).Streets formed monumental axes giving a Baroque approach to city planning.

Munich (Germany): Glyptothek
1816 – 1830, destroyed, reconstructed 1964 – 1972, Leo von Klenze

The Glyptothek was Germany's first independent museum building. It manifested a new understanding of antiquity: The focal point was no longer the self-appointed ruling family, but art itself. Only the best exhibits were displayed – among which only twelve from the royal collections. With the Glyptothek, Klenze transformed from the French academic to the archaeologically founded classicism. To achieve this, however, was a hard undertaking: For the competition of the academy in 1816 Klenze submitted his design in three equal stylistic versions – Greek, Roman, Italian. Since the jury had not awarded a prize, Klenze and Carl von Fischer had to draw new plans. Klenze's revised version got the award. But the single-storey building which was completed in 1830, and encloses a square inner court, was the result of a tough struggle between architect and commissioner, the prince regent Ludwig. The main façade overlooking Königsplatz is on a stepped base. The entrance is composed of a portico supported by eight smooth Ionian columns, the width of which each amount to a third of the façade that is structured by one principal moulding and three figure niches. While the principal moulding ends abruptly, the figure niches are continued along the side façades. A reserved entrance for the king and two Venetian windows form the rear facade. The room layout and arrangement were completely harmonized with the exhibits, and the single rooms were connected by enfilade.

Often misunderstood by its contemporaries, the Glyptothek today joins Schinkel's Building Academy and the Altes Museum as one of the best Classical buildings of Europe. Although destroyed in 1944 it was reconstructed by Josef Wiedemann in a simplified form (1964-1972)

left:
Koenigsplatz arose as part of the expansion of Munich on the street linking the residency and the Baroque Nymphenburg Castle. First was the Glyptothek with its Ionic order. After that, just opposite, came the Art and Industry Exhibition Building from G. F. Ziebland with a Corinthian order (1838–1848). Last of all came the Propylaea, also by von Klenze, with a Doric order (1846–1860).

London (U.K.): Houses of Parliament
1840 – 1852, Charles Barry

The old palace area of Westminster went up in flames on the 16th October, 1834. The fire presented a unique opportunity to create a parliament and government building appropriate for the most powerful colonial power of the world at that time. No fewer than 97 architects participated in the contest which stipulated a building in the Elizabethan or Gothic style. The architect, Charles Barry, who was essentially a classicist, was declared the winner in 1836. As a precaution he had secured the collaboration of Augustus Welby Pugin, an undisputed authority and champion in the field of Gothic architecture and ornamentation which thus ensured his victory. The enor-

mous rectangular building complex of the new parliament which stretches for a distance of 275 metres (303 yds.) along the Thames and comprises about 1100 rooms, is divided into numerous, asymmetrically consecutive sections. The western front overlooking the Thames is dominated by Victoria Tower, the north side by Big Ben. The centre and main entrance of the building is the central lobby. Barry's layout is both functional and clear, relying on classic construction principles. Pugin's façades, on the other hand, reveal small, repetitive adornments in Gothic ornamentation – a return to the perpendicular designs of the English late Gothic where vertical ele-

above:
The Houses of Parliament are covered by a filigree web of tracery. The typical three-dimensional volume of a Gothic building is completely missing here; in its place, the pilasters of a (Neo-) Renaissance building have sprouted into pier buttresses. The symmetry of the overall composition is interrupted by two towers ("Big Ben" Clock Tower and Victoria Tower).

ments were accented and surfaces gridded. Pugin should have commented to his contractor on these opposites like this: "All Grecian, Sir; Tudor details on a classic body".

Pugin, whose influence lasted up till the arts and crafts movement at the end of the nineteenth century died, aged only 40 years old in the year that the building was completed. Barry died in 1860 as the last work on Victoria Tower was completed. A formal inauguration of the Houses of Parliament never took place; it simply went smoothly into operation.

Bexley Heath (Great Britain): Red House
1859/60, Philip Webb

left:
The Red House clearly tries to arouse the impression of a conglomerate building: extensions, jumping roof ridges, the converted corner tower as the core of an annex that seems to have developed over centuries. The false hip roof on the right is a typical rural form. Such rural growth was seen as ideal by the Arts and Crafts movement.

In the middle of the19th century, Bexley Heath, a small town in the county of Kent, was a long way from London. The fact that the young reformer William Morris made his home there, and not in the metropolis, can be regarded as a programmatic decision: a vote against living in the big city and for life in the open countryside. He was able to win over his friend Philip Webb to do the architecture. Like Morris, Webb had also been an assistant to George Edmund Street, an exponent of Neo-Gothicism in Oxford. Webb designed an L-shaped building, which was given the name "Red House" on account of its unplastered red brick walls and red roofing. The design of the house was not determined by the demands of social representation, but rather by a use of space that accorded with the life of the inhabitant. A look at the irregularly placed windows shows the extent to which the exterior reflects the interior. By and large, the building dispenses with any form of decoration or ornamentation, or any airs and graces. In this way, the "Red House" marks the beginning of a movement that was eventually to lead to Functionalism in the 20th century. At the same time, it clearly draws on the tradition of simple, rural architecture, as championed by the English Neo-Gothic movement. Much the same applies to the plain, simple appointments of the interior, which Morris had made with the help of his artist friends. The rejection of contemporary industrial production led in 1861 to the founding of their own company (Morris, Marshall & Faulkner; later Morris & Co.), which manufactured not only furniture according to his principles, but also fabrics, wallpaper and stained-glass windows. Yet although Morris adhered to an enthused form of Socialism, he was unable to solve an intrinsic problem: his high-quality hand-made products could not be afforded by the broad masses.

The theories of John Ruskin and the reformer William Morris led to the Arts a Crafts movement in the second hald of the 19 th century in England , which propagated the idea of quality products made by craftsmen as an alternative to industrial production, the latter having become bogged down in a tasteless historicism. The aim was to reunite art and craft. The movement caught on in both continental Europe and the USA, where it influenced a number of reform architects, including Henry van de Velde, and ultimately led to the founding of the Deutscher Werkbund in Germany.

Paris (France): Opera, 1862 - 1875, Charles Garnier

left:
The opera, formerly the forum of bourgeois representation, is provided with ornament and sculpture all over. Worth highlighting here is the left group on the base of the projection on the right side: the dance of Jean Baptiste Carpeaux (1827–1875). A flat dome conceals the stage house, which always presents the greatest composition problem for theatre buildings.

The "Cathedral of the Bourgeoisie," a "Monument to the Upstanding Citizenry" - Parisian society fittingly celebrated the opening of this Neo-Baroque building in 1875. It not only offered an ambiance well suited to the performance of works of music, but also the ideal surroundings for the bourgeoisie to present itself. The idiosyncratic plan for the building, submitted by an architect who was at that point unknown, surprisingly triumphed in two rounds of competition against colleagues as famous as Viollet-le-Duc. It drew on French and Italian Mannerist and Baroque traditions, existing styles of theatre construction and - in its lavish decorations - on palace architecture. Garnier impressively combined all of these elements in a style of his own. "This is Napoleon III!" was the answer he gave the empress when she accused it of being neither Greek nor Louis XV nor Louis XVI, of ultimately having no style at all. It was the emperor who had decided to finally move the opera from the temporary location it had occupied for decades, on the Rue Le Peletier, by commissioning the construction of a building at a prominent location in downtown Paris.

The architect copies the stairways, and other elements from Victor Louis' theatre in Bourdeaux (1780) but the decorations are more entertaining in the motifs they display. Chandeliers, paintings, sculptures and works by well known artists.

Schwangau near Füssen (Germany) Neuschwanstein Castle

1869 – 1892, Eduard Riedel (until 1874), Georg von Dollmann (until 1884), and Julius Hofmann

left:
The King of Bavaria had this complex, built in a style reminiscent of the Middle Ages and imbued with a romantic spirit of chivalry, overlooking the Pöllat canyon near Füssen in the Allgäu. It nevertheless seems to refute a sense of defensive readiness, as would have befitted the eve of the Franco-Prussian War of 1871 as well as the looming unification of Germany (Ludwig II was obliged to acknowledge the German Kaiser). It became a private dream house, far removed from the reality of politics.

Originally, Ludwig II of Bavaria only planned to have the ruins of a medieval fortress in the Allgäu region renovated. It ended up becoming a new place: Neuschwanstein. This castle is the embodiment of Romantic architecture, going far beyond the formal retrospective ideals of Historicism. This sort of homage to the past can otherwise only be found in literature or painting, hardly in architecture, which is intended to fulfil practical purposes. Construction was begun in 1869 on the basis of plans drawn up by Eduard Riedel. In 1867 he had originally only planned a purely Neo-Gothic building, but then added Neo-Romanesque elements before it was built. In 1874 Georg von Dollmann took over, and work was completed in 1881. Julius Hoffmann was responsible for furnishing the interior, which was subsequently undertaken. In this conjunction every object that would be needed, from the door handles to the hairbrushes, were especially and lavishly designed in an attempt to create a total work of art. The interior decoration was, however, interrupted when the king died in 1886. Until 1891 the castle was called Neu-Hohenschwangau after the castle that Maximillian II. Joseph had had rebuilt between 1833 and 1837. The castle provided a model, along with some others in the Loire valley, for Walt Disney's fairy-tale castle.

In addition to Neuschwanstein, Ludwig II had Dollman build the castle at Linderhof and the Herren-chiemsee which was built on an island in the style of the Baroque ensemble at Versailles. They provided the king with an opportunity to flee from every day politics, as was the case with Richard Wagner's operas. These operas not only provided the motifs for the interior decoration, but also for actual parts of the building, like the Wagner Grotto with its big lake at Linderhof.

Paris (France): The Eiffel Tower
1885 – 1889, Gustave Eiffel

left:
The (64,000 tons) symbol of the World Exposition, which took place in Paris exactly 100 years after the French Revolution, was originally termed simply "tour 300 mètre" (the height without the more recent broadcasting mast). The four legs converge to form a pointed tower. Still located in the arches and consoles are strongly historiated forms, and originally the first platform had Art Nouveau galleries.

The "tower of Babel ... the gigantic and laughable column," such were the comments on this bone of contention measuring over 300 metres (985 ft.) in height at the end of the 19th century in Paris. At the beginning the controversy was tremendous, and shortly after construction was begun there was a petition in the magazine Le Temps. Even the authors Guy de Maupassant and Emile Zola signed it. Those who lived near it were afraid of the catastrophic consequences of it crashing down. Its builder, Gustave Eiffel, even had to assume personal liability for any and all possible damages that might result from the tower. Yet all the resistance come for nought, in 1889 the tower was completed in time for the International Exhibition in Paris. The innovative structure designed by the Parisian engineer, Gustave Eiffel, was dedicated to the 100th anniversary of the French Revolution. For decades the Eiffel Tower was the tallest structure in the world and embodied the realization of many 19th century architects' greatest dreams. (The English architect Richard Trevithick had drawn up a plan for a 1000-foot tower as early as 1833.) In addition, the construction of the tower marked the transition from Neoclassicism und Historicism to a more pragmatic, rational form of architecture in France.

The way Gustave Eiffel used iron as a building material is still quite overwhelming today. His criteria in designing the tower, which was to provide a grand entrance to the exhibition grounds, were not dictated by architectural style but by the laws of wind pressure. He had the awe-inspiring total of 10,000 tons of iron put into the structure. There were 2.5 million rivets and iron mountings used to keep approximately 15,000 girders together. Originally the tower was planned as a temporary structure. It was only in 1910 that the decision was finally made to keep it standing, and today the Eiffel Tower is a landmark without which one can searely imagine Paris.

The Twentieth Century

The Twentieth Century

Without any doubt, architectural history has taken place in the last hundred years. At the beginning of the 20th century, structural advancements like cast iron and reinforced concrete held centre stage. Although the first two decades were characterized by the last big building projects in the overladen style of Historicism, which was expressed differently in every country, parallel developments were already beginning to exhibit more diverse tendencies. Around the turn of the century it was Art Nouveau. In Paris, Nancy and Brussels, a new movement emerged featuring decorative, floral elements, with which even the skyscrapers in Chicago were decorated. In Spain, Antoni Gaudí created bizarre organic architecture. In Moscow it was the Constructivists who rejected the principles of Formalism. They sought a radical technical and expressionist approach, while in Italy Antonio Sant'Elia created the urban visions of Futurism. It was a period of transition marked by the anticipation of something new. International Style stood for the liberation from the formal obligation to Classical architecture that had existed for centuries. For the first time an innovation of truly epoch-making importance emerged. The protagonists were Adolf Loos, Tony Garnie, Walter Gropius and, in the USA, Frank Lloyd Wright. Le Corbusier, Rietfeld, Oud and many others followed. The Bauhaus in Dessau taught the new language of architecture, it was the most important art school in the 20th century. It was closed down when the National Socialists came to power. They propagated monumental state architecture as a sign of their power. In Italy, Rationalism, which was to produce a series of important buildings, was developed by Giuseppe Terragni and others in the 1930s. The 1950s were characterized by the application of the ideals of International Style, which was often simply called Modernism. In the USA, where many architects had arrived as immigrants, big building projects were created, like the Seagram Building by Mies van der Rohe. Richard Neutra, Louis I. Kahn and Philip Johnson also made decisive contributions in this period. It was, however, Le Corbusier, who determined the development of architecture in this period like no one else. His work ranged from the Chapel at Ronchamps, through the Unité d'Habitation in Marseille, to the buildings in Chandigarh, India. Japan opened its doors to influences from Europe and the United States for the first time. Kenzo Tange built a number of major projects. Oscar Niemeyer developed a style of his own in Brazil that would have been inconceivable without Le Corbusier. In the 1960s architects like Pier Luigi Nervi in Italy, Alvar Aalto and Eero Saarinen in Finland and Hans Scharoun in Germany, developed highly elegant, sweeping building forms based on modern thought and paired with innovations like poured concrete and other new methods of construction. With the belief in progress, common in this period, many planners saw the future of humanity in prefabricated cities made of spatial structures located on bodies of water or in the desert. International Style led to macro-structures some of which were executed in the "beton brut" (Brutalism) making them seem like "cement fortresses." In every important European country, in the United States, in the former Eastern Bloc and Japan, as well, there were examples of such developments. A critical reaction came at the beginning of the 1980s when a new and differentiated understanding of the real qualities of the city and urban space emerged. Architects like Aldo Rossi, Oswald Mathias Ungers, Hans Hollein, Charles Moore, Robert Venturi and Rob Krier called, each in their own way, for a more retrospective view. This tendency was reflected in the concepts of "New Rationalism" and "Postmodernism." In the 1990s, this led to the development of "New Urbanism" in the United States. A countermovement can be seen in the work of architects and engineers like Ove Arup, Peter Rice, Renzo Piano and Richard Rogers. The Centre Pompidou in Paris – built in the 1970s – is a milestone on the road to this altered view of architecture determined by the structural considerations. Other architects, ranging from Sir Norman Foster to Günter Behnisch, also proposed daring, innovative architectural projects while never losing sight of ecological concerns. At the beginning of the 21st century the picture is quite varied: ecological building and High-Tech have entered a liaison and retreated from their pedantic claims, now serving as tools that are inevitably employed in every new construction. Daniel Libeskind, for example, considers the surroundings and the intent as the conceptual tangents in planning a building; Rem Koolhaas seeks the disorder created by organic growth; Frank O. Gehry opens up a whole new world of forms with the aid of computers. Along with Santiago Calatravas lightweight and expressive engineering architecture, Mario Botta's weighty geometry and the differentiated surfaces created by Herzog & de Meuron, a wide variety of approaches to an architecture of tomorrow are clearly indicated.

Brussels (Belgium): The Hôtel Tassel

1893–1897, Victor Horta

Horta started his career working in Alphonse Ballat's office, taking it over when the latter died. In designing the Hôtel Tassel he developed Art Nouveau from a basis in Historicism: He drew lines in a manner which differed from those found in historical models, created forms that seem vegetal. This free floral delineation was most easily realized with iron elements, of the type E.E. Viollet le Duc had proposed.

The disposition of space in the floor plan was also new on the Continent. Instead of using corridors, Horta grouped individual rooms – as was done by the English Arts and Crafts Movement and in Domestic Revival – around a spacious stairway, which is extended spatially on various levels. There are neither floors, in the narrower sense, nor is there a symmetric floor plan. The space requirements, and not the composition of the façade, determine the location and size of the rooms. Hence the façade and the order of the windows are "free," i.e. not imposingly symmetric in their grid nor in their rhythm, but rather sculptural in their composition with a variety of arches.

When Héctor Guimard (entrances to the Paris Métro stations) came through Brussels on his trip to England (1894), there were very few other Art Nouveau buildings (another one of Horta's Hôtels and the Hankar residence).

However, he was so impressed that it triggered Parisian Art Nouveau.

The English painter William Hogarth (1697–1764) had suggested the curving S-line in his treatise "The Analysis of Beauty" (1753). As the "whiplash curve" it was destined to become the most important motif in Art Nouveau in Belgium and France, while it is not found at all in the strict geometric form of Art Nouveau in Austria and Germany, the "Jugendstil."

Uccle near Brussels (Belgium) "Bloemenwerf" House

1895–1896, Henry van de Velde

left:
The strict sequence of gables, already visible on the exterior of Huis Blomenwerf, was the most important influence on van der Velde. Its was already applied in the English Arts and Crafts movement, in particular by Charles Francis Annesley Voysey. The exclusively vertical half-timbering also suggests Normandy or England.

Like a number of the protagonists who, around 1900, sped on the departure from historicism and eclecticism, Henry van de Velde, born in 1863 in Antwerp, was an architectural dilettante. A trained painter who was fairly dissatisfied with a living as an independent artist, he turned in 1892/93 to arts and crafts. In keeping with the spirit of the English Arts and Crafts Movement, van de Velde taught applied art at the Academy in Antwerp, and became increasingly known for his theoretical texts. After his marriage to the artisan Maria Sèthe, the young couple built "Bloemenwerf" House in Uccle, a suburb to the south of Brussels, as their own abode. The house is a work from a period of transition: with its three gables and its chamfered corners – so typical of van de Velde – it is the work of an artisan who has taken the first step towards practical architecture, and encountered a number of difficulties in the process, as is demonstrated by the rather clumsy arrangement of the rooms. Nor is it clear what kind of house it represents: it is too showy for a country house, but too plain and conventional for a villa. It is apparent that he failed to achieve a real synthesis of English country house, prestigious Villa and artist's house. Yet the building of this house marked a turning point in van de Velde's life, for it was the first time that he managed to combine all art forms in one building. The artist designed not only the building, but also the whole interior. Even if the family was only to live in "Bloemenwerf" for a few short years, it is a vivid example of the ideas of form and life that van de Velde championed. The artist was able here to meet up with a number of influential people, without whom his career between 1900 and 1917, chiefly in Germany, would not have been conceivable.

Through the mediation of Harry Graf Kessler, in 1902 Henry van de Velde was made artistic adviser for industry and crafts in the grand duchy of Saxony-Weimar. In this capacity he advised the local trade and opened the Kunstgewerbliche Seminar (Department of Arts and Crafts), which expanded in 1907 to a School of the Applied Arts. After the First World War, in 1919, the school and the former Art Academy became the Bauhaus in Weimar, under the direction of Walter Gropius. The collaboration between artists, artisans and factory owners that was advocated by the Bauhaus had already been set in motion 20 years earlier by Henry van de Velde.

Amsterdam (the Netherlands)
Amsterdam Stock Exchange
1896–1903, Hendrik Petrus Berlage

left:
With the Stock Exchange, we can clearly recognize how Berlage uses cut stone to both emphasize the decisive, static moments (arch crown, springing), but at the same time subordinate this to the flatness of the façade. The gutters, on the other hand, become emerging, structuring elements.

In the Netherlands Hendrik Peter Berlage is considered a type of father figure of modern architecture. His significance can be compared to that of Louis Sullivan in the USA. As a theorist and extremely successful practitioner, he managed to overcome the prevailing eclecticism, as represented in particular by the Neo-renaissance, and moved towards a more constructive-rational architecture. The Amsterdam Stock Exchange, situated in the heart of the city between the central station and the town hall, is considered his main work. Between the first draft and the start of construction work in 1898, the design changed tremendously; the formal reduction compared to the first drawings is astonishing. As a result, Berlage's work is evolutionary rather than revolutionary. In the centre of this building complex, composed of brick and accented by a tower in the southwest corner, is the large hall of the produce exchange covered by a glass roof. The fundamental arrangement of a large area surrounded by arcades is rooted in a tradition dating back to 17th-century Dutch exchanges: a predominantly open square hemmed by colonnades. The real innovation does not lie in the visible beams of the glass roof; these had already been found in functional buildings of past decades for example, in train stations or Parisian libraries by Henri Labrouste. However, while these constructive elements were mainly ornamental, Berlage works chiefly with unprofiled steel girders and unplastered brick walls. Building stones and ornamental details are not distributed arbitrarily, but to support the visualization of the construction. This also applies to the exterior, where a historicizing structuring was suspended in favour of a flat view of the façade.

Berlage not only made his mark on Amsterdam with noteworthy, dominant buildings such as the stock exchange, but first and foremost as a city planner. Of great importance for the development of the city are his two urban extension plans for southern Amsterdam (1900-05 and 1914–17), which remained valid up until the 1930s. After the First World War, large areas were built based on the expressionist forms of the Amsterdam School.

DER·ZEIT·IHRE·KVNST·
DER·KVNST·IHRE·FREIHEIT

VER·SACRVM·

Vienna (Austria): Building of the Sezession
1897–1898, Joseph Maria Olbrich

left:
German Jugendstil was both more geometric in the total construction and also more repetitive with its forms of decoration than Franco-Belgian Art Nouveau. Clear forms and stringing dominate and the only free floral design of the dome is subordinated to the semi-circle.

The exhibition pavilion of the Viennese Sezession is one of the most important examples of European architecture at its turn from historicism to modernism. With this, Joseph Maria Olbrich the architect, artist and painter created not only a key building of Viennese architectural history, but also a main work of the whole Art Nouveau period. His design for this "temple of art" was inspired and influenced by Gustav Klimt and Otto Wagner. The building rests on 8-metre (26 ft.) high concrete pillars and rises above a central outlay. As a result of the walls that are closed towards the outside it appears as if it has been built of massive cubes. The functional exhibition hall was constructed as a neutral enclosure with a skylight to diffuse light equally. Thanks to adjustable inner walls, the space could be adapted to various exhibition requirements. Gustav Klimt originally created the bronze front doors. The fascination of the building is based primarily on the rhythm of the big structures with their simple geometrical forms. Protocubism was the forerunner of twentieth century architecture and led directly to the new functionalism. Professionalism was not the main aim for Olbrich as for Adolf Loos. In spite of a radical departure from contemporary architectural principles, his form of Art Nouveau still employs the artistic concepts of late historicism, according to which a structure consisting of geometric forms like cubes and cylinders can be altered with decorative elements. The cost of construction of approximately 60,000 guilder was mainly raised by the artists themselves. The city of Vienna donated the development site, but did not hold to their other promises. Thus the avenue that should have led from the axis of the building up to Karl's church was never implemented.

The ornamentation of tendrils and trunks rising up the building is crowned by a wrought iron dome clamped between pylons. Their gilded, pierced leafwork lent the building its jocular name "Krauthappel" (cabbage).

Glasgow (Scotland)
The Glasgow School of Arts
1897–1899 and 1907–1909, Rennie Mackintosh

left:

At the entrance to the Glasgow School of Art, its asymmetrical construction immediately catches the eye. Mackintosh adopted this element from Arts and Crafts. Completely alien to this, though, are the castle-like heavy masonry and the artistic filigree metal work contrasting with this. This contrast between original and artificial can frequently be found with Mackintosh.

When he won the competition staged to find a design for Glasgows new art school in 1896, Charles Rennie Mackintosh was working as a draughtsman in the office of the local architects, Honeyman & Keppie. His plan took special consideration of the institutions transformation, from an arts and crafts, to a full-fledged art school under Newberys direction. The execution of the project, which was decisively influenced both by rationalism and by Art Déco, took place in two steps (for financial reasons). The main building was completed between 1887 and 1899, while the library annex was built between 1907 and 1909. The structure combines traditional and modern, as well as typically Scottish and universal elements. Hence, the architect uses the natural stone found in Scottish castles while also making references to the country house style of the English architect Charles Francis Annesley Voysey. The clear lines of the main granite façade are interspersed with Art Nouveau elements made of metal. Shifting the entrance slightly out of symmetry served to reduce the monumentality and severity of the building. Located on a slope, the impression the building creates varies according to the perspective from which it is viewed. From the east it looks like a hermetic fortress, for example, while from the north it looks like an industrial plant.

The two-storey library, completed in the second building phase, is nearly as impressive as the calculated variation of the different façades. The library can be recognized from outside by virtue of its unusually high windows, measuring 7,5 metres (25 ft.). They are flanked by stones that were originally supposed to be sculpturally formed. The furniture and the all wood in the interior are designed to suggest lattice-work. Often, Mackintoshs combining of buildings and interiors in this manner can be seen as a form of architectural protest against the the kind of Victorian conformism that, for example, Oscar Wilde also satirized.

New York (U.S.A): The Flatiron Building
1901–1903, Daniel Hudson Burnham

left:
On the ground floor of this skyscraper you can recognize why the modern architects of the 20th century were to turn against historical façades. The thin columns are quite obviously not capable of carrying the stone masses of the upper stories. It needed to be a modern construction, but the building did not wish to confess this.

Where Broadway and Fifth Avenue intersect, there is a particularly prominent and daring example of one of the earliest skyscrapers: the Flatiron Building on Madison Square in New York. On it narrowest side its measures just 1.85 metres (6 ft.), on its widest side 18 meters (59 ft.). This floor plan, culminating in a narrow angle, is shaped like an iron. Hence, the "Fuller Building" was soon renamed. The lack of space in the centres of big cities coupled with new technical developments, like telephones and lifts, as well as the solid ground on the building site, encouraged the development of skyscrapers. Of course the optimal use of a limited piece of property was also no small economic concern. Hence the 20-storey building, erected using a steel frame, pointed dramatically towards the future with its height of 87 metres (285 ft.). On the vertical plane there is, similar to a classical pillar, a clear separation of a building in its base, shaft and capital. In addition to making this reference to the pillar as the prototype of a vertical structure, this separation is also related to the immediate functional distribution within the building. In the base, with its large windows, there were stores white uniform floors of the shaft were used for offices and the floor on the capital level provided space for the technical infrastruc-

ture. At first many feared that the wind would be channelled to such speeds that it would soon bring the idiosyncratic building to fall, however the biggest problem ever to be reported was caused by womens skirts being blown up in the air. The façade, with its historical references, is given character by limestone and richly ornamented terra-cotta tiles. It is the oldest skyscraper in Manhattan still standing today.

"Form follows function" was the motto of the Chicago School, around Louis Henri Sullivan, from which the architect Daniel Hudson Burnham came. Despite his modernity, he adhered to a classical sense of order.

Paris (France)
Apartment block Rue Franklin No. 25
1903–1904, Auguste Perret

The name Perret is inseparably linked in France with the triumphal march of the "Béton armé." Auguste Perret was an architect, building contractor and town planner. His late work included the market square at Amiens and the reconstruction of Le Havre town centre, which was almost completely destroyed by the Germans. This eight-storey apartment building in Paris marks the beginning of a new epoch in architecture: although Auguste and Gustave Perret had already employed the newly developed material reinforced concrete five years earlier for the Casino Municipal in Saint-Malo (1899), it had not been outwardly visible in that building. It was only used to construct the façade. The building on rue Franklin was the first occasion on which Perret began to explore the material's structural possibilities and make the design principles visible: the supporting reinforced concrete frame is no longer concealed, but clearly discernible. From this moment on, architecture needed to pay no more regard to the traditional constraints of statics. The new method of construction allowed wall surfaces to be almost completely dispensed with. This also meant that the apartments in this building, which were constructed on a long, narrow plot, could be provided with the best natural light. This new material was also to prove revolutionary for the design of the floor plan: the reinforced concrete frame at last allowed the creation of the flat roof, the complete elimination of supporting walls, and together with that, the so-called "open plan." It was left, however, to Auguste Perret's former employee, Le Corbusier, to truly exploit the freedom of design that this permitted.

Even if Perret viewed exposed concrete as the equal of sandstone and marble, and thus ennobled it, he remained constantly faithful to a traditional grammar of forms: the prefabricated partition walls in rue Franklin were decorated with Art Nouveau floral faiences.

Helsinki (Finland): Central Station
1904–1919, Eliel Saarinen

Although founded in the middle of the 16th century by the Swedish king Gustav Wasa, Helsinki is a comparatively young city. The layout was only developed at the beginning of the 19th century when Czar Alexander I allowed the establishment of a capital city, which until 1917 had formed an autonomous principality within the Russian Empire. This was implemented by Carl Ludwig Engel, the czar's architect who came originally from Berlin. He was supposed to establish a "white city" of the north. The economic expansion between 1890 and 1914 went hand in hand with a trebling of the number of inhabitants. The result was the creation of new districts largely characterized by Art Nouveau buildings. These districts did not express the delicacy and elegance of Art Nouveau, but rather a more durable and monumental variant referred to as National Romanticism. The award-winning design for the main railway station in Helsinki by architect Eliel Saarinen falls within the category of National Romanticism, of which he was a protagonist. During the buildings execution, however, the architect was inspired by German reform architects such as Peter Behrens and Alfred Messel. The extended, strictly functionally arranged ensemble which, in addition to the station, also includes the buildings for the administration and goods dispatches, is fascinating due to the rhythmical separation of its constituent parts and the convincing arrangement. In spite of its relatively modest dimensions, the granite façades and imposing gate-like main entrance facing the city appear especially enormous. Helsinki's central station set standards. It not only influenced future railway-station architecture, but is also considered an important work within the Saarinen oeuvre. With his award-winning design for the Chicago Tribune Tower (1922), the Finn transferred his idea of the graded tower into larger dimensions, thereby significantly influencing the debate on skyscraper architecture in the USA.

Eliel Saarinen, Herman Gesellius and Armas Lindgren were among the leading proponents of Finnish National Romanticism when they shared an office between 1897 and 1905/1907. Their main work of what is known as Nordic variations of Art Nouveau was the internationally acclaimed Finnish Pavilion at the Paris World Exposition of 1900. The pavilion was oriented to medieval Finnish buildings and influenced by the American architect Henry Hobson Richard.

Barcelona (Spain): Casa Milà
1905–1910, Antoni Gaudì y Cornet

left:
Thanks to a system of supports that worked independently of the walls, Gaudí was able to arrange the flats of his "Quarry" – as the building was called – very freely. This is noticeably reflected by the asymmetrical arrangement of the windows. The prescribed chamfering of the corners is scarcely noticeable due to the building's animated lines. The ventilation shafts and chimneys on the roof terrace have been adapted to the flowing yet angular style of the building.

The influences found in Gaudís architecture can be identified as Moorish, Moroccan and Gothic as well as Rococo and Art Nouveau. However, its abundance in terms of décor and its unbridled forms are thoroughly unique. His late work is so closely associated with nature that it defies architectural comparisons. The Casa Milà, also known as "La Pedrera" (The Quarry), is the last secular building Gaudí completed before devoting himself exclusively to his cathedral, La Sagrada Familia. At the same time, it was his first multi-family dwelling. Although it is surrounded by other buildings, the Casa Milà with its round corners, seems as if it is standing by itself. The façade, made entirely of the same light-coloured sandstone, quotes elements for which he had become famous: the wrought iron balconies from the nearby Casa Batlló, the meandering benches from the Park Güell and the bizarre chimneys decorated with coloured glass and ceramic tiles. With its ongoing series of swells, waves, niches and asymmetric windows it reminds one of sand dunes, a beehive, or cliffs. One loses sight of the tectonic quality of the building in the face of its overwhelming organic impression. As grotesque as the building may seem from outside, the luxury flats within catered successfully to current tastes. In addition, the principle underlying its construction proved to be an important innovation; there are no supporting walls because everything rests on supports and girders. This allows for different floor plans on every level. Two light shafts that are very wide at the top and like a funnel, become narrower from floor to floor, provide excellent lighting and ventilation.

To this day Gaudí's stylistic vocabulary remains a source of inspiration. It has influenced such diverse artists as Santiago Calatrava, Salvador Dalí, Max Ernst, Niki de Saint-Phalle and Friedrich Stowasser (better known as Friedensreich Hundertwasser).

Berlin (Germany)
AEG Turbine Factory/Montagehalle
1908–1909, Peter Behrens

From 1907 to 1914 Peter Behrens served as artistic adviser to the electronics and machine manufacturing concern GEC (General Electricity Company) based in Berlin. The German Labour Union called for artists, craftsmen and manufacturers to cooperate in the design of quality German products that could be marketed worldwide. Behrens' studio was responsible for all visual aspects, be it printed matter, advertisements, typography, product organization or the architecture of manufacturing sites. For the first time, the concept of "corporate design" was used for the identity of a company. The assembly shop of the turbine factory, which was established by Behrens in 1908/09 in the Berlin suburb of Moabit, is considered the cradle of modern industrial architecture. He endowed an engineering construction with a memorable, monumental form. The triple-joint beams resting on foot joints are clearly revealed in the lengthwise eastern elevation and harmonious façade. The intention was to create the image of a "temple of work." While the staccato of the pillars reminds one of a column arrangement from Antiquity, the blind pylons and the tympanum with the company logo on the front create the impression of an overwhelming, Egyptian-like might. The most modern construction is represented in the smaller hall, located on the western side, whose court façade was designed by Ludwig Mies van der Rohe, who worked in Behrens' office. The glass façade is strongly characterized by flatness, appears more abstract, and already points to the later American buildings by the architect whose façades are divided by double T-beams. Originally 110 metres (361 ft.) in length, the building was later extended to 207 metres (679 ft.).

The "new style" that German reform architects called for around 1900 expressed itself most convincingly in industrial architecture. Different factors influenced this development. On the one hand, the economic position of prospering companies promoted the establishment of new production plants. On the other, broadminded entrepreneurs broke with the Wilhelminian representation of culture and saw – in keeping with the wishes of the German Labour Union – the form that best suited their own self-representation as being based on professionalism and monumentality. In addition, due to its emphasis on functional operations industrial architecture favoured purpose-oriented construction.

left:
At the side of the functional construction of the hall you can clearly see and recognize how little it has to do with the aesthetic treatment Behrens gave the façade. A huge wall mass was added to the filigree skeleton. It creates the illusion that there are two pylons carrying a gable.

Vienna (Austria)
Loos House on Michael's Square
1909–1911, Adolf Loos

Alfred Loos arrived via a roundabout route to building: after reading architecture at the Technical College in Dresden, he worked from 1893 to 1896 in the United States as a structural draughtsman, bricklayer and parquet layer. He gained his initial reputation in Vienna as the author of astute polemics against purely decorative ornamentation, which he regarded as being no longer in the spirit of the times. This led him to fall out with the leading architects of the Vienna Secession, Josef Hoffmann and Joseph Maria Olbrich. Loos' career as an architect began with work on conversions and extensions: the Café Museum, Joseph Knize's bespoke tailoring establishment, and the Kärntner Bar, the first American Bar in Vienna. In 1908, he published his infamous text "Ornament and Crime." The house on Michael's Square for the firm Goldman & Salatsch gave him his first opportunity to build as he wished. And in the best of locations: the first district, directly opposite the Imperial Palace. A simple building, the ground floor, which was used for business, was clad with green Cipollino marble and simply interspersed with Tuscan columns, while the upper (residential) floors were plastered with lime stucco and the windows left unframed. Today the "Loos House" is an essential part of any tour of the city, but at that time it created a scandal. Loos' opponents disparaged it as a "house without eyebrows" and as the "dirt box on Michael's Square." He almost almost never built it: he declined down the invitation to take part in the competition, and only received the commission because none of the submissions met with satisfaction.

With this building, Loos succeeded in forging the first link to the Modern movement: he was a forerunner of the International Style. Yet it was not his intention to create a new style; the founder of Purism renounced style of any kind. Before it became a listed building in 1947, the house was worked over a number of times. In 1987 it was bought and restored by the Raiffeisenlandesbank Niederösterreich-Wien.

Stockholm (Sweden)
The Woodland Cemetery
1915–1934, Sigurd Lewerentz and Erik Gunnar Asplund

left:
Asplund returned to reduced neo-Classicisms with the Crematory (1935–1940) of the Southern Cemetery and its column positions, which already characterized his Stockholm Library. With the latter he clearly stood in succession to Revolution architecture, but here the portico shows itself as a modern construction with its broad span.

It was in 1914 that the young architect, Erik Gunnar Asplund, met Sigurd Lewerentz at an exhibition in Malmö, where the latter was presenting his model for a crematorium. In finding a solution to this previously neglected building task he employed a language rich in metaphor. The mourners were to take leave of the deceased in the hall of death, then ascend into the hall of life, in order to await singing, and finally accompany the urn out into an open courtyard. Lewerentz and Asplund decided to work together on an entry for a competition to extend a cemetery in Stockholm and won the first prize. Unlike their competitors, they were the only ones who made use of the natural conditions of the landscape – the woods and the topography – while playing again upon the motif of going from darkness into light. During the ensuing twenty-year partnership on the project, which did not hinder either of them from realizing other projects on their own, the design was transformed under the influence of Functionalism, which, however, Asplund and Lewerentz interpreted in a very unique manner. The first buildings on the terrain, the Woodland (Asplund 1920) and the Resurrection (Lewerentz, 1925) Chapels employed a stylistic vernacular of "Nordic Classicism," consisting of axial paths and elements from antiquity,

in a very direct manner. The design of the entrance area and the main chapel (Asplund, 1934) are, by contrast, much more subtle and abstract. The path taken by the mourners leads from the entrance into an open landscape in which individual elements, like the cross, a hill crowned by a growth of trees, the altar and the portico of the main chapel (to which the crematorium is attached), are arranged in free composition.

Lewerentz and Asplund would never have received the commission, if there had not been a number of new developments, particularly in Germany, that had a determining influence in an international competition. The Waldriedhof (Woodland Cemetery) in Munich and the Ohlsdorf Cemetery in Hamburg had already refuted the 19th century model of "industrialized" cemetery plans, with their endless rows of grave stones. When he was young, Lewerentz had worked in Munich for Theodor Fischer and Richard Riemerschmid, who were members of the German Werkbund, founded in 1907, and which maintained close contacts to the movement for cemetery reform.

Potsdam (Germany): The Einstein Tower
1920–1921, Erich Mendelsohn

left:
The Einstein Tower can be traced back to sketches Mendelsohn made while he was still serving in the First World War. These were executed in the free-flowing gesture of Art Nouveau. Only very few buildings were ever constructed in this sweeping "organic" form. The flowing walls of the Einstein Tower make it look like poured concrete, yet it was built of brick.

Even before the First World War, Erich Mendelsohn started making the first sketches for his visionary Einstein Tower near Potsdam. The physicist Erwin Freundlich had discussed his idea of constructing a series of experiments, designed to prove Einsteins theory of relativity, with the architect. In mid-1918 Freundlich outlined a precise building programme: he needed a tower 15 metres high and beneath it a long, underground laboratory in which the light fall from above could be redirected by mirrors in order to perform spectral analysis. However, Mendelsohn did not confine himself to the design of the "external architecture" required by his client. With the exception of the purely technical spaces, he designed the entire interior as well; above all, however, he gave the building such a significant form that it is now considered one of the rare examples of expressionist architecture. "Iron combined with concrete – 'iron concrete' – is the material with which we can express our determination to create new forms, to create a new style," wrote Mendelsohn as early as 1914. Indeed the sculptural form of the tower on the telegraph hill overlooking Potsdam evolved out of this materials characteristic of going from liquid to solid. However, problems resulted from the fact that materials were not yet available with which forms could be built for the unusually shaped surfaces. Contrary to the architects plans, only the lower parts were actually made of poured concrete; the stucco surface of the tower only conceals a conventional brick surface. It was to take several decades before technical processes were so refined that nearly any form could be poured. Formally, however, Mendelsohns experimental construction in Potsdam can be seen at the beginning of a series of sculpturally expressive architectural projects ranging from Eero Saarinens TWA terminal in New York through to buildings by Frank O. Gehry.

However, due to a lack of financial backing only very few Expressionist buildings were constructed before a more sober stylistic vernacular began to prevail around 1922. Expressionism only continued to be influential into the 1930s in the somewhat muted Northern German regional variation of 'Brick Expressionism'.

Dessau (Germany): Bauhaus

1925–1926, Walter Gropius

left:
The workshop wing is
the most famous part of
the Bauhaus. Originally
the floors ended on each
story some distance from
the large glass curtain
wall that made the buil-
ding an icon of
International Style.
Clearly recognizable is
the way in which the individual elements of the
building are distinguis-
hed by the use of white,
gray and black. It can
also be seen that the
corners have no supports
– as is typical of the New
Building style.

A manifesto of modern architecture, a major work of "New Objectivity": with the Bauhaus in Dessau Gropius built efficiency, austerity, smoothness, and transparency. His idea of building a school in the style of a factory has found many imitators. Furthermore, the skeleton of this building was made of reinforced concrete and indicated the direction that industrial pre-fabrication was going to take in its future development. As in the Bauhütten (the original Masonic lodges) of the Middle Ages, the ideal was for all of the artistic abilities and the craftsmanship necessary for the completion of a building to come together. The term Bauhaus expresses the connection to tradition and emphasizes the desire that architects, artists and craftsmen work together in the realization of buildings in the future. Walter Gropius, who had directed the Bauhaus since it was established in 1919, began around the middle of the 1920s to propagate the idea of industrialized production more and more and called for a shift from a craft based to a more industrial emphasis. The move to the German industrial town of Dessau in 1925 was precipitated by politics. It also provided an opportunity to express changing attitudes in a new building. The coordinated programme of teaching, working and living at the Bauhaus was expressed in three L-shaped building complexes that were connected to each other: the technical institute or workshop wing with high walls of mirrored glass on three sides, the vocational training school wing with long bands of windows, and the atelier building or dormitory with a number of additional floors. The vocational school building was originally intended to house the Dessau arts and crafts school which, however, never moved into the space. Gropius was able to use curtain walls over three storeys by setting back the supports of the building.

When viewing the building, it becomes necessary to walk around it, because there is neither a main façade nor any view that allows one to see all of its parts at once. At best from a birds eye view, as Gropius states, since he also considered this perspective. One can only get an impression of the entire building when viewing it from above.

Berlin (Germany): The Residential Development Berlin-Britz (The Hufeisensiedlung / Horseshoe Development), 1925–1930, Bruno Taut

left:
The Hufeisensiedlung is surrounded by ribbon development and seems like one last triumph of block border construction. However, in contrast to traditional block construction, the yard here is clearly larger and open on one side so that light and air can flow in.

In 1924 Bruno Taut left his position as the city building commissioner of Magdeburg in order to go to Berlin where he had been engaged by the 'Gehag' as an artistic consultant. This organization, the union-owned "Gemeinnützige Heimstätten-, Spar- und Bauaktiengesellschaft" (Co-operative Homestead, Savings and Building Corporation), was one of the most important initiators of social housing projects at the time; ultimately Taut built around 10,000 units of housing for the Gehag before moving to Moscow in 1932. Two-storey terraced houses and three-storey housing blocks determine the outward appearance of this development in southern Berlin that had a total of 1000 units. At that time one of the most important tasks facing local authorities in areas of urban concentration was the alleviation of the housing shortage, and Tauts development was one of the earliest to provide an exemplary solution to the question of how social housing should be constructed. The most remarkable feature of the development is the horseshoe shaped housing block at the centre, built around a previously existing pond. This not only allowed Taut to succeed in establishing a connection between the landscape and the architecture, it also provided the development with a centre around which it could become a unified whole. Even though the architect is referring back to concepts that previously determined the identity of residential areas here, very few developments built in the Weimar period exhibit a similarly striking form. The radical construction of parallel housing blocks, such as Ernst May realized a few years later in Frankfurt-Westhausen, was better suited to reducing the cost of building by employing prefabricated elements.

The black and white photographs of buildings from the classical modern period are misleading; modern methods of colour analyses have proved that many of the buildings were even more colourful than had previously been assumed. The balconies of the Bauhaus in Dessau were, for example, painted orange, and the white façade was really grey. Bruno Taut had already used bright colours in housing developments before the First World War and during his tenure in Magdeburg he published an "Appeal for colourful building." In his developments he used colour extensively in order to differentiate buildings or to create a particular impression.

Rotterdam (Netherlands): The Van Nelle Tobacco Factory

1925–1931, Johannes Andreas Brinkmann
Leendert Cornelis van der Vlugt with Mart Stam

left:
There is still no agreement on the authorship of the Van Nelle Factory. Stam's works shortly beforehand were not yet so radical (Maats Monument in Purmerend). On the other hand, the works of Brinkmann and van der Vlugt (school in Groningen with Wiebenga) were. The only thing that is certain is that Stam designed the round pavilion on the roof. It served as the tearoom.

In the mid-1920s, Soviet Constructivism began to influence European architecture. Along with Theo van Doesburg, Walter Gropius and Hannes Meyer, Mart Stam played an important role. From 1923 to 1925 he had worked with El Lissitzky, one of the founders of the Constructivist International on the Moscow "Wolkenbügel" (Cloud Iron) project for an office skyscraper. The project for the new Van Nelle Tobacco Factory consisted of a number of well proportioned and detailed buildings distributed on a spacious site. The entrance consists of a free-standing, three-storey office building designed on a dynamic curved floor plan. The height of the 230 metres (ca. 750 ft) long main building is staggered from eight, to five and then to three storeys. An extended form was the result of the desire for natural lighting. Employees were supposed to be able to look outside in two directions from wherever they worked. The transparency and clarity of the building were supposed to promote Van Nelles's image as a progressive employer. These buildings, with their many windows, are connected by an extensive network of open, highly visible, and dramatically designed stairways, ramps and so-called "clip-ons," i.e. openly displayed conveyor belts that run diagonally in hollow-profile bridges. They facilitate the flow of people and raw materials between the slab-like production tract and warehouses located on the canal. The machine aesthetics that resulted and the programmatically visible construction employing exposed supports make the Van Nelle Tobacco Factory one of the most outstanding examples of Constructivism in Europe. To the disappointment of the committed Constructivist, Stam, the building was to go down in history as a prime example of formal composition.

On the basis of the reputation Stam established with this building, he was invited by Ludwig Mies van der Rohe to erect a row of houses at the Stuttgart Weißenhofsiedlung. Ultimately Stam became most famous for the S43 chair he designed in this conjunction.

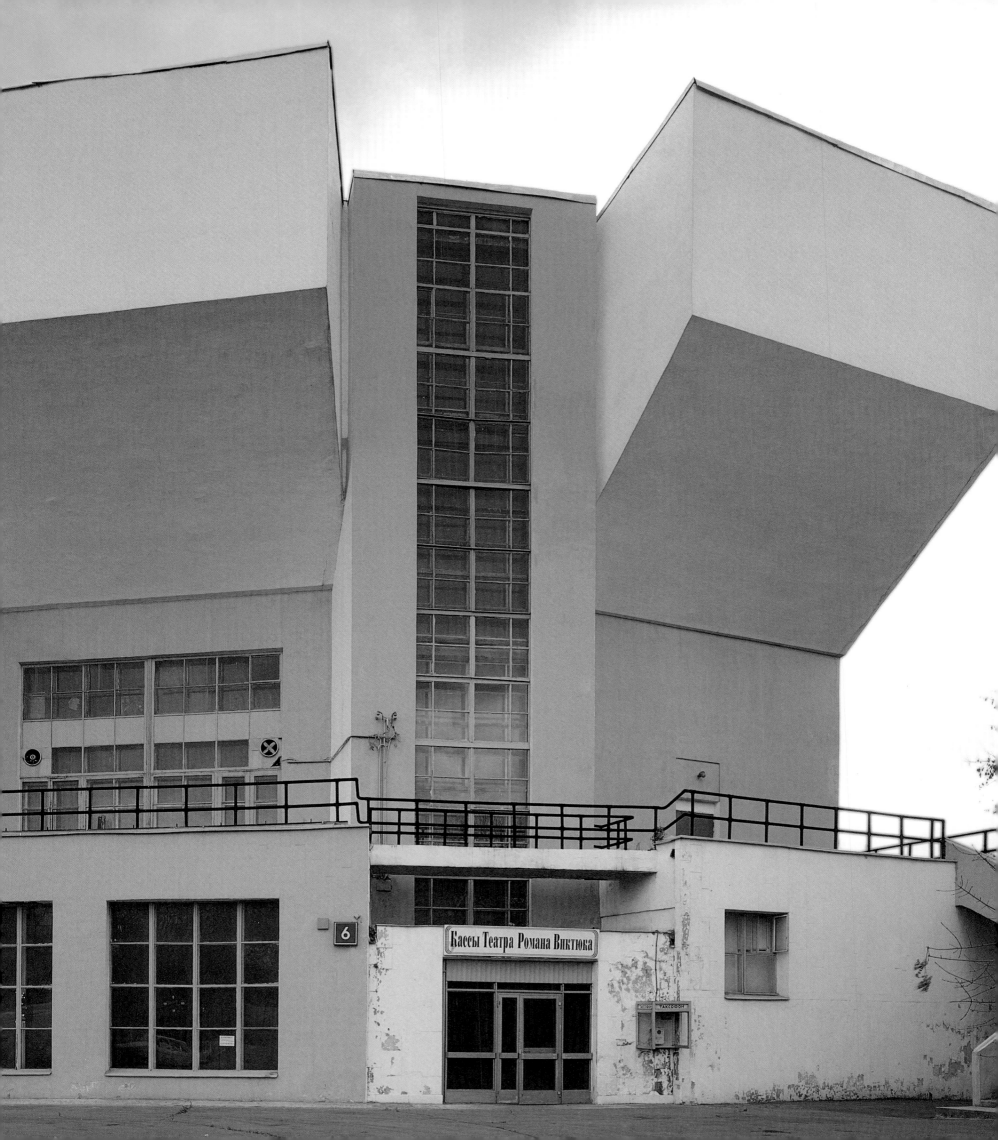

Moscov (Russia)
Rusakov Workers' Clubhouse
1927–1928, Konstantin Stepanovich Melnikov

left:
The Rusakov Club for municipal employees is one of 45 clubs with more than 300 seats, which were built in Moscow between 1926 and 1928. These clubs were part of the Cultural Revolution and served, in the words of the artist El Lissitzky, as a "social power station" and as a replacement for the churches and palaces of capitalism. Melnikov's three cantilevering auditoriums could be used individually, or by folding back the walls, together with the main hall.

Melnikov's works – he died in 1974 at the age of 84 years – are limited to the period between 1922 and 1934, before he came into conflict with orthodox Stalinism and was only allowed to paint, apart from smaller jobs with private patrons. Internationally he became known for his design of the USSR pavilion at the Paris "Exposition des arts décoratifs et industriels modernes". Melnikov's workers' clubhouses in Moscov, the best known of which is the Rusakov club, are built manifestos of Russian Constructivism. His undertaking was to eliminate the traditional contrast of art and life in favour of technique. The new building method was developed in the middle of the 1920s as an expression of the socialist way of life. It was intended to equally illustrate and promote the new unity of leisure activities and education as "socialist power". As with most Constructivists, Melnikow understood architecture as a category, settled between machine technology and biological structure. His Rusakov club, which was assembled from block-like cubes, best illustrates his architectural language – movement frozen into dynamic form – with its massive concreted, overhanging auditoriums. While the façade of the wedge-shaped building is determined by rhythmic change from plastered wall surfaces to horizontal glass strips, internal space is provided for political, cultural, mental and physical activities.

After the formalism debates at the beginning of the 1930s, the Communist Party of the USSR determined socialist realism as an obligatory style direction. This meant the abrupt end of Constructivism in the USSR. In Europe it found a later resonance in High-Tech architecture.

New York (U.S.A.): Chrysler Building

William van Alen

left:
Art Deco building comprised a synthesis of motifs from the "old" and the "New Building" styles: the dressed stone and verticalism of the central rows of windows are elements of the Chrysler Building that originate from older highrise architecture; while horizontal sweeps of windows and metal façades were a sign of the "New Building." When the Bank of Manhattan building threatened to top Chrysler by 60 centimetres (24 inches), architect Van Alen added a 55 metre (180 ft.) tall needle to its peak.

At the end of the 1920s everyone in New York wanted to make his or her way up: a virtual competition to build the highest building in the world began. Half of the approximately 400 skyscrapers in the United States with more than 20 storeys stood in New York. The 319-metre (1046 ft.) tall "Chrysler Building," named after the automobile king Walter Percy Chrysler, outdistanced the Bank of Manhattan in height (282 metres or 925 ft.) in 1929. Although it only held the title of the "highest building in the world" for a very short time (until 1931 when the Empire State Building designed by Shreve, Lamb & Harmon reached 381 metres [1250 ft.] and remained the tallest building in the world until 1977), is still considered the king of the skyscrapers and the cathedral of capitalism because of its elegance and stylistically impressive vernacular. Wheels, shining chrome hub caps and eagles heads, like those on the coolers of Chrysler automobiles, as imaginary water spouts characterize the ornamentation of the facade of this steel frame structure consisting, otherwise, of brick and marble. Another special feature, drawing attention to the building, is the top of the tower that crowns the 77th floor. The staggered, shimmering silver steeple made of stainless steel seems like a helmet set on top of the building.

Stainless steel, as the material for facades, was still a rarity then. Inside of the building, movable steel walls allowed for the individual adaptation of office space. Some 30 lifts and 200 stairways were put into the building, as well as almost 4,000 windows and 3,000 doors.

The architect, William van Alen, had learned his trade at the Ecole des Beaux Arts in Paris and brought with him his experience with Art Deco, which was characteristic of skyscraper architecture in New York at that time. In the Chrysler Building this form found its penultimate expression. In 1950 the 32-storey Kent Building was added.

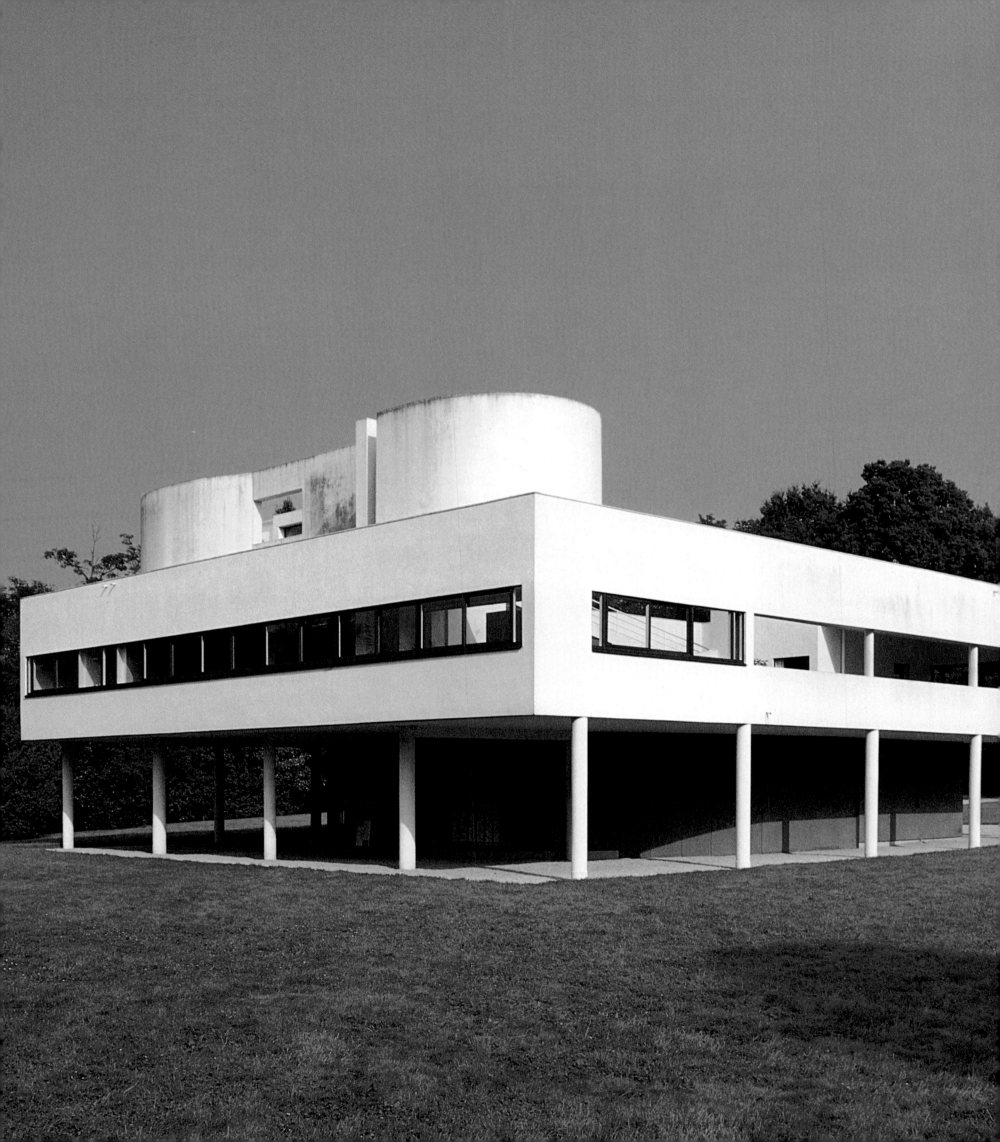

Poissy (France): Villa Savoye
1928–1931, Le Corbusier

Giving the architect "carte blanche" in designing this house ultimately cost the client a tidy sum in budget overruns; he was, however, compensated with a masterpiece that takes a very special place in Le Corbusier's series of white villas. In Poissy, roughly 20 kilometres (approx. 12 miles) west of Paris, Le Corbusier created a "living machine" or, as he called it, "an object on the lawn," Designed without a clearly defined frontal view, the ground floor offers visitors a space they can drive up to, or in which they can wander between the supporting columns. The main floors are connected to each other primarily by ramps that are intended to create a spatial continuum. All the way down to the windows in the salon and the metal doors on the built-in closet cabinets, everything has been planned with stringency and elegance. An extravagant roof serves to complete the villa. Set on a rectangular site with a quadratic floor plan, the building has been compared to the work of the Italian Renaissance architect Andrea Palladio. The Villa Savoye represents a milestone in the Modern movement or International Style, as the case may be. Threatened with demolition in the 1950s, it was taken over by the state in 1965 and listed as an historic landmark.

In 1926 Le Corbusier formulated a five-point programme for a new architecture. And as is the case with many architects, building smaller residential structures an opportunity for experimenting with new ideas. His five-point programme foresaw the use of exposed supports on the ground level, floor plans and facades that were not predetermined, wide horizontal bands of windows and fully landscaped, multifunctional roof gardens. In 1927 he also applied these concepts to the design of the Villa Stein in Garches, near Paris, as well as to his houses for the Weißenhofsiedlung in Stuttgart.

left:
This villa also clearly demonstrates the way Le Corbusier conceived of architecture: columns as supports and planar surfaces as roofs and floors. Apart from the seven points that Le Corbusier formulated, the building's (roof) terraces also show the glassless "windows" that typified the International Style.

Paimio (Finland): A Sanatorium
1929–1933, Alvar Aalto

In constructing this sanatorium for 50 individual municipalities, Aalto adhered more rigidly to the international style than with all his other buildings. In many places, it was precisely with buildings for the health system or education that such new style construction was able to establish itself. It was not just that these buildings offered air and light in the battle against tuberculosis, they moreover symbolized this hygienic involvement as well.

It was to be healthy and modern - the sanatorium in Paimio, 30 kilometres east of Turku and it is one of the few buildings Aalto designed uncompromisingly in International Style. Winning the competition for this project in 1928 catapulted the 33-year-old architect, who was at that point unknown outside Finland, into a league with internationally famous architects. Aalto even designed the Artek furniture for the sanatorium together with his wife and colleague, Aino Marsio. The plan for the two wing sanatorium, situated in a forest, took consideration of the common method of treating tuberculosis - fresh air, sun and nature - as well as of the daily rhythm of the patients. It is highly stylized and functional, influenced by Johannes Duiker's sanatorium Zonnestraal in Hilversum (1928). The sanatorium, with its white stucco façade defined by horizontal bands of windows, consists of a six-storey tract for the patients and a four-storey hotel zone with dining and recreation rooms, as well as offices, to the north. By planning the building to face the southeast, it was possible to ensure that every one of the 145 patients rooms had the morning sun. At the eastern end of the patients tract there are fresh-air terraces and common balconies facing the south. The two main tracts are connected by a transport and service zone, the

kitchens are located in an adjacent structure. All of the other facilities needed to run a hospital - flats for the doctors, housing for the nurses and the technical infrastructure - are located in external buildings of their own.

The strict functional segregation, the innovative reinforced concrete skeletal construction and the high standard of the furnishings (rooms with only two beds, windows with integrated ventilation, infra-red heating elements on the ceilings and acoustically insulated walls to the corridor) make Paimio an icon of classic Modernism.

Barcelona (Spain): The German Pavilion
1929, Ludwig Mies van der Rohe with Lilly Reich dismantled reconstructed 1986

A jewel of classic Modernism - the "German Pavilion at the International Exhibition in Barcelona in 1929", as it was officially called, is considered one of the key buildings in Modern architecture, although it only stood for eight months. Numerous publications, from the very same year as it was built, described it as the single most outstanding example of International Style. Yet it was almost not built at all! Budgetary problems had forced the project to be temporarily put on hold during the planning period. Six cross-shaped supports made of chrome-plated steel hold up a roof that seems to float in the air above a large pedestal covered with travertine. The

pavilion, which is flanked by bushes and trees on three sides, presents an open façade of glass to the street. It seems almost as if there is no real view of the outside of the building. The optical focus of the pavilion is on a free-standing wall made of red onyx. Walls, made of reflecting glass and green porphyry held in place by chrome-plated metal frames, define the perimeter of an open, asymmetric room. The transition from the interior to the exterior of the building is optically suspended by a roof extending far beyond the outer walls. Two reflecting pools complete the ensemble. The principle on which the structure is based foresaw a clear separation of the supports and the

above:
The present building was reconstructed in 1985 by Ignasi de Solà-Morales, Ferran Ramos and Cristià Cirici. It is striking here how Mies van der Rohe – inspired by De Stijl – materialized individual slices in theoretically endless planes of space. The building was viewed in its day as demonstrating the return of Germany to the democratic world after the end of the First World War.

walls. It is expressed in an extremely reduced composition made up of horizontal and vertical planes, the effect of which is amplified by the ascetic furnishings. With the exception of the Barcelona chairs designed by Sergius Ruegenberg and Georg Kolbe's sculpture "Der Morgen" ("The Morning") the pavilion was virtually empty.

In January 1930 the pavilion was taken down and its individual parts sold. Since its reconstruction (1983 - 1986) by Ignasi de Solà-Morales, Cristian Cirici and Fernando Ramos it has served as the seat of the Mies van der Rohe Foundation.

Como (Italy): Casa del Fascio (now Casa del Popolo)

1932–1936, Giuseppe Terragni

left:
In contrast to the stucco commonly used in International Style, the House of the Fascists is faced with white marble. Although the construction is thoroughly modern, the material used on the façade is drawn from Antiquity, as were many of the models emulated by the architects of the Gruppo 7. The raw cement on the interior was, on the other hand, intended to add an archaic element. Como was a centre of Fascist architecture.

The works and person of Giuseppe Terragni are replete with widespread prejudice: that classical modernism should always be equated with the value canon of liberty and democracy. Although his buildings are in no way inferior to the highlights of International Style, he remained a convinced fascist right up till his early death. The Casa del Fascio is considered a masterly example of rationalism. It is not only historically important as a building, but also as an indicator of the extent of fascist cultural policy: Modernism reached Italy at a time when both it and fascism were already established – and, in contrast to Germany, the avant-garde in Italy did not displace industrial building. The marble-clad building is built on a square of 33 metres (36 yds.) lengthways and half this length in height. It complies with a strictly rational geometry, which not only exposes the logic of its beam construction, but also that of the facade structure. Like all his buildings, Terragnis considered his main work in the historical context of its location and interprets it by means of the New Building: From the first sight of the ground plan of a Venetian Renaissance Palazzo, the Casa del Fascio also refers, by means of its three-part organization around a covered courtyard, to the inner court house of the Como. The solidum takes up items of the medieval city tower, the front overlooking the Piazza del Popolo reflects the outline of the town of Comos, established in Roman times. A complex façade covers the historical elements which – although based on a uniform modular system – is unique in modern architecture.

For a long time Terragnis' works remained unconsidered in Europe and without resonance. In contrast, his influence on American architects such as Richard Meier, Michel Graves and Peter Eisenman were important.

Bear Run, Pennsylvania (U.S.A.): Fallingwater
1935–1937, Frank Lloyd Wright

left:
This house, built right over a brook, had a great influence on the development of architecture, although it was known almost solely from illustrations in professional journals; only very few architects actually saw the completed building at that time. The house's stone walls underline a natural component, while the concrete surfaces, which extend out daringly, emphasize man's role in its creation.

If an architect has ever sought to achieve a symbiosis with nature, then this is where it was realized. In designing "Fallingwater" in Pennsylvania, Frank Lloyd Wright succeeded in a stroke of genius. He was commissioned to build a weekend house. The architect, who was quite taken with his own work, was able to live out his fantasies here and, in doing so, created a work of art in complete harmony with nature. Located over a waterfall on the Bear Run River, the building engages in a self-confident dialogue with the waterfall and the rocky landscape that surrounds it. Since Wright was able in this house, as in no other, to unite organic architecture with Rationalism and International Style. Concrete, natural stone and glass, as well as right angles and natural forms, all come into their own. Masonry walls of Pottsville sandstone rise up vertically to support the horizontal slabs of reinforced concrete that form the terraces. On the roof there is a glassed in belvedere that is used as an exhibition pavilion. In the main living area, plate glass is set into the floor providing a view of the water. The three floors are, owing to the slant of the ledges, not set directly one over the other, but staggered. The terraces seem to melt in with the natural surroundings, and the stairway that connects the different levels of the house with one another echoes the form of the waterfall.

The Kaufmann family, who commissioned the house, were, like many others, at first shocked because the house seemed more like an architectural sculpture than a place to inhabit. Yet the house to be seen as one of the major works by a man who was perhaps the most important American architect of the 20th century.

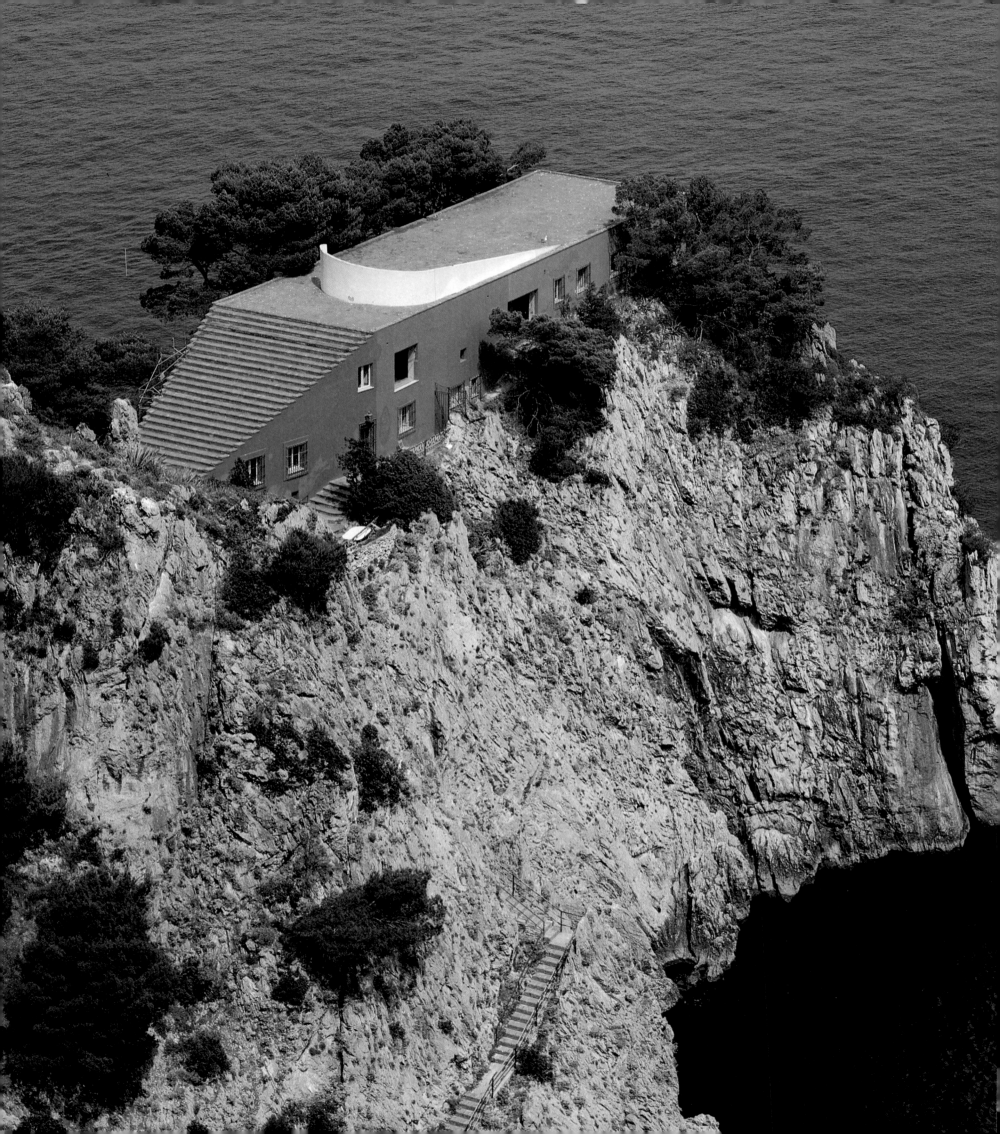

Capri (Italy): Casa Malaparte
1938–1943, Adalberto Libera

One might say that eccentric people build in eccentric places. This may not always be the case, but it was certainly true of the poet Curzio Malaparte. Born as Erich Kurt Suckert, he secretly saw himself as Napoleon Bonaparte's antipode, hence he called himself Malaparte. He was able to purchase a piece of property on the Italian island of Capri for a very modest sum, and then he had an idiosyncratic house designed for the spot by the architect Adalberto Libera. Set up on a cliff, it offers views so dramatic they seem staged. In order to better realize his ideal of building a house that mirrored his own character, Malaparte reworked the design himself. He described the fundamental characteristics as: sad, hard and severe – although with some measure of coquetry. The central room in this two-storey building is a salon measuring roughly 100 metres (328 sq. ft.) with a terrace set in front of it. In addition, there were bedrooms and workrooms for the poet and a flat for guests with another four rooms. The list of guests is impressive and includes the names of such famous colleagues as Albert Camus, Jean Cocteau and Alberto Moravia. Writers, artists, fashion photographers and architects all equally admired this unconventional house, the Casa Malaparte.

left:
The Casa Malaparte on Capri interprets the building forms of the Mediterranean area in a new way by breaking up the conventional arrangement. Its flat roof is reached by a large open flight of stairs, which can almost be interpreted as a roof slope.

The owner of the house is reported to have enjoyed riding his bicycle up on the roof, and it even served as a heliport. In 1963 scenes for Jean-Luc Godard's film Le MÈpris, starring Michel Piccoli and Brigitte Bardot, were also filmed there.

Marseille (France): Unité d'Habitation

1947–1952, Le Corbusier

left:
The housing shortage after the Second World War was intended to be reduced by means of "machines for living," like the Unité d'Habitation, which would also decrease the amount of space required by normal residential buildings. These high-rise constructions allowed the countryside to be preserved, which should then be accessible to the community rather than be parcelled into separate private gardens. Large residential complexes are back in discussion, if only because of the increasing hindrance to rain capture posed by detached family housing.

Le Corbusier operated on the assumption that the man-made world was better than the natural one. By concentrating on high-rise housing, he wanted to create more space to move around out of doors. These criteria led him to a concept that was brand-new at that time. The first example of his altered opinion is the Unité d'Habitation in Marseille. Massive concrete segments and a fantastically shaped roof are the outer features, flexible floor plans and skeleton construction are the interior features. Any one of 23 possible floor plans could be set into the rectilinear ferroconcrete grid "like bottles into a wine rack", as le Corbusier put it. In this building measuring 57 metres (187 ft.) in height, 135 metres (443 ft.) in length and 20 metres (65.6 ft.) in breadth, there were 3,337 units for between one and 20 inhabitants. Altogether almost 1800 people could take up residence here. The majority of the units were maisonette apartments. Shops and laundries, child-care facilities, a roof garden, an athletic track and a swimming-pool were all intended to make it possible to lead a life within the boundaries of the building. In his radicalism Le Corbusier could imagine that buildings of this kind would one day be able to replace entire city districts. Although Le Corbusier was commissioned by the Ministry for Reconstruction and Urban Planning to fight the massive housing shortage after the war, it was not possible to turn this concept - despite the intentions stated - into a type of standard housing.

The idea of this system was developed by Le Corbusier in the period between 1942 and 1948. Based on an assumed body height of 1.83 metres (6 ft.) the architect developed a complex system of proportions for construction. The starting point for these calculations were the human form and the golden section. The result was an optimal room height of 2.26 metres (7.4 ft.) and a room width of 3.66 metres (12 ft.).

Moscow (Russia): Lomonossov Moscow State University

1948–1952, Lev Vladimirovich Rudnov, Sergei Tchernisev, Pavel Abrossimov, Andrei Rostkovski, Alexander Chrikov, Vsevolod Nassonov

left:
As with the New York skyscrapers, here too a modern construction has been provided with a historicist façade. In the 1920's, modern architects had been supported in Moscow. However, around 1930 a gradual but total change of direction took place, one manifesting in the result of the competition for the Palace of the Supreme Soviet.

The free combination of architecture and sculpture connects the Lomonossov University to the unrealized Palace of the Soviets; on the other hand, the Stalinist "gingerbread style" is not dissimilar to some of the New York gothic art deco skyscrapers. But due to an excess of sculptural detail, the building appears overloaded. The Moscow State University is part of an ensemble of eight apartment houses that were projected in the course of the reconstruction of Moscow and its 800-year anniversary in 1947. Seven of these were realized. The aim of the construction was to lend form to the collective dream of a new world and new people as quickly as possible. The importance of the apartment houses lie in their embodiment of a uniform town planning ensemble intended to encompass the whole city: As compositional elements they returned the concise silhouette to the Moscow city structure which had been lost with the reconstruction plan of 1935. At that time the majority of churches were torn down, among them, the cathedral of Christ the Redeemer. The architect's group established under the direction of Rudnov in a park on Moscow's Lenin Hill erected a severely symmetrical university as its most important building for the new Moscow development. In the style of socialist realism, the establish-ed complex consists of a main building with a heavy soaring, central projection and four cubic stepped towers which are connected by means of an extensive ten storey "landscaped border" containing four corner towers. The octagonal form of the central spire was done in compliance with an instruction from Stalin.

After the reorganization of the dictatorial Soviet regime (from 1931/32), the architecture in Stalin's totalitarian state was also targeted by party dogmatists. "Progressive" socialism had embarked on a U-turn away from a style of building that was satisfying the social requirements towards that of a megalomaniacal self-representation of a people-despising regime.

Ronchamp (France): Notre-Dame-du-Haut
1950–1954, Le Corbusier

The pilgrimage church "Our Lady on High" is set on a rise in the Vosges Mountains. After the two previous churches there were both lost to fire, it was decided to have a new church built out of cement. In Le Corbusier's work, this church represents the transition from Brutalism (1952 - 1956, Maisson Jaoul in Neuilly) to a more sweeping style already be sensed in the roof constructions of the "Unité d'habitation" in Marseille. The building can be seen as a reflection of the Neo-Expressionist tendencies current in the 1950s and 1960s. These can also be found in Oscar Neimeyer's work and in Jørn Utzon's Sydney Opera House in the same period. While the building features all of the main elements that traditionally dominate every church - solid walls, stained glass windows, a tower and a large roof - here they all take on unusual forms. The glass in the wide variety of windows is set into deep openings in the wall, sometimes further forward, sometimes further back and sometimes at an angle. The tower seems as if it is made of mud, and the roof seems to have been put on the wrong way around, whith being too big and too heavy. Seen from inside, it seems to float over the walls. Yet within the church it is the windows that have the greatest effect. In a very thick wall, that becomes thinner towards the top,

the window openings become tunnels in which the glass seems much darker than most of the painted glass windows in early Gothic churches. While the interior of the church accommodates only about 200 visitors, thousands can participate in the outdoor services for which there is an additional altar under the roof that extends far beyond the building. The figure of Mary on the wall above the altar, that has always attracted pilgrims to the site, can be seen both from inside and out.

In order to create massive sculptural elements in cement (sculptural cement architecture) one needs highly adept carpenters able to build the necessary forms into which the cement can be poured or sprayed.

Rotterdam (Netherlands): The Lijnbaan

1954, Johannes Hendrik van den Broek and Jacob Berend Bakema

Like a small town, a vending machine, a shopper's paradise – the opinions concerning the first pedestrian shopping mall in Rotterdam, and in the Netherlands, were and are highly divergent. In 1949 Johannes Hendrik van den Broek and his much younger partner Jacob Berend Bakema were commissioned by businessmen who viewed the arrangement of their stores one next to the other as a democratic form of construction and as a means of strengthening their position. When completed, in 1953, the big plate glass windows of 65 two-storey shops faced onto a pedestrian mall. Since the reinforced concrete skeleton only influenced the basic dimensions, the size and the distribution of room within the shops could be determined individually. The big glass fronts attract window shoppers who come into the stores from the central path which is lined with flowers, benches and art. The centre of this promenade is also partly covered by a roof. Goods are delivered to the stores over a back street delivery zone. The construction of housing units up above, common in retail sites then, was restricted to separate apartment blocks. Anyone expecting this project to provide a greater variety of uses in the inner city was mistaken. Pushing the apartment blocks back, made it possible to refrain from the traditional design of façades, allowing greater density to be realized. "The building will … seem like a closed city system and, due to its greater height, seem even more massive than other, closed housing blocks, which are limited in their height by the profile of the street."

On 14 May, 1940 the German Luftwaffe destroyed the centre of Rotterdam. The Lijnbaan is one of the symbols for post-war reconstruction. It was the first pedestrian shopping mall in the Netherlands and the model for many similar projects all over the world. The functions of business, traffic and housing were clearly separated. This reflected one of the central thoughts behind the rebuilding effort in Rotterdam. On the other hand, the city was not supposed to be hierarchically designed on a drawing board, since that would have seemed totalitarian, but rather grow in the sense of a city organism.

New York (U.S.A.): Seagram Building
1954–1958, Ludwig Mies van der Rohe

left:
The Seagram Building founded the New York tradition of steel frame and glass skyscrapers. Unlike many of its banal successors, clear attempts were made here to achieve beauty of proportion: as in a column, the base (ground storey) and capital (upper section) are clearly varied, and the surfaces are separated at the corners by groins. They alone appear to act as filigree supports.

Due to its elegance, the Seagram Building, situated on Park Avenue in Manhattan, ranks among the most important apartment buildings in the world. It was built by Joseph E. Seagrams and Sons to serve as the headquarters of the Canadian Rum Distillery. They came into contact with Mies van der Rohe (who had emigrated from Germany in 1938), thanks to Phyllis Bronfman Lambert, the daughter of the company's president, who was interested in architecture. On account of Manhattan's so-called "zoning law," most apartment buildings had been established as "set backs": these "set backs" had to be matched with increasing height. The alternative was clearly discernible obliquely opposite: the Lever House (1952) built by Gordon Bunshaft of Skidmore, Owings and Merrill, an apartment building disc which rises above a horizontal podium. Mies van der Rohe, however, built a severe, vertically organized 38-storey stele striving towards the sky. The geometrical clarity of the edifice, which has a bronze curtain-wall façade, appears in the main façade, distanced from Park Avenue by means of a public plaza. An examination of the rear façade reveals that in reality the building is designed in the form of a T and possesses two annexes of six and ten storeys. Van der Rohe was not concerned with function-

alism, but rather with its image; this is also evident in his dealings with wing unit and façade. The steel skeleton, encased in concrete for reasons of fire protection, is coated with bronze in the lobby zone, which appears Egyptian-like due to the travertine-clad elevator shafts. The skin refers visually to the invisible bones. This is repeated in the curtain-wall facades with their rhythmically repetitive double T-beams, which visually articulate the function of load bearing, but are in reality decorative and only form an exterior, in the vertically ascending skin.

Ludwig Mies van der Rohe, who had created two masterpieces of New Building in the service of the home-protection movement emigrated to the USA in 1938. His many years of work at the Illinois Institute of Technology (IIT) in Chicago had a profound influence on his views concerning rationalist architecture. The architect frequently varied two fundamental construction types: the open pavilion (Crown Hall of the IIT, 1950-56; National Gallery of Berlin, 1962-68), and the apartment building in skeleton construction (Lake Shore Drive Apartments, Chicago, 1948-51), through the labyrinth and, hence, to consciously confront the past.

New York (U.S.A.)
The Solomon R. Guggenheim Museum
1956–1959, Frank Lloyd Wright
Extension 1992: Gwathmey Siegel & Associates

left:

With his exhibition rotunda, which opens upwards in a spiral, funnel-shaped manner, Wright was able to free himself from one of the seeming givens of architecture: the storey. Although the idea of the extended floor had already been touched on (see for instance Maison Tassel), Wright's spiral, which ignores the idea of levels, goes far beyond.

What architecture enthusiasts celebrated as a stroke of genius, more critical contemporaries dismissed with ridicule and scorn: "coffee mill," "salad bowl" or "washing machine" were some of the more common epithets for the gigantic spiral made of reinforced concrete. Frank Lloyd Wright never lived to see this, his most spectacular and undoubtedly his most elegant building, completed. He had been awarded the commission in 1943, but construction did not begin until 13 years later, hence the Guggenheim Museum was only opened shortly after his death. The hermetic building in the form of a spiral that widens towards the top, radically calling into question all museum architecture known at that time. The building put demands on the technology of its day which the latter was not able to fulfil. The monolithically conceived form of the spiral had to be built in a number of segments, the balustrade that had been planned as an integral part of the ramp had to be poured separately. During this process the cement did not harden evenly, causing unintentional ripples. On the inside of the building, an elevator takes visitors to the top floor, where they begin to make their "way around" the exhibition on a gently sloping spiral ramp that leads downward to a kind of white-washed cement arcade winding around an inner court covered by a glass dome. It can also be seen as a continuous room with no interruptions. The organic architecture of the museum encourages comparison with the Abstract Art, for which it was planned, from the outset.

The building drove most curators to desperation. The natural lighting is uneven and unreliable, the walls, that are tilted outwards, force the visitor to lean forward when viewing a painting, their modest height only allows the exhibition of artworks of limited size. Yet despite the functional shortcomings, the Guggenheim Museum is architecturally impressive. When it was augmented by a ten-storey tower, which included four exhibition levels, in 1992, waves of indignation concerning the "desecration of a landmark" arose; in the meantime this "tide of fury" has settled.

New York (U.S.A.)
The Trans World Airlines Terminal Building
1956–1962, Eero Saarinen

The TWA arrival terminal at New York's Idlewild (now John F. Kennedy) Airport is one of the major works in the neo-Expressionist sculptural style that emerged around the middle of the 1950s as a counter-development to the obligatory right angles and quadratic shapes of International Style. This building, that evolved through a number of model studies, was supposed to symbolize the dynamism of flying and inevitably reminds one of a bird with extended wings. The roof construction rests on massive Y-shaped supports. It consists of quarter segments of reinforced concrete which are arched at the outer edges and meet on the two inner sides at right angles where bands of skylights line the seams. Under this umbrella-like roof, the curved band of windows tilt out slightly creating a dynamic space in which architectonic design and engineering achievement enter a symbiotic relationship, creating an impressive union.

Going into the building is like entering a sculpture, all of the details – stairways, ramps, waiting rooms and check-in desks – seem to flow from one to the other. The sweeping forms remind one of European Art Nouveau, particularly the works of Hector Guimard, Louis Majorelle and Antoni Gaudí.

This is where Saarinen's training as a sculptor came to play a role – before studying architecture he had been a student at the Académie de la Grande Chaumière in Paris.

The TWA arrival building marks Saarinen's departure from an attitude towards design closely aligned with Mies van der Rohe's, and the orientation towards more subjective solutions developed individually for every new building and function, solutions that were capable of stark sculptural expression and a certain measure of stylistic pluralism.

Jerusalem (Israel): Shrine of the Book
1957–1965, Frederick J. Kiesler

The scrolls of Qumran were discovered shortly before the state of Israel was established in 1948 – the oldest written testimony of Jewish culture. They belonged to the library of a religious Jewish community dating from the 2nd century BC. The finding paved the way for a new textual criticism of the Old Testament and the scrolls serve as a new source for the history of the Hebrew and Aramaic languages. The location of the discovery on the Jordanian side of the Dead Sea complicated the clarification of its ownership. Thus it took ten years for the manuscripts, which were sent to the USA in 1948 by the metropolitan of St. Mark's monastery in the old Arab quarter of Jerusalem, to be returned to Israel, in 1958, for the then astonishing sum of 250,000 dollars. The Gottesman Foundation approached the New York architect Armand P. Bartos in 1957 with orders to design a shrine for the archaeological treasure. Bartos passed on the task to his senior partner, Frederick Kiesler. While the first draft envisaged a domed building on the top floor of the Hebrew University library that would not be visible from afar, the implemented version is part of the Israel Museum, located on a hill above a monastery dating from the 12th century. The domed building's exterior is tiled in white, while the interior gradates from bright to darker colours and is partly dressed in roughly hewn limestone half-sunken into the cliff and open at the top for climatological reasons. A fountain spraying water from the interior through the open dome into a square basin also serves as air conditioning. The scrolls themselves are housed in a double-parabolic vaulted dome in the centre of the building, flanked by two exterior stone staircases.

left:
The shrine is similar to the lid of one of the vessels in which some of the scrolls were found. True to this image, a large part of the building is buried. Inside, we find the amorphous room shapes with which Kiesler had already occupied himself previously. The ceilings, floors, and walls appear as a unit like a natural cave.

With this project Kiesler was able to realize for the first time in architecture the avant-garde concept of a dramatic, continuously flowing space he developed as a stage designer (he taught at the Juilliard School of Music from 1933 to 1956).

Sydney (Australia): The Sydney Opera House
1965–1973, Jørn Utzon

left:
In Sydney, the shells of the ceramic roofs of the Opera House rise up on an inconspicuous terraced foundation. In the context of the water surrounding the peninsula, they are also reminiscent of both sport boats' sails and mussels, without currying favour with these forms.

The new cultural centre in Sydney was supposed to be a landmark expressing the growing importance of culture. A prominent site, on a peninsular in the harbour, was provided as its location. The design by the Danish architect Jørn Utzon won out over 234 competitors. The construction period extended from 1957 to 1973, the costs exploded, increasing from a planned four to a final total of 57 million dollars. In 1966 the architect turned his back on the project in discord and his Australian colleagues, Peter Hall, David Littlemore and Lionel Todd, completed the building. Therefore, the interior does not correspond with Utzon's plan. Utzon foresaw a high degree of separation between the work behind the scenes, which takes place below the ground, and the area for the audience, located above the ground and characterized by a very impressive exterior form. The spaces for rehearsals and for the infrastructure, as well as the theatre, are below the ground where rational, clean-lined design dominates. In the buildings above the ground, shell-shaped roofs enclose a large concert hall, the opera stage, as well as two foyers and a restaurant. Hence it is by no means just an opera house, but rather a cultural centre. It is said that the architect was inspired by an orange peel. The organic forms of the roof structures also remind one of waves or clouds, sails or shells, helmets or hoods. The roofs are between 40 and 60 metres (130 and 197 ft.) high. The engineer Sir Ove Arup developed a solution to ensure the structural stability. The gigantic shells are made of pre-fabricated concrete segments with Swedish ceramic tiles affixed to them.

Utzon gave International Style decisive impulses with this design. He loosened the constraints of strict functional rationalism by introducing symbolism that serves no specific purpose. This organic structure is also considered one of the pioneering works of Postmodernism.

Brasilia (Brazil): The National Congress
1958–1960, Oscar Niemeyer

left:
The parliament in Brasilia looks like a huge sculpture of the contemporaneous Minimal Art.
Simple, elegant forms are composed to form arrangements. Here are two preformed sections, which are arranged on a thin surface. It is also typical of that time that the columns seem to be too thin for the slabs and sections weighing heavily on them.

Both in a law drafted in 1823 and in the constitution of Brazil proposed in 1891, plans for the establishment of a new capital named Brasilia were intended. Yet a site was not chosen until President Juscelino Kubitschek de Oliveira was elected in 1956. It was then decided to have the capital, that was inaugurated on 21 April, 1960, located on a highland plane near the centre of the country. The new city was laid out according to a plan by Lúcio Costas. From the air it appears to be modelled on an airplane. The "Plaza of the Three Powers" is located where the cockpit would be. On each of the three corners of the plaza one finds the Presidential Palace (the executive) the Place of Justice (the judiciary) and the National Congress (the legislative). The National Congress is part of a comprehensive expression of the state's organization manifested in both architecture and city planning. Niemeyer illustrated the balance of power between the senate (dome) the house of representatives (dish): two forms that mirror each other on a flat-roofed building that only seems to serve as a pediment. Between these two institutions, the two slender administrative towers, housing the representatives' offices, maintain the "balance." The wide drive in front of the building is characteristic of Brasilia, which was completely orientated towards automobile traffic. This is endemic of the euphoric view of the future in the post-war period, when neither dangers for the environment, nor the negative social effects of automobile traffic and building sprawl were recognized.

The Don Bosco Cathedral in Brasilia (as are almost all of Niemeyer's public buildings) is just as impressive and symbolic. It is built above the ground in the form of a gigantic Crown of Thorns. The Italian priest and teacher, Don Bosco (1815 - 1888), was the first person to suggest establishing a capital at this location far from the densely populated coast.

San Diego (U.S.A.)
Salk Institute for Biological Studies
1959–1967, Louis Isidore Kahn with August Komendant (extended in 1994)

Architecture as idea: Louis Kahn stands in the history of 20th-century architecture as the person who called for a return to form as a major factor in its own right. As a result, he went against the dogma of "form follows function." The Salk institute, founded by the developer of the polio vaccine, Dr. Jonas Salk, is located directly on the Pacific coast. Kahn began work in 1959 on his first drafts for a laboratory, a meetinghouse and living quarters for the scientists. The final plans were agreed on in 1962, and comprised two symmetrical laboratory wings grouped round a courtyard facing the ocean. They consist of two fully glazed storeys without supports; the window-

less service departments located in between form the supporting construction. Set in front of the laboratories are studies and research rooms that resemble monks' cells. They are offset from the laboratories by one storey (so that they are of the same height as the service departments), and are linked with them by bridges and stairways. The courtyard with its fountains and pools was only finalized in 1967, the meetinghouse and living quarters were never constructed. The former entry to the site, a copse of eucalyptus trees, was sacrificed to allow for extensions in 1994. The main motif of the design is the centre. Since the unsupported laboratories are the main

rooms in functional terms, and allow little scope for architectural freedom, Kahn concentrated on the "service" elements of the ensemble: the studies, the development of the surrounding site and the courtyard itself, which he placed on equal standing in his architecture.

A particularly noteworthy aspect of this construction is the exceptional quality of the materials that Kahn employed – travertine, concrete admixed with volcanic ash, teak and glass – as well as the enormous attention that was paid to treating the surfaces.

Berlin (Germany): The Philharmonie
1960–1963, Hans Scharoun

left:
Scharoun had a major share in the reconstruction of Berlin after the Second World War with his plans for rebuilding the city. His first public building commission was the Philharmonic Hall. After that, he was also able to realize the German Embassy in Brazil (1963–1971) and the City Theatre in Wolfsburg (1965–1973).

"In the valley the orchestra, in the terraced vineyards the audience; and the heavens form a tented roof." The architect conjured the image of a landscape in which man, space and music were to become one. Even sceptics had to admit that here, listening to music became a shared experience. "When buskers play, a circle of listeners always forms around them."Hans Scharoun cited this observation as the inspiration for his approach to planning the concert hall. The audience surrounds the orchestra. The seating in the auditorium is arranged in terraces, one higher than the other until they almost reach the ceiling, which takes the form of a number of sails for acoustical reasons. The arrangement of the interior space gives the building's exterior its form. The pronounced segmentation in the layout of the main concert hall, the complex foyer, and the spaces for the administration and auditions, all come together creating a homogenous impression. The Berlin Philharmonie is Hans Scharoun's most important building and a masterpiece of organic design in which Expressionist ideas were echoed. This becomes apparent as soon as one begins making one's way up the uniform, angular stairways and culminates in the perfect acoustic conditions in every one of the 2,200 seats. At the opening ceremony Berlin's Senator for Culture, Adolf Arndt, claimed that "Democracy played the role of the builder here."

The Philharmonie was later augmented by the Neue Nationalgalerie, designed by Mies van der Rohe, also the Musikinstrumentenmuseum, the Staatsbibliothek and the state-owned museums of Berlin.

Tokyo (Japan): Olympic Stadiums
1961–1964, Kenzo Tange with Yoshikatsu Tsuboi and Uichi Inoue

Spectacular and elaborate, the roof construction of the Olympic stadiums in Tokyo not only astonished visitors to the 18th Olympic Games, it remains breathtaking to this day. It constitutes the logical development of a constructional principle that was known in the 1950s (Le Corbusier's Philips Pavilion at the World Exposition of 1958 in Brussels; Eero Saarinen's Hockey arena in New Haven/USA, also 1958). Kenzo Tange and his engineers Yoshikatsu Tsuboi and Uichi Inoue constructed the lower roof anchoring (two curved concrete arches) to act simultaneously as supports for the tribunes. Suspended by massive steel cables from two enormous concrete

piers – in the small stadium these are replaced by a single pier and frame-like struts- – the weight of the membrane-like roof is borne by a net of tensile steel. Attached to this are welded, enamelled steel plates. The span of the large stadium was hitherto unmatched. The side rooms are integrated into a sunken system of paths, passageways and green spaces that link the two stadiums. The ground plan of the swimming stadium is formed by two semi-circles that are slightly displaced in relation to one another, while the ground plan of the small stadium, which staged boxing matches, is circular. The entrances are all located to the south on the ground level, while the

above:
The two stadiums for the 18th Olympics are linked underground. The smaller one is dominated by a mast, which is not in the centre. From there, its roof descends. Both roofs bend outwards to the edge, reminiscent of Buddhist temples. Nevertheless, Tange claims he wanted to use every means to prevent his buildings from being labelled traditional.

actual sports arenas are sunken. The interior of the large stadium is dominated by six diving platforms; the swimming pool could be covered over for judo and other sports by means of an extendable floor slab.

A convincing synthesis of Japan's past and present: the Olympic stadiums designed for the 1964 Summer Olympic Games are representative of the vivid, expressive formal language Kenzo Tange employed during the 1950s and 1960s.

Apeldoorn (Netherlands): Central Beheer (CB1)
1968–1972, Herman Hertzberger

The client told the architect Herman Hertzberger that the employees were supposed to feel "right at home" in the new building. The utopia sought after was nothing less than a workplace free of alienation. Hence, hierarchical barriers were done away with – everyone was given a space, that they could decorate as they chose, in a room that was open to all sides. A wide array of terraces, hobby rooms, corners for coffee breaks and playgrounds were supposed to motivate employees to view work as a natural part of their self-realization. Soon after the building's completion a jungle-like plethora of greenery filled the three-storey courtyards of the Central Beheer insurance

company. During the 1970s some say it almost became a "swamp" in which the building began to seem more and more like a "grotto". Despite his tendency to favour rather staid building materials (cement blocks, prefabricated elements), Herman Hertzberger can still be called the hippie of the Dutch architectural scene. His designs always start with human beings, and their need to communicate with each other is always given the highest priority. Hertzberger became acquainted with this "structuralist" attitude while working on the editorial board of the magazine "Forum" with Aldo van Eyck and Jakob Bakema. They had come to criticize modernism as too rigid and

above:
The exterior of Herzberger's building reveals its modular construction. This form alone is a tribute to the concept of democratic architecture. It also corresponds with the wide range of uses (which are far from arbitrary) to which people can put the space on the inside. The structure of the building is intended to create a gradual transition from a purely private sphere to a public space.

dogmatic, and attempted to take its development a step further. Hertzberger applied the results of these efforts to actual building practice. Using prefabricated elements, he created a fortress-like complex, made of series of staggered towers that each had a footprint measuring 9 by 9 metres (ca.30 by 30 ft.) and accommodated 12 work spaces on each level. They were in turn connected to each other by a series of bridges. A planned pedestrian bridge to the city centre was never realized. Hence, the building, which seems like a labyrinth inside, is cut off from its surroundings by four highways.

The attitude that life should not be reduced to functions like "living, working and travelling" led to the establishment of a countermovement, the CIAM (Congrès internationaux d'architecture moderne). Within its context, "Structuralist" architecture was developed. "Structuralist" designs are usually like cities en miniature, urban density and overlapping functions within individual buildings were intended to help overcome the reservations many had toward Modernism, particularly the Modernism of the post-war reconstruction period in Europe.

Munich (Germany): The Olympic Stadium
1968–1972, Günter Behnisch, Frei Otto

left:
With their translucent tent roofs, the sports buildings at the Olympic Park fit in the parkland made from deposited war debris. The choice of transparent acryl for the tent roofs ensured a natural lighting of the sports buildings after the PAL television system had been introduced in Germany in 1967.

The games were supposed to be a happy event, celebrated amidst verdant surroundings and human in their dimension. In keeping with these aspirations, the architecture was intended to be somewhat whimsical. The second Olympic Games to be held in Germany were meant to differ fundamentally from the rigidly organized event in Berlin in 1936. The latter had involved a brash display of Monumental architecture put on by the National Socialists (Nazis). Munich's Olympic Park was considered fascinating the world over, particularly thanks to its wide tent-like roof. Frei Otto had already created a similar tent-like roof for the German Pavilion at the Montreal Expo in 1967. In Munich nearly 60 pylons support the construction. A network of steel cables is spanned to support plexi-glass panels measuring 9 m (ca. 30 ft). The stadium, athletic centre and swimming pool are all connected by the "roof without shade." The German architects, Günter Behnisch and Frei Otto won the competition staged in 1967 for the commission to design the park. The stadium, the Olympic hall, the swimming-pool, the Olympic lake and the Olympic hill were all created around the centrally located Coubertinplatz . The terrain was planned by the landscape architect Günther Grzimek. A look back at history leaves no doubt, the stadium, which offers seating for 70,000 spectators, refers back to structures like the Amphitheatrum Flavium, the Colosseum, in Rome. It also reminds one of the idea of a theatre nestled into the slope of a mountain, as in Epidauros, for example.

The Olympic grounds in Munich represent a particularly successful example of the amalgamation of High-Tech Architecture, using vast amounts of glass, and organic architecture. It is already listed as a sight worthy of historic preservation. Unfortunately it also reminds us of the Arab terrorist attack that led to hostages being taken and the killing of Israeli athletes. Yet the architecture bears witness to the intention of peaceful cooperation for which it was built.

Washington D. C. (U.S.A.)
East Building of the National Gallery of Art
1968–1978, Ieoh Ming Pei

left:
From outside, the Museum appears as a massive closed group of forms with just a few glass surfaces. The broad entrance recedes far behind the building line, so that its function does not impose itself. Instead, it seems to be nothing more than a hollow form in the urban development sculpture.

The ground plan of the US capital is dominated by axes and radial roads, and was created on the drawing board according to the plans of French engineer and architect Pierre Charles L'Enfant. It is not surprising, then, that the extension of the National Gallery on a trapezoid plot at the end of the mall had to comply with these specifications. Pei incorporated the diagonal alignment of the location to Capitol Hill by constructing the building from two complementary triangles, which are connected by a similarly triangular courtyard. Like the original National Gallery building, now called the West Building, the exterior walls of the East Building are clad in pink marble from Tennessee. The courtyard is covered by a glass dome-like construction, which is supported by 25 tetrahedrons that form a steel framework in space. The lobby inside is dominated by a mobile by Alexander Calder, which is suspended from under the dome. The three exhibition areas are prism-shaped and subdivided into hexagonal spaces to allow fuller usage. Stretching between the old and the new wings of the museum is a plaza with a subterranean café. Its pyramidal skylight anticipates the idea that Pei was to perfect three years later for the entrance to the Louvre in Paris. Although the language of form from the 1960s and 1970s that Pei employed for the building seems to harmonize with the principles behind L'Enfant's design from the 19th century, this building is less concerned with the context of urban construction and far more with geometric abstraction. For this he convincingly picks up on a theme that is reflected by the majority of artworks on display.

During the decades spanning the 1970s and 1990s, there was a veritable boom in building new museums and converting old ones. As visible signs of the power and success of the cities, they came to replace the mighty sacred buildings of yore as symbols of wealth. Pei made two very important contributions to this: the East Building of the National Gallery in Washington D. C. and, as the culmination of his work, the pyramid at the Louvre in Paris.

Newcastle-upon-Tyne (England)
Byker Redevelopment
1968–1981, Ralph Erskine

left:
The Byker
Redevelopment consists
of a high protective wall
and lower buildings
behind it. All that there is
on the closed north side
of the "wall" are the kit-
chen, bathroom, and box
room together with the
yellow and red air condi-
tioners. The future resi-
dents had a say as
regards the colours,
materials, and develop-
ment of the ground
plans.

In 1968 the architect Ralph Erskine, who then lived in Sweden, was commissioned by the northern English city of Newcastle-upon-Tyne to redevelop Byker, a working-class neighbourhood to the east of the city. In a survey, 80 per cent of the population had voted in favour of the area being razed. Only those buildings that had served the community at large - pubs, churches and a swimming-pool - were preserved as islands of tradition. The 7,850 residents of this area, that became a textbook example of participatory design, only needed a few minutes to travel between their homes and the city centre by underground. Initially, visitors are confronted with a massive wall measuring nearly one and a half kilometres. This 'Byker wall' protects the area from wind and traffic noise from the north. The meandering, snake-like housing block rises to as many as nine storeys. Bastion-like construction in the foreground suggests something like an inhabited city wall of archaic proportions. If one enters the interior of the development through one of the narrow entryways, the hermetic compactness of the exterior gives way to the openness of the southern façade: balconies, entryways and stairwells are fitted with revetments of colourful wooden slats and roofed with transparent corrugated plastic. Set in front of the wall, they give the ensemble a provisional touch. While the flats in the Byker wall provide housing for approximately 20 per cent of the area's population, the remaining residents live to the west of it, in smaller, mainly two-storey buildings. Automobile traffic has been excluded from Byker altogether, at the request of the residents, and a system of pedestrian walkways, paths and narrow passageways provides access to the landscaped development. With its colourful houses and the provisional character of the wooden revetments the whole estate seems like a cross between a Scandinavian suburb and an English Garden City.

The way building was approached in Byker, as a form of step by step urban redevelopment, allowed the residents to take part in the planning process. Erskine established a branch office on the site that was a clearinghouse for questions and complaints. The future residents were able to express their opinions on a number of issues. Decisions on the configuration of buildings as well as the colours and materials were made in cooperation with the users.

Chicago (U.S.A.): Sears Tower

1971–1974, Skidmore, Owings & Merrill (SOM) with Fazlur Rahman Khan

left:
The Sears Tower, here in the background, was designed by Bruce Graham in the SOM Office. He belonged to it from 1951 to 1989, as a partner from 1960. Graham explains that, "Towers have historically been not only the pride of their temporary owners, but of their cities as well." In this way, he sees the Sears Tower in the tradition of the family towers in San Gimignano in Italy.

In 1974, the city of Chicago, in which the first "genuine skyscraper" – the Home Insurance Building – had been built in 1895 by William Le Baron Jenney, became home for almost 25 years to the world's tallest building: the 442 metre (1,418 ft.) tall Sears Tower, an administrative building for captains of commerce Sears, Roebuck & Co. Since 1997 it has had competition: the 452 metre (1,450 ft.) tall Petronas Twin-Towers designed by Cesar Pelli in Kuala Lumpur. Yet there has been no end to the discussion as to which of the two building deserves this accolade, for the height of the twin towers in Malaysia includes the pointed antenna at its apex, whilst the version installed on the Sears Tower apparently does not count. The construction consists of nine tubes that are enclosed by a steel frame and clad in black aluminium and bronze-tinted glass. Although they are discrete structures, together the tubes go to make up the whole building. In constructional terms, the tube cluster forms a kind of "mega-tube," which is aimed at compensating for the wind pressure that comes from the side. Each of the nine tubes has 49 storeys, where they end on the southeastern and north-western corners. The rest of the building ascends over the next 16 storeys in the form of a "Z," and from there on in the shape of a cross, up to the 90th floor. This brings the remaining tubes to an end; but upwards from here is a rectangular structure 20 storeys high, which forms the zenith of the Tower. This pattern of smooth surfaces and stepback construction is strongly reminiscent of the skyscrapers of the 1920s and 1930s.

The building is an outstanding achievement in both architectural and constructional terms. Scarcely another skyscraper offers so many different views to look at. It also leaves an interesting acoustic impression: the squeaky sound it emits in high winds is a regular source of confusion.

Paris (France): Centre Pompidou
1971–1977, Renzo Piano and Richard Rogers

left:
Usually, the utilities of a building are to be found in a compact core on the inside for reasons of cost. However, with the Centre National d'Art et de Culture Georges Pompidou, they were put on the "façade," consisting in turn of just stands with cantilevers and beams (spanning 47 metres – 154 ft.) along with a cross-support system.

The second president of France's Fifth Republic, Georges Pompidou, expressed the desire for a cultural centre in the capital that would be open to people from all walks of life. In 1970, 681 architects and architectural offices took part in the competition for the construction of a "Centre National d'Art et de Culture". The decision in favour of the Italian-British architectural duo, Renzo Piano and Richard Rogers, was made by a prominent jury, which included Philip Johnson and Oscar Niemeyer, and it was highly controversial. It was claimed that their high-tech architecture, consciously exposing the technical infrastructure by putting it in front of the façade, did not fit in with the surroundings. Indeed, the impression created by the exposed pipes, tubes and cast-iron supports, featured in front of a glass façade, is absolutely unique. Colours indicate each pipe's function: blue is for ventilation, green for water, yellow for electricity and red for the lifts. From outside, the building looks like a "Culture Factory", and because the infrastructure has been moved to the outside of the building, there is more flexibility inside. Yet everything is not solely intended to be functional, as the architects emphasize. What is most important is that an environment is created in which culture can be produced and not just consumed. Indeed, the

Centre Pompidou, or Beaubourg as it is named after the district in which it is located, has been able to convince even many of its harshest critics by presenting a widely varied and vital programme since it opened in 1977.

Not only the Musée National d'Art Moderne and its library, but also the special exhibitions, the fascinating view from the roof, and sometimes simply just the restaurant all attract a large number of visitors every year. The culture machine works! Not least of all thanks to the tubes containing the lifts that extend out in front of the façade. So criticized in the beginning, they now seem to personally invite every visitor to enter the building.

Modena (Italy): San Catoldo Cemetery
1971–1978, Aldo Rossi with Gianni Braghieri

left:
The large cube with the perforated façade as a house of the dead is only part of a complex that was supposed to be built in different phases. It is surrounded by a Columbarium. Architectural archetypes are combined to form a universal backdrop. The so-called perforated façade is also an archetype: the openings in the wall to let in light cannot be reduced any further.

Along with an apartment house in Milan's Gallaratese 2 district, San Catoldo is considered Aldo Rossi's most important early work. A major proponent of Rational Architecture, up until that point he had been more famous as an author and theorist ("The Architecture of the City"). In designing the cemetery he virtuously employed a repertoire of forms that was typical in his work, and which he drew from French Revolutionary Architecture - the cube, the cone, the triangle and the cylinder. The design with which Rossi won a national competition held in 1971 was for a western extension of an existing neoclassical cemetery. Like the older one, this new cemetery is built on a geometric grid. In the middle there is a series of parallel sepulchres ensconced in colonnades that look like an equilateral triangle when viewed from above, but increase in height as they progress from south to north. At the top of the triangle there is a conically shaped chapel, built over a mass grave. Across from it, at the base of the triangle and connected to the chapel through a middle axis like a backbone, the cubically shaped ossuary with a memorial for the dead of both World Wars. Without windows in the openings or a roof on top the monumental cube reminds one of an unfinished or deserted house. The cone across from

it reminds one of a gigantic, inactive chimney - two metaphors for death and, at the same time, a built-up painting in the style of Giorgio de Chirico and the Pittura Metafisica.

The exterior appearance of the cemetery is determined by aluminium roofs of the colonnades that are painted blue and the stucco outer walls that are pink. The interior is dominated by grey cement and the steel visible under the roofs and in the open stairways.

Tôkyô (Japan): The Nagakin Capsule Tower
1972, Kisho Kurokawa

left:
The Nagakin Capsule Tower was clearly constructed modularly. This simple and consistent system can be used to put up buildings with very different heights and widths. The only thing that does need adjusting is the core. It is currently experiencing a revival in simple automatized hotels.

The Nagakin Capsule Tower was designed according to the so-called metabolic architectural paradigm. One of its leading proponents in the 1960s was Kisho Kurakawa, who formulated the "Proposal for a New Urbanism" as follows: "We view human society as a lively process ... the reason for the use of the biological word 'Metabolism' is the belief that designs and technology should characterize human vitality. In this conjunction, the underlying principle of the exchangeability and modification of the parts, which should not be confused with disposability. On the basis of metabolic cycles only those parts should be replaced that have lost their usefulness." Kurokawa's Capsule building, erected in 1972, consisted of 144 housing units equipped with a whole array of appliances and a floor plan measuring 2.30 by 3.80 metres (7.5 by 12.5 ft.) and a height of 2.10 metres (7 ft.), that contained all of the functions and furniture needed in a housing unit. Whereby every capsule could be pieced together in twenty cells, ranging from the bathroom to the television, in whatever combination suited the needs of the individual. The "housing units" were prefabricated and suspended on steel shafts. The beehive-like form of the building that was screwed together in this manner allows its internal structure to be recognized from outside. In Kurokawa's metabolic tower a conscious version of a perfectly equipped minimal apartment with full technical infrastructure was built. Le Corbusier's housing machines with the standard of an automobile became reality here. These one-room cells were mainly purchased by companies for their employees. The concept, however, was never a great success. The expansion of the building was then undertaken in a more conventional manner.

Extracts from Kisho Kurokawa's "Capsule Declaration: 1. The capsule is cyborg-architecture. 2. A capsule is an apartment for the homo movens. 3. The capsule is an indication of a pluralistic society. 4. The capsule intends to erect a new family system. 7. The capsule is the ultimate form of industrialized construction. 8. The capsule mentality rejects uniformity and systematic thought.

New York (U.S.A.): The AT&T Building
1979–1984, Philip C. Johnson and John Burgee

left:
After the see-through high-rise buildings of the postwar era, the AT&T shows a return to a closed-in building, but without the typical stepback in the region of the roof. This characteristic of the first half of the 20th century was determined by the regulations regarding light access. These were rescinded around 1980: so long as the ground floor is publicly accessible, the building can be made as tall as desired.

In 1978, Philip Johnson was commissioned to build an impressive new company headquarters for AT&T in New York. The company did not want a plain glass tower, like Mies van der Rohe's Seagram Building, for their central office, but rather a building that would figure as prominently in the skyline as William Van Alen's Chrysler Building, one set up on a massive pedestal with an unusual roof. Here Johnson again demonstrated his flexibility and sense of Zeitgeist, and it led him to create the first Postmodern skyscraper in New York. Postmodernism emerged at the end of the 20th century as an alternative concept to Modernism, with its ever more obvious shortcomings, and was distinguished by its references to the architecture and the decorative forms of antiquity. The tower-like building, measuring 197 metres (647 ft.), brought about the world-wide breakthrough of Postmodernism with its pink granite façade and Chippendale gable. Like almost all Postmodern buildings, it represents a paradox: as a skyscraper it belongs to the modern period, while as a building type, with its pilaster-like façade and its split gable, it is obviously inspired by antiquity. The 37-storey steel frame and cement slab building stands on supports that are almost 20 metres (60 ft.) high and which form an arcade. The main entrance is marked by a high arch, measuring 35 metres (115 ft.), which is located in this arcade. 13,000 tons of granite were used for the traditional stone facing of the building. In the meantime, it is now called the Sony Building and the arcades at its base have been enclosed by windows and transformed into retail space.

Philip Johnson is regarded as a chameleon within the context of 20th century architecture and played a key role in the process of designing a number of new forms. He coined the term International Style, along with Henry-Russel Hitchcock, and was one of its most important proponents, earning himself the nickname "Mies van der Johnson". He was, however, just as dedicated to clearing a path for Postmodernism and also paid homage to Deconstructivism.

Chicago (U.S.A.): State of Illinois Center

1979–1985, Helmut Jahn for C. F. Murphy Associates

left:
The two lowest floors of the Center house restaurants and shops, the upper ones the offices. These are glazed and so, according to a German architecture theory, are to be interpreted as democratic, since citizens can watch their civil servants at work. The atrium is illuminated by a trellis-like cylinder.

Of all the buildings constructed in Chicago during the latter half of the 20th century, the State of Illinois Center has been by far the most controversial. It was later renamed after the state governor of the day, and thus personified its client: James R. Thompson. Wicked tongues claim that it exactly reflects his blatant political ambition and increasingly spectacular squandering of material resources. Others, however, would view this as patronage. Regardless of which position is correct, the building's location alone is quite remarkable. This governmental building, which can house 3,000 employees on 17 storeys, stands directly opposite the Chicago City Hall and the Daley Center, and extends along an entire block. It has the shape of an oversize cylinder flattened off at an angle, and in this alone differs from the penchant for right angles that dominates the city's skyline. The glass façade, which is supported on slender stilts, curves backwards and is stepped back every five storeys by 50 centimetres (ca. 20 inches). The outer façade is largely created by coloured strips of glass and a facing of alternating white and salmon marble. Say what one will: the Center is an experiment in municipal architecture, whose importance lies in the serious attempt to transpose to a public building a style that, until then, had been the exclusive preserve of the private sector. The sloping-topped glass cylinder that juts out of the roof forms the inner hall, which has the form of a rotunda. This spacious atrium with its galleries running around its sides and its see-through lift shafts and staircases, serve as visual compensation for the building's functional weaknesses. Above all, the noise levels in the open-plan offices inside are a problem that has yet to be solved. Compared to them, the sometimes extreme differences in temperature are almost a side issue.

The German-born and Chicago-based architect Helmut Jahn is regarded as a protagonist of a romanticist hi-tech style. His design for the State of Illinois Center made a sharp break with the city's architectural traditions, and triggered a debate about architecture that was fierce by present-day standards.

Paris (France): Opéra de la Bastille
1983–1989, Carlos Ott

During the era of Francois Mitterand, who became president in 1981, the so-called Grands Travaux, or prestigious architectural projects, received substantial material and financial backing. The new opera house on the Place de la Bastille was one such project. There were fierce debates about where the building should be located. Finally, the Gare de la Bastille as well as some buildings dating back to the 16th century were razed to make room for the structure. Equally spectacular was the contest that was organized. Carlos Ott, a Uruguayan-Canadian architect who was virtually unknown until then, won the competition against 756 other design entries. The jury saw Meier's style in his plans and wished to recognize his "established professionalism." The intention was to establish a "people's opera" that would serve as a substitute for the over-used Garnier Opera at the site where the French Revolution began. In addition, the slightly dilapidated quarter in the east of Paris was to be revitalized. Though this has undoubtedly been achieved, the building itself looks like a foreign body amidst the traditional architecture of this quarter. Ott's structure consists of numerous glass and marble slabs attached to a circular façade facing the square. The marble cladding at the main entrance follows the ascending motion of a staircase. But the building misses its mark architecturally due to its arbitrariness, nonconformism, and obtrusiveness, reminiscent of many office buildings erected in the 1980s. However, from a functional point of view the building is successful, with its good acoustics, large auditorium, and technical equipment. Unfortunately, structural faults soon became apparent and netting was put up to protect passers-by from occasionally falling marble slabs.

Mitterand's rule from 1981 to 1995 had a lasting influence on the world of architecture. During that time, 15 billion francs (approx. 2.3 billion euros) were allocated to Grand Travaux building projects. Although some projects, including the Opéra de la Bastille, did not meet their objectives, the architecture of the outgoing 20th century received important impetus, and talents such as Jean Nouvel and Christian de Portzamparc emerged.

left:
The Opéra de la Bastille is located on the spot where the Bastille fortress, which once served as an ignominious prison, stood. This is where the French Revolution began. In keeping with the historical importance of the site, the new opera – in contrast to the bourgeois Opéra Garnier – was supposed to be a people's opera.

Weil am Rhein (Germany)
Vitra Design Museum

1986–1989, Frank O. Gehry

left:
Gehry's style became more unified in the surface construction with the Vitra Museum in Weil am Rhein, even if the rugged form remained. In this way, differentiated illumination arises on the inside. The spiral staircase forms a large curve on the exterior, similar to that on Scharoun's building in Weissenhof (Stuttgart 1926–1927).

Weil am Rhein, a German border town directly north of Basle, is located between the Rhine river basin and the edge of the Black Forest. The major employer there is a Swiss company, Vitra. Its plant includes buildings designed by a number of prominent international architects and almost seems like an open-air museum of contemporary architecture. Rolf Fehlbaum, the owner of the company, which produces chairs and office furniture, commissioned the California-based architect Frank O. Gehry, who was then hardly known in Europe, with the construction of a museum on the site. The commission included not only an exhibition building, but also a gatehouse and a production hall, which were all to fit into the grid of the already existing plant buildings designed by Nicholas Grimshaw. As a contrast to the high-tech aesthetic of the British architect's factory buildings with their metal façades, Gehry proposed a white building with clean lines and spiralling rampways on its northern corners as their sole expressive accent. This side of the production hall also serves as a backdrop framing the Vitra Design Museum set out on a lawn in the foreground as a free-standing pavilion. This building marks a turning point in Gehry's oeuvre: it was his first building in Europe and, simultaneously, it showed the breakthrough in the deve-

lopment of a style combining complex arrangements of architectonic elements. Gehry's stylistic vernacular developed in the 1960s and 1970s, emerging from California's often seemingly makeshift collage-style architecture. While some of the earlier private homes he designed in America almost look like chance arrangements of individual building elements, he achieves a real synthesis in Weil am Rhein: the museum is both architecture and sculpture.

After the Second World War Vitra entered a license agreement with the U.S. firm Herman Miller Inc. securing the rights to produce furniture designed by Charles and Ray Eames. In the 1980s and 1990s internationally renowned architects were called upon to design buildings for the company's plant in Weil am Rhein. Hence, there are production halls designed by Nicholas Grimshaw, Alvaro Siza and Frank O. Gehry, a fire station by Zaha Hadid and a conference pavilion by Tadao Ando. Gehry's museum was planned to exhibit the collection of chairs owned by the company's proprietor.

Rotterdam (the Netherlands): Kunsthal

1988–1992, Rem Koolhaas/Office for Metropolitan Architecture

left:
At the end of the Museum Park, the Kunsthal forms a bar to a busy road. The strict basic form of the building is reminiscent of Mies van der Rohe's New National Gallery in Berlin (1963–1968). Koolhaas' pluralistic approach produces a variety of individual forms, such as the various columns.

New solutions for a new millenium: Rem Koolhaas' Office for Metropolitan Architecture (OMA) aligns itself strongly with the functional design of shopping centres, promising interesting building commissions for the future on account of its functional mix. Although a particular interest of the office is a kind of anonymous "generic architecture" on the periphery of cities, notable individual buildings do make an appearance. Koolhaas' critical dealings with the architecture of the Modern age manifests itself with particular clarity in the Kunsthal in Rotterdam, which can be interpreted as an unorthodox paraphrasing of subjects by Mies van der Rohe and Le Corbusier. Located in the centre of Rotterdam, the Kunsthal has two main views; in a southerly direction it is turned towards the elevated, very busy Westzeedijk; while in a northerly direction it overlooks the museum park, which is situated at a lower level and whose end encompasses the Dutch Architectural Institute and the Boijmans van Beuningen Museum. This townplanning situation took Koolhaas to the starting point of his design: a public footway leads through the building from the idyllic park to the Magistrale. But the ramp utilizes the connection system of Le Corbusier's Villa Savoye in Poissy, while simultaneously serving as a space-dividing principle. The walkway through the halls and rooms marginally descends and ascends alternately. Lecture hall, café and a small studio gallery are located on the west side of the passage, with both exhibition rooms in the east; the one oriented towards the park and the other to the Magistrale. Observed from the Westzeedijk, the Kunsthal is undoubtedly a paraphrasing of the rationalism of Mies van der Rohe's National Gallery in Berlin. However, the imaginative combination of banal and decorative material breaks with the dogma of material reduction.

Just as the Office for Metropolitan Architecture (OMA) influences contemporary architectural-theoretical discourse in the Netherlands, the Basel-based architects Herzog & de Meuron (H&deM) influence it in Switzerland. In 1999 OMA and H&deM embarked on a joint project. Their first result was a design presented in 2001 for a hotel in Manhattan. In the interim, the contract has been withdrawn and awarded instead to Frank O. Gehry. However, the two firms are expected to continue to cooperate on other projects.

London (U.K.)
Waterloo Station International Terminal
1988–1993, Nicholas Grimshaw & Partners

Ten international architectural offices were invited to take part in the competition to build a train station at the end of the Channel Tunnel, Nicholas Grimshaw & Partners won. During the five years that followed, around a third of his employees were involved in the development of the train station. Grimshaw compared the task with the construction of an inner-city airport, while nevertheless respecting the archetype of the train station. The organically formed, transparent hall solves the space problem sovereignly – the site is completely utilized by the track viaduct and the station below it. The linchpin of the design is the roof, an asymmetrical arched construction made of three pin arches, that support the load with a minimum of material. Since the 400 metre (ca. 1,300 ft.) long, irregular curve of the track would have necessitated 2,000 different glass sizes, standard glass elements that overlap each other, like the scales of a reptile, form the skin of the roof, which moves up and down in waves. The individual glass panels are held in place by the same stainless steel rotating joints Grimshaw used in earlier buildings. This clear structure contributes to the functionality of the terminal. The west side that leads to the "old" Waterloo Station is made completely of glass, allowing a clear view of the trains and providing the arriving guests with a first view of the Thames and London Inner City. The brick vaults that already existed under the station are used for shops and support services.

The international terminal designed for the Eurostar takes its place in the long tradition of Victorian train stations, while at the same time symbolizing a new age in which trains compete with airplanes as the most efficient means of transportation.

Berlin (Germany): The Jewish Museum
1989–1999, Daniel Libeskind

left:
The unusual shape of the museum led to numerous associations with lightning, a broken Star of David, or even a derailed train. Their only common denominator is force. The building is far too large for the collection, but it can hold its own as usable sculpture. Libeskind's stele garden is reminiscent of the Peter Eisenman design for the Berlin Holocaust Memorial.

There is hardly another city in the world that experienced such a high volume of construction as did Berlin at the end of the 20th century; in no other metropolis were there so many internationally famous architects at work as in the old and new German capital. Nevertheless, very few of the newly created buildings are more than mediocre. There is only one building that rises above this potpourri, a building that is absolutely incomparable and justly considered a masterpiece of the period: the Jewish Museum by Daniel Libeskind. "Between the Lines" is what the architect called his prize-winning design in 1989, before the fall of the wall. The title is an indication of the idea behind his concept, which is most clearly expressed by the floor plan or in aerial photography. The museum consists of a building arranged in a zig-zag form and faced with galvanized sheet metal. The building's graphic façade, which is interspersed with openings in the form of lines, crosses or triangles, does not reveal how the floors are distributed within. The zig-zag line intersects another – invisible – line which is perfectly straight. This line is formed in the basement and cuts through the entire building in the form of impassable, sometimes even invisible, hollow spaces (so-called "voids"). The bolt of lightening and the straight line are therefore related to each other in various ways. The jagged line stands for the turbulent course of history – including that of the city of Berlin, the straight line represents the almost invisible tradition of Jewish life after the Holocaust. This "non-existence" can, however, always be sensed in the "voids" that block the way. Libeskind, who is seen as one of the most important proponents of Deconstructivist architecture, created a building that is, intellectually, highly complex and fascinating in a use of space that appeals directly to the senses, sometimes almost stunning them.

With the new Jewish Museum, the architect enters into a dialogue with Berlin's Jewish history. By avoiding superficial associations, while nevertheless leaving traces for interpretation, he encourages the visitor to seek his own way through the labyrinth and, hence, to consciously confront the past.

Weil am Rhein (Germany): The Fire Station
1990–1993, Zaha Hadid

left:
The building is no longer used by the Fire Department, but with its top sticking out so far it transposes into constructed form the idea of a fire-extinguishing vehicle rushing out as fast as lightning for action. Considerable doubts were raised about the feasibility of the 30 metre (98 ft.) high roof sticking out so far.

Vitra sought to create an alternative to the dreary architecture of industrial plants. Consequently, an architectural park has been in the making on the furniture company's production site, in Weil am Rhein north of Basle, since 1981. After a major fire, Vitra commissioned the English High-Tech architect, Nicholas Grimshaw, with the reconstruction of the furniture factory and the development of a master plan of the entire grounds. Different buildings were supposed to distinguish the plant with their vitality and singularity. Hence, Vitra commissioned a different architect for each building. For the Iraqi-British architect, Zaha Hadid, the Fire Station at the Vitra plant, built between 1990 and 1993, was her first major project. Her explosive drawings had been exhibited all over the world, but no builder had yet dared to build one of her Deconstructivist designs. Hadid's building lies at one end of the site's main axis. Instead of designing the building as an isolated object, it was developed as a part of the landscape zone, picking up on patterns of the surroundings and continuing them in the building itself. The core of the building is a series of staggered wall panels. Between these walls lie the different functional areas. A big opening serves as the exit for the fire trucks. Between further panels lies a series of rooms in a linear arrangement. A stairway at the intersection of two girders leads to two terraces from which one has a view of the plant buildings and the countryside. Since the company no longer maintains its own fire department, the building is now used as an exhibition space.

The Vitra Design Museum by Frank O. Gehry and the Conference Pavilion by Tadao Ando are accessible from outside. There are also regular architectural tours of the, otherwise not publicly accessible, plant grounds. In conjunction with such tours, the production halls by the Portuguese architect, Alvaro Siza, and by the British architect, Nicholas Grimshaw, are also presented.

Tokyo (Japan): Asahi Beer Hall – "The Flame"
1991, Philippe Starck

left:
Starck's flame on the new building rises up from the beer-coloured glass of the brewery's skyscraper. At night, the 295-ton-heavy metal flame seems to float when it is illuminated. This is because then you can hardly still see the foundation made of polished black granite.

The site on which the Asahi company has brewed its beer for over a century stretches along the River Sumidagawa, in a district of Tokyo that has seen better days. This setting makes Starck's futuristic construction seem all the more unusual and impressive. This architectural symbol of the Asahi Brewery stands with its eccentric style and use of colour in clear contrast to the normative grey of most of the other buildings in Tokyo. Consequently, the number of its deriders is large, and it has already gained a number of unflattering names. The building curves gently down from the roof, and is clad in black polished granite that lights up far and wide in the shine of the surrounding spotlights. It is surrounded by a "dramatic" stairway, which has all the glamour of a Hollywood musical set. The windows are no more than small portholes that are scarcely distinguishable from a distance. Not that any of this is of great importance, for the building is in any case simply the pedestal for the sculpture on the roof, and that gives the whole its name: "The Flame." It is the trademark of the designer-cum-architect, and is a frequent motif of his in his designs for sconces and door handles. It is, however, singularly unique in this monumental form. The over 300 ton metal construction has a gilt surface that makes it glisten far beyond the grounds. The gold is repeated in the panel on the main entrance, where it punctuates the otherwise black façade. It goes without saying that Starck also designed the interior. The lobby alone is quite typical of his work: the curved walls are clad in grey velvet, and the twisting columns vaguely resemble human forms.

Philippe Starck, who is chiefly known as a designer of furniture and interiors, has realized a number of object-like constructions in Japan that show a natural connection to his other, futuristic design objects. It is precisely through this distinctive approach that Starck has come up with a number of interesting definitions of architectural forms.

Bilbao (Spain): Guggenheim Museum
1991–1997, Frank O. Gehry

left:
The Guggenheim
Museum reveals itself to
be more uniform than
the early buildings Gehry
"put together." This was
also already the case
with his museum in Weil
am Rhein. The flowing
and fragmented forms
enable a very differentiated lighting for the
modern art inside, which
includes a sculpture of
his friend Richard Serra.

In October 1997, the spectacular new Guggenheim Museum, built according to plans by the Californian architect Frank O. Gehry, was opened in Bilbao. The building stands at the mouth of the Nervión River, which is spanned by a bridge at that point. The new building was intended to help bring a new sense of order into a run-down industrial quarter full of deserted factories and cut off from the central city by a train line. The museum's unusual form reflects Gehry's working method. He makes sketches and models by hand, then enters the forms into a computer, technical and structural problems are solved by means of special computer programmes. His Guggenheim Museum consists of a number of building segments that are connected to each other and arranged around a roughly 50 metres (164 ft.) high atrium with glass skylights. The main entrance, which is at the end of a long stairway, leads into this atrium. The exhibition spaces, on various levels, are connected by bridges, glass elevators and stairways. The permanent exhibition is in the southern part of the building, a collection of contemporary art can be found in seven galleries in the western wing, and special exhibitions are featured in a big hall extending to the east. Three different materials give the building its character: stone, steel and glass. The forms vary according to the material: sandstone is used for cubes, glass for the curved windows, sheets of titanium form the scales of the winding outer skin. Popular expression has produced a number of nicknames for the building, most of them inspired by the shimmering façade, for example the "silver artichoke" or "titanium fish". The initial reservations that some had, at the idea of spending 23 billion pesetas (ca. $ 138.25 million) on the building, have in the meantime dissipated, since Bilbao has advanced to a Mecca of art. 80 per cent of the works exhibited come from the holdings of the Solomon R. Guggenheim Foundation.

The Guggenheim Museum is a tourist magnate. Around a third of the visitors come from abroad, mainly from France, the United States, Germany and Japan. Brad Pitt, Robert de Niro and Oliver Stone have already been there – a completely new situation for Bilbao. In the high season, the city's hotels are completely booked.

Prague (CZ): "Ginger and Fred"
1993-1996, Frank O. Gehry and Vladow Milunic

left:
Large vertical windows in regular patterns are typical for the architecture of residential buildings before the advent of International Style, which preferred oblong format right-angled windows. Here, Gehry used the older window type but removed its rigid regularity and turned some of the window crosses upside down.

The office block at 80 Rasínovo nábrezí is probably the most spectacular new building since the Velvet Revolution in the city. The design phase goes back a long time. In 1986, the author and later State President Václav Havel gave the assignment to architect Miluniã to reconstruct the house next door on the Vltava river. Both men lived in the house, which had been built by an ancestor of Havel with the same name. In 1990, Miluniã drew up the first plans for the end house, which was to become "Ginger and Fred." Already in this design we find two complementary forms, one dynamic and one static. In 1992, a Dutch insurance company took over the site for the building and started looking for a well-known architect. Nouvel turned it down. Gehry accepted and continued work together with Miluniã. An end building arose, one side of which is completely covered in glass and metal, and the other, visible from the riverbank, is a concrete building with windows suitable for its surroundings from the start of the 20th century. Two corresponding towers form the corner. The one on the left appears to lean on the right one with its upper half, so revealing the view from the street building line. The one on the right is crowned with a dome made of lead, one remotely reminiscent of the sphere on Havel's House. Here we can see how well deconstructive architecture can also integrate itself into block boundary construction.

The nickname "Ginger and Fred" refers to Ginger Rogers and Fred Astaire, a pair who made a total of ten musical films together between 1933 and 1949. The light "Ginger," on the left with her skirt sticking out, nestles on the somewhat larger "Fred." The latter still stands very solidly, even on just one leg. It is a pas des deux in architecture.

Cologne (Germany): Neven DuMont Building
1994–1998, HPP Hentrich-Petschnigg & Partner KG
Design: Duk-Kyu Ryang

It all began when the Cologne-based media concern M. DuMont Schauberg realized that their familiar offices in the city centre, where the company had been located for around 150 years, no longer met the demands of a modern enterprise. The company's relocation from a number of office buildings in the city centre out to the northern district of Cologne, Niehl, was of great importance, because it meant that all of the employees would again be united on one site. In 1994 HPP was commissioned with planning a new building with the aim of creating a structure in which the diverse departments and editorial offices could be brought together with the

actual production in the printing plant. HPP's architect, Duk-Kyu Ryang, submitted a design, which featured two chamber-like office wings connected by an atrium. The building is clear, transparent and inviting. The limited range of materials that were used - glass, raw concrete, wood, steel and aluminium - are all clearly visible and contribute to this impression. The form of the building also clearly demonstrates that transparency was a primary concern for both the client and the architect. A remarkable feature is the glass tower that rises up over 40 meters (131 ft.). It is visible from a great distance and Cologne natives have already become fond of this new

above:
The 48 metre (158 ft.) tower and the sweeping concave, glass façade, measuring 155 metres (509 ft.) in length and 20 metres (66 ft.) in height, characterize the building. Its exterior is completely enclosed in glass encompassing 27,000 square metres (88,583 sq. ft.).

accent in the city's silhouette. Yet the building is not only integrated into a local scheme of things. Numerous other aspects also played a role for the Korean architect. In his view, the concern is embedded in a worldwide network. Consequently, he drew on Asian and European as well as ancient traditions. The construction of the Neven DuMont Haus, which was supervised by HPP, created a symbol made of glass and concrete, a symbol for establishing communication, for striving for clarity and for helping to inform public opinion.

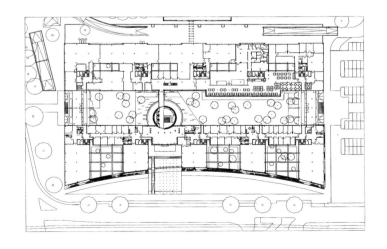

Vals (Switzerland): Thermal Bath

1994–1996, Peter Zumthor

left:
According to Zumthor, this bath is intended to convey "the direct experience of skin, water, stone and space – the way it all smells together and maybe even tastes." The building is characterized by stone from the Vals valley in a strictly regimented form that seems as if it was made up of blocks shoved together, whereby small light shafts remain between the individual elements. The pools are not set into the ground; they seem more like a part of the room that is filled with water.

For centuries Graubünden, nowadays the easternmost canton in Switzerland, had been the country's poorhouse. With the development of tourism in the Alps, the region became more attractive: former villages like Davos, Pontresina or St. Moritz were developed as spas or ski centres. The apartment and hotel complex built in Vals, a village 40 kilometres southwest of Chur, attests to this fact. During a later period, when tourism in the Alps was in a crisis, Vals took the initiative and had a thermal bath built in the middle of the hotel complex by the architect Peter Zumthor. This decision was an expression of resistance against the prevailing trends. Vals's thermal bath sees itself neither as a fun nor as a public pool, but rather as a bath for the senses. Half of the rectangular building that houses the thermal bath is dug into the slope of a mountain and its roof is planted leaving merely a façade of local stone (Vals gneiss), interrupted only by openings of various sizes, exposed to view. The layered slabs of natural stone form the central motif in the bath's design: massive blocks of stone outline the interior and exterior pools, as well as the relaxation zones. They also support the roof, a cascade of massive cement slabs separated by seams to let in light. The stone blocks themselves are, however, hollowed out; behind unassuming entryways there is a series of intimate special baths that account for the real charm of this thermal grotto: the fire bath or the flower bath, the sweating stone or the cave of springs. Within the surroundings of rough stone these chambers seem like shimmering geodes. This allowed the architect, despite his rather austere stylistic vernacular, to create a number of impressive and highly meditative spaces by using accents of colour sparingly and choosing materials wisely. Water, however, is the central medium in this thermal bath - whether it comes trickling, splashing or surging.

In the 1980s and 1990s the canton of Graubünden opened its doors to contemporary architecture. The fact that it is, in the meantime, one of the most interesting architectural landscapes in Switzerland is an achievement of which regional decision makers, who did much to support modern building concepts, can well be proud. The major protagonist of new architecture in Graubünden is Peter Zumthor, who was originally employed by the historic preservation authorities. His buildings, which fascinate us with the sensuality of their materials, represent very contemporary sensibilities in terms of form, yet respect both tradition and the landscape.

Berlin (Germany)
Glass Dome – Reichstag Building
1997–1999, Sir Norman Foster

Eight hundred architectural practices from 54 countries participated in the 1992 competition to redesign a building with an extraordinary history: the Reichstag in Berlin. After much discussion, the competition was finally won by the frequently reworked design done by Sir Norman Foster, who originally wanted to make the superstructure on top of the already extensive building a great deal larger. The result is a historic building with modern features that come very close to the original structure. The building is surmounted by a glass dome whose final shape – long since familiar to the whole of the world – was originally the object of fierce debate. Foster offered some 50 different designs before the Council of Elders at the German Parliament finally decided in 1995 on the version that came to be constructed. It was promptly dismissed by the critics as an "egg-shaped something." Yet the shape and size of the dome constitute a successful compromise between the proportions of the building and its own significance for urban construction, and the gesture of state power that it signals. With a diameter of 40 metres (131 ft.) and a height of 23 metres (75 ft.), it is only half as tall as the original dome dating from 1894. But far more important is the fact that contrary to its historical situation, the dome now also makes direct reference to the parliamentary chamber. It not only provides the latter with natural light and ventilation, but can also be walked up by means of spiral ramps inside. The shape inside the dome is determined by a mirror-surfaced funnel, which conducts diffuse daylight into the parliamentary chamber ten metres (33 ft.) below. Despite all the criticisms and objections to the dome, it has advanced to become the building's main draw for visitors. It offers not only a magnificent view across the city, but also a glimpse into the workings of parliament. Possibly some people will find this interpretation of "democratic transparency" a little too forced.

The Reichstag building was built between 1884 and 1894 according to the plans of architect Paul Wallot. The burning of the Reichstag in 1933 left the inside almost totally destroyed. The first overhaul of the building was done in 1961 by Paul Baumgarten. In 1995, it was wrapped in a spectacular action by the artists Christo and Jeanne Claude, and presented to the world at large as an object of art.

left:
The funnel in the centre of the dome doesn't just reflect into the plenary hall, it also fulfils air-conditioning tasks. This combination of inconspicuous high tech and aesthetic form is typical of contemporary architecture. Visitors can climb up the spiral-shaped ramps in the dome.

Hanover (Germany): "Holland is Creating Space"
Expo 2000 Hanover, MVRDV

The Dutch Pavilion was certainly the most stimulating at the World Exhibition in Hanover. The world's most densely populated country preoccupies itself with the theme "Holland is Creating Space." In the process, only ca. 920 square metres (9,903 sq. ft.) was actually built on of the almost 8,360 square metre (89,450 sq. ft.) available. The rest was covered in plants. The building itself is open in all directions. On its various floors there are typically Dutch rural scenes. On the roof there is a coastal strip with wind turbines. In the stories we find a flower-growing area with insects on video monitors, a forest with tree-trunks support the ceiling and roots forming a narrow path system (infrastructure) in the floor below, in pot-like recesses. The way in which the rural scenes are stacked allows the architecture to have a greater use density and so prevent the surrounding pavilion area from being sealed. It is not just roads that cause this ground sealing, but buildings as well. More specifically, it is private house building (detached houses) and their access roads. It has become a key question in environmental protection. Thus, in the Netherlands, Utrecht, Amsterdam, The Hague and Rotterdam have increasingly merged into a continuously constructed arch around the country's so-called "green heart." The Dutch contribution to the Expo raises this question about ecological damage caused by extensive, low settlement within the fair's theme of sustainability. The MVRDV building shows how architecture can be both funny and profound simultaneously.

Since the first World's Fair, almost all Expos offered sensational architecture. In London in 1851, it was the Crystal Palace in succession to the glasshouses from J. Paxton. In Paris in 1889, it was the Eiffel Tower, and in 1900 the Art Nouveau Metro Stations by Guimard. In 1937 there the Soviet pavilion (by B. Iofan) and its National Socialist counterpart (by A. Speer senior) stood opposite each other meaningfully. In Brussels in 1958, A. Waterkeyn constructed the Atomium. In Montreal in 1967, R. Gutbrod and F. Otto constructed the German Pavilion. And in Hanover, the national pavilions by MVRDV, P. Zumthor, Sh. Ban, and A. Siza stood out.

Sendai (Japan): Mediatheque

2001, Toyo Ito

It is a mere two-hours trip by Shinkansen high-speed train from Tokyo to Sendai (one million inhabitants, 350 kilometres northeast of the capital). For visitors to Japan, the city might just as well have been a transit station, for Sendai had nothing worthwhile disembarking for. However, this changed in 2001 when Sendai excited attention by erecting a building that has set worldwide standards: the mediatheque by architect Toyo Ito. The architect, who was born in 1941, has been a leading Japanese avant-gardist since he designed a reinforced concrete building in the form of a U (1976). In the process, he succeeded in devising a comparatively new construction technique. He created a building that reacts without appearing to be exerted in any way – programmatically according to contemporary architectural-theoretical discourse by forming a synthesis between minimalism and formal wealth. The mediatheque functions firstly as a minimalist cube: the building, which measures 50 x 50 metres (164 x 164 ft.) lengthwise, is glass-fronted on three sides and divided into seven floors by reinforced concrete bases. The children's library, the library, the exhibition centre and the actual mediatheque are stacked on top of one another. Unusually, the load-bearing of the building is not performed by a reinforced concrete skeleton, but rather by 13 lattice-shaped tubes of differing dimensions which extend through all levels and house the elevator shafts or supply lines, or simply provide light in the lower levels. The grid towers change their forms from floor to floor and can be interpreted as an expressive aspect, in contrast to the minimalism of the volume. Large open spaces appear between the steel girder structures on every floor. Toyo Ito consulted a number of designers, each of whom was responsible for a particular level and lent it his own unique style.

For a long time, libraries have no longer collected and lent out only books, but are increasingly turning to electronic media – whether CD-ROM, audio-CD, videocassette or data bank. They are being transformed into information centres, which place the diverse media at the disposal of their users. Thus the architectural library is being replaced by the mediatheque.

left:
The floors of the Mediatheque are conceived as use-neutral surfaces, in order to serve its diverse tasks (e.g. exhibitions). This idea already lay behind the Centre Pompidou, but the building conception is the complete opposite of that. Whereas in Paris the supply cores were done away with, here the tubes also take on a constructive aspect.

Biographies

Aalto, Hugo Alvar Hendrik
*3.02.1898 in Kuortane
†11.05.1976 in Helsinki
Aalto studied in Helsinki. After a short Classical Revival phase, he turned toward International Style (the Library in Viipuri, begun in 1927). After the Second World War he combined the latter with simpler materials that he had used previously (brick and wood) in order to create a very individual style that caused him to be very much in demand. His buildings are asymmetrical and sweeping, and their floor plans already exhibit expressive tendencies. Despite their size, they seem dynamic even in their vertical projection. His last project, the Aalto Music Theatre in Essen, was opened in 1988.

Adam, Robert
*3.07.1728 in Kirkcaldy, Fife
†3.03.1792 in London
In Rome, Robert Adam, the son of the leading Scottish architect William Adam, became acquainted with the Neoclassical architect Ch. L. Clérisseau and the engraver G.B. Piransi, whom he befriended for life. While Piransi only came to recognize the virtue of Greek antiquity later, Adam became a mediator between English Palladianism and Greek Revival. He is noted not only for his buildings, but also for his work as an interior decorator, which reflects the impressions he gathered on a trip to Italy (Pompeii). Among his later works there are numerous castles, for example the Neogothic Culzean Castle in Ayrshire (1777 – 1790). Adam's influence spread rapidly, being felt as far away as America and Russia.

Adler, Dankmar
*3.01.1844 in Langenfeld
†19.04.1900 in Chicago
Adler was one of Louis Sullivan's partners.

Alberti, Leon Battista
*14.02.1404 in Genoa
†04.1472 in Rome
Alberti was trained in the humanities in Padua and studied ecclesiastical law in Bologna. He was interested in mathematics, physics and optics and was first noted as a writer ("Libri della famiglia" 1433). He served as a secretary to a number of popes. In Florence he became acquainted with Brunelleschi as well as Masaccio's works using linear perspective. Back in Rome he published his "Treatise on Architecture" (ca. 1452) as a critique of Vitruv's own architectural treatise. It combines architectural theory with thoughts on political philosophy. This treatise not only informed his own building – which produced model examples of Renaissance architecture – it also influenced others, among them Palladio. Following Brunelleschi's example, he sought a closer tie to antiquity. His "Treatise on Painting" was also important to Mantegna. Involved in a wide variety of activities, he embodied the ideal of Renaissance man.

Anthemius of Tralles
The son of a doctor's family in Lydia, Anthemius was not only an architect and sculptor, but above all a mathematician (geometry) and physicist (statics, kinetics). He viewed architecture as "the application of geometry to solid materials." Apart from Hagia Sophia, no other work of his has been verified as his.

Asplund, Erik Gunnar
*22.09.1885 in Stockholm
†20.10.1940 in Stockholm
Together with Sigurd Lewerentz and Osvald Almquist, Asplund established an architectural school of their own in 1910, as an alternative to the Stockholm Academy, where techniques of draughting stood in the foreground. However, the new school existed only for a year. In 1915 he and Lewerentz won a commission for the expansion of the Stockholm's Woodland Cemetery (Woodland Chapel 1918 – 1920). The Stockholm Library (1918 – 1920), with its architrave at the entrance and round hall, reveals a reductive aesthetic ideal typical of the monumental Egyptian Revival style found in French Second Empire Architecture. It also proved to be an influence on Alvar Aalto. Asplund's restaurant designed for the Stockholm Exhibition of 1930 has walls of glass while the building and the terraces are set on pediments. It is one of the purest examples of International Style. In the design of the crematorium for the Woodland Cemetery between 1935 and 1940 this evolves toward the austerity of Neoclassicism. In the 1930s, he also influenced Arne Jacobsen.

Bähr (also Baehr), Georg
*15.03.1666 in Fürstenwalde
†16.03.1738 in Dresden
Bähr first trained in carpentry and became the Master Carpenter of the City of Dresden in 1705. His churches in Schmiedeberg (1713 – 1715) and Forchheim (1719 – 1726) already reveal his interest in central-plan architecture augmented by galleries, which was to find its penultimate expression in Dresden's Frauenkirche. Here he combined the late baroque central-plan church architecture with the gallery church preferred by Protestant parishes and a dome that was to become a landmark in the city, and that in the face of stiff resistance. Bähr's most important secular building was the Palais de Saxe that is just as markedly structured.

Bakema, Jacob Berend
*8.03.1914 in Groningen
†20.03.1981 in Rotterdam
Bakema, who worked for Cornelis van Eesteren as a student, became Johannes Hendrik van den Broek's partner in 1948. Together they built the Lijnbaan in Rotterdam between 1949 and 1953, a thoroughly user-friendly (pedestrian) city centre, as was called for by the C.I.A.M. with which Bakema was involved. Bakema later became a member of the Forum Group and of Team X, both of which were concerned with the reforming post-war architecture in order to make it more human. The two partners once more gained some notoriety with the extension plans for Amsterdam-Pampus (1965) which provi-

ded for a programme to enlarge the city by building oversized landings on the water. In 1965 Bakema became a professor in Hamburg.

Barry, Charles
*23.05.1795 in London
†12.05.1860 in London
After completing his studies, Barry made a tour of the Mediterranean (including Syria and Egypt) which lasted from 1817 to 1820. His first buildings were Gothic Revival, but subsequently he introduced Neorenaissance architecture to England (The Travellers' Club in Pall Mall, London 1829 – 1831). He also began planning the Houses of Parliament in London as a Neorenaissance building, however, he then brought in Pugin to collaborate, and the latter designed the ornamentation and furnishings in Gothic Revival style. These two architects had already worked together on a school building in Birmingham (1834 – 1837). In designing the Pentonville Prison, Pugin introduced J. Haviland's American form of prison architecture, with its radial floor plan, to Europe (1841 – 1843).

Behnisch, Günther
*12.06.1922 in Lockwitz
Behnisch studied in Stuttgart. He became internationally famous with the construction of the Olympic Stadium in Munich (along with Frei Otto). The fundamental idea behind both his buildings and his architectural office is "building democratically". This can be seen particularly in the plenary assembly hall that he designed for the German Bundestag in Bonn. Here, a sense of openness between the people and their representatives is expressed in the extensive use of glass. This attitude – along with Behnisch's predilection for industrial materials – led to a controversial discussion with regard to the Post Modern Neue Staatsgalerie in Stuttgart (by Stirling) and the reconstruction of the Reichstag in Berlin. In the 1980s Behnisch turned more and more toward Deconstructionism (Hysolar Research Institute at the University of Stuttgart).

Behrens, Peter
*14.04.1868 in Hamburg
†27.02.1940 in Berlin
Behrens began as a painter and craftsman in Munich Art Nouveau circles. The first house he built was in the artists' colony on Darmstadt's Marienhöhe, it was his own. From 1907 to 1914, he was an artistic advisor to the AEG in Berlin. He designed products, typography and advertisements for the company in the style of the German Werkbund, as well as a number of buildings, among them a turbine factory (1909). Although he was later celebrated as one of the forefathers of the Modern Movement, the building still proves – in comparison with American factory buildings from the period – to be monumentally representative. In designing the German embassy in St. Petersburg (1911 – 1912) Behrens employed an oversized façade featuring half-columns. In this period L.

Mies van der Rohe, W. Gropius and Le Corbusier were all in his employ. His design for the administration of the Farbwerke Hoechst (1920 – 1924) was Expressionist and focussed on the company's products (paints and dyes) in its colourful interior. In 1922 he became a professor in Vienna, where he contributed to two of the "roten Wohnhöfe" (red housing courts).

Berlage, Hendrik Petrus
* 21.02.1856 in Amsterdam
† 12.08.1934 in Den Haag
Berlage studied in Zurich. After his first Neo-Renaissance designs for the stock exchange, done together with Th. Sanders, he produced a number of buildings for insurance companies in a tempered Art Nouveau style. During his work on the stock exchange he drew on Romanic, Italian and American models to arrive at a highly reduced style, which emphasised the "honesty" of the construction. This was the point of departure in the Netherlands for the representatives of the New Building style, while the architects of Berlage's Amsterdam School admired perfect craftsmanship and plain monumentalism. Berlage also wrote architectural history with his designs for the extension of Amsterdam to the south (1900 and 1914-1917), for he drew up the first ever framework plan.

Bernini, Gian Lorenzo
*7.12.1598 in Naples
†28.11.1680 in Rome
Gian Lorenzo learned to be a sculptor from his father, Pietro Bernini. After Maderna's death, he took over the construction of St. Peter's Cathedral and the completion of the Palazzo Barberini, thereby becoming Borromini's rival. Under Pope Urban VIII, Innocence X and Alexander VII, Bernini clearly enjoyed a more influential position and was able to complete numerous works of decisive importance to the city (the Colonnades on St. Peter's Square). The plan for the renovation of the eastern façade of the Louvre, which was never undertaken, had great influence on the development of architecture in France. Also a celebrated sculptor, he created the Cathedra Petri (1657 – 1665) for St. Peter's Cathedral and dynamic ensembles of figures, like his "Apollo and Daphne" (1622 – 1625), for his patron, Cardinal Scipione Borghese. As an example of religious sculpture his "Ecstasy of Saint Therese" (1645 – 1652) can be seen as a highpoint in the symbolic depiction of faith, to which the Counterreformation aspired.

Borromini, Francesco
*25.09.1599 in Bissone
†2.08.1667 in Rome
Borromini, whose real name was Francesco Castelli, trained as a stone mason in Milan. In 1619, he presumably began to work within the lodge, involved in the construction of St. Peter's in Rome and under the direction of one of his relatives, C. Maderna. He also worked with Maderna on the construction of the Palazzo Barberini. Both projects were taken

over by Bernini after Maderna's death in 1629, which led to the life-long rivalry between Bernini and Borromini. Even Borromini's first commission, S. Carlo alle Quattro Fontane (from 1638), illustrates his pronounced interest in combining and contrasting convex and concave forms. This dynamization was of decisive influence for transalpine Baroque, yet it was only during Pope Innocence X's pontificate (1644 – 1655) that Borromini was able to win more attractive commissions than Bernini. He died by his own hand.

Bramante, actually Donato d'Angelo
* 1444 near Urbino
† 11.03.1514 in Rome
It is possible that Bramante's first contact with painting was at the court of the Montefeltro in Urbino. In 1477 he worked as a façade painter, and in 1479 at the court of the Sforza in Milan, where he constructed his first buildings. He developed his predilection for central-plan buildings while working with Leonardo da Vinci. With the construction of the Tempietto, Bramante became the foremost architect of the High Renaissance. In 1503 he became the principle architect of the new St. Peter's in Rome, but only a small fraction of his ideal central-plan construction was realized.

Brinkman, Johannes Andreas
*22.03.1902 in Rotterdam
†6.05.1949 in Rotterdam
Brinkman studied in Delft and took over the office established by his father, Michiel Brinkman, in 1925. Leendert C. van der Vlught, who became his partner until 1936, was already working there. The partners were initially influenced by Frank Lloyd Wright's architecture, but went on to build the most famous example of International Style: the Van Nelle Factory in Rotterdam. The Functionalist Mart Stam, whom they employed to oversee the construction of the project, eventually criticized the building as having too much emphasis on style. The buildings they designed for the Theosophs in Amsterdam (1927) and the Krishnamurti in Ommen (1930) demonstrate the partners' interest in spiritual works. Along with van Tijen they built the Bergpolderflats in Rotterdam in 1934: one of the few minimal housing projects built before the Second World War and, as gallery apartments, one that opened a new perspective for Dutch housing construction after 1945. These buildings are more functional than those created previously. This is also true of the Feyenoord Rotterdam football stadium (1934 – 1936), from which 65,000 spectators can exit in just 6 minutes using 22 external steel stairways.

van den Broek, Johannes Hendrik
*4.10.1898 in Rotterdam
†6.09.1978 in Rotterdam
Van den Broek studied at the Technical University in Delft. He began working in Delft in 1927 where he started with simple brick buildings. During a trip to Germany in 1928, he met Ernst May and gravitated more and more toward Functionalism (Mathenesserrlaan 1933) until he became

Johannes Andreas Brinkman's partner from 1937 to 1948. In 1948 he entered a lasting partnership with Jacob Berend Bakema.

Brunelleschi, Filippo
*1377 in Florence
†15.04.1446 in Florence
The work of Brunelleschi, a goldsmith from Florence, marks the beginning of the Renaissance. It was immensely important not only for the development of sculpture (the competition for the bronze doors of the Baptistery, 1402), but also for painting (the discovery of linear perspective) as well as architecture. His architectural work was based on the Tuscan tradition, particularly the Florentine Proto-Renaissance (Romanesque, 11th – 12th century) from which he developed a reduced, completely new architectonic system. The commission in charge of the construction of the cathedral in Florence sought out his advice in 1404, and in 1417 he started on a project that was to become his life's work: the dome of the Florence Cathedral. While in this context he was restricted by older plans, in the Ospedale degli Innocenti (1419) one finds a clearer break with the traditional vertical axes of Gothic architecture. With his Sacrestia Vecchia for the Church of San Lorenzo, the language of Renaissance architecture finds its way into a central-plan church architecture. A typical feature is the contrast formed by geometric patterns of dark grey stone against light stucco walls. In the case of S. Maria degli Angeli, Brunelleschi developed an ideal high renaissance floor plan as early as 1435.

Bulfinch, Charles
* 8.08.1763 in Boston
† 15.04.1844 in Boston
Bulfinch received his doctorate at Harvard, and on the recommendation of Jefferson went on a study tour to Europe. His impressions there were to leave their mark. The sacred buildings of Wren and the profane buildings of Adam inspired his Palladianism. In Boston, Bulfinch planned a system of streets with rows of houses according to the English model. As one of the architects of the Capitol he was responsible for the central section with its original flat dome.

Burgee, John Henry
* 28.08.1933 in Chicago
Burgee studied at the University of Notre Dame, Indianapolis, and at first worked for C.F. Murphy before joining Philip Johnson and subsequently becoming his partner in 1968. Burgee brought to the partnership the experience in tackling large contracts that he had gained under Murphy. For their commercial projects they employed a style using motifs along the skyline to create a historical effect.

Burnham, Daniel Hudson

* 4.09.1846 in Henderson
† 1.06.1912 in Heidelberg

Burnham, who initially tried out a variety of professions, teamed up with John W. Root in Chicago. Their practice played a significant part in the development of the Chicago School (Masonic Temple, 1891, with the newly invented steel skeleton frame). When Burnham, in 1893, became chief architect for the World's Columbian Exhibition in Chicago, Classicist buildings came to replace the rationalism of the Chicago School.

Callicrates

Callicrates not only designed the Nike temple at the Acropolis, but also – according to Plutarch – was the master builder of the Parthenon before Iktinos.

Chelles (see Jean de Chelles)

Corbusier (see Le Corbusier)

de Cotte, Robert

*1656 in Paris
†15.07.1735 in Paris

Initially, de Cotte trained under J. Hardouin-Mansarts, whose colleague, brother-in-law and successor as Premier architecte du roi he later became. In this office he undertook the work on the Palace Chapel and on the Grand Trianon in Versailles. His buildings mark the transition from the splendid style of Louis XIV to the elegant-cosy salon and boudoir style of Louis XV.
De Cotte worked on many palaces at home and abroad (Madrid, Tivoli, Bonn, Poppelsdorf) and was also active in urban planning (Place Bellecour in Lyons, Place Royale in Bordeaux). He also designed interior decorations, furniture, metal work and goblins (as head of the Parisian manufactory).

Dollmann, Georg

*21.10.1830 in Ansbach
†31.03.1895 in Munich

Dollmann was trained by L. von Klenze. His castles for Ludwig II of Bavaria (Linderhof 1869 – 1878; Herrenchiemsee 1878 – 1885) made him famous. He completed the construction of Neuschwanstein.

Eiffel, Alexandre Gustave

* 15.12.1832 in Dijon
† 28.12.1923 in Paris

Eiffel was an engineer and not an architect. He studied in Paris, before working for a Belgian firm (railway equipment) and founding his own company in 1864. Apart from his achievements as a constructional engineer – above all bridges – he was also known for his wrought-iron lattice structures.

Erdmannsdorff, Friedrich Wilhelm von

*18.05.1736 in Dresden
†9.03.1800 in Dessau

Erdmannsdorff studied in Wittenberg and was appointed by Prince Franz to his court in Dessau. The Prince was guided by the ideas of Humanism, creating not just a liberal climate, establishing hospitals, poor houses and libraries, but also draining marshes, renewing the street network and reforming the farming (crop rotation). An integrative component of all this redesigning was the grounds of a scenic area in Dessau-Worlitz incorporating various parks and buildings that are only partly preserved. The parks were linked with fruit avenues and designed according to the then-modern understanding of the English landscape garden. Both the Prince and the architect had come to know the latter on their travels. The palace and park buildings arose as important early works of classicism and the (early Italianizing) Neo-Gothic. Erdmannsdorff later worked for the Prussian king in Berlin. Eyserbeck, the gardener at Worlitz, also did, allowing his work to become a model for the parks of the next generation (Lenné).

Erskine, Ralph

* 24.02.1914 in London

Erskine studied first in London and then in Stockholm, for Sweden seemed to him to be the country where he could best realize his ideas of a social, modern form of building. Together with the Dane Aage Rosenvold, he frequently devised experimental buildings that are marked by the great consideration they give to the climate and inhabitants ("Arctic towns": Svappavaara in Lapland, 1963-1964).

Fischer von Erlach, Johann Bernhard

*20.07.1656 in Graz
†5.04.1723 in Vienna

Fischer von Erlach was trained as a sculptor by his father and as an architect by C. Fontana in Rome. Back in Vienna he was named court architect in 1704. In contrast to von Hildebrandt, Fischer von Erlach was more involved in the construction churches. His buildings combine the vocabularies of the Italian high baroque period and French Classicism. The basilica and central-plan architecture enter into a synthesis in his floor plans. The façades of his churches reveal an interest in convexly and concavely sweeping dynamization. His most important secular works are the Schönbrunn Palace in Vienna and the library at the Viennese Hofburg, which was completed by his son Joseph Emanuel. As an architectural theorist ("Entwurf einer historischen Architektur" [A Plan for Historical Architecture] 1721) he made a sizeable contribution to the revival of Egyptian and Chinese fashions during the Rococo period.

Foster, Norman Robert
* 1.06.1935 in Manchester

Foster studied in Manchester and Yale, and initially worked for Buckminster Fuller. Together with Rogers, Roger's wife Su, and his own wife Wendy, he founded Team 4, whose buildings demonstrate a stylistic mixture derived from the two architects: Foster's rigorous simplicity and Rogers' emphasis on technical aspects. Foster's office block for the insurance agency Willis, Faber & Dumas in Ipswich (1971-1975) is – with its frameless glass façades and open-plan spaces – the second prototype for modern office building beside Herzberger's Centraal Beheer. Thanks to his enormous practices (400 employees in London, with additional branches in Berlin, Frankfurt, Glasgow, Hong Kong and Tokyo), Foster is able to work simultaneously on numerous projects. In 1999 he was awarded the Pritzker Prize.

Gabriel, Jacques-Ange
* 23.10.1698 in Paris
† 4.01.1782 in Paris

Jacques-Ange, the son of the Royal Architect Jacques Gabriel V, grew up on the court of Louis XV. After the death of his father, he was made in 1742 "Premier architecte du Roi" and continued working on the enlargement of Versailles (Opera house, interior conversions). With the Petit Trianon (1764-1768) in Versailles, he built one of the earliest Classicist buildings, whose stringency can be read as paralleling the logic of the Enlightenment. In 1755 he was commissioned to design the present-day Place de la Concorde in Paris, to which Vignon was later to add gables.

Garnier, Charles
*6.11.1825 in Paris
†3.08.1898 in Paris

Garnier was trained at the École des Beaux-Arts in Paris. He was working as a draughtsman for E.E. Viollet le Duc, and had hardly built anything himself, when he won the competition for the design of the Paris Opera in 1860. In the wake of this building Neobaroque became the predominant style under Napoleon III. The clear separation of functional areas became a characteristic of theatre construction. Garnier also built the Casino in Monte Carlo.

Gaudí y Cornet, Antonio
*25.06.1852 in Reus
†10.06.1926 in Barcelona

Gaudí, the son of an engraver, was trained by Francisco de Paula del Villar and began by finding his own stylistic vernacular in wrought iron. Starting from Eclecticism, he developed his own very individual interpretation, expressed even in his early works which include Moorish elements. This is already apparent in the case of the Casa Vicens (1878 – 1888), a house he built for the owner of a tile factory and which he decorated with ceramic tile. This is also reflected in the buildings he designed for his patron, Eusebi Güell, particularly in the never completed garden city (Park Güell). Gaudí's bizarre vegetal forms influenced Modernisme, the Catalan form of Art Nouveau. The basic form of Gaudí's buildings became more and more amorphous in this conjunction. The construction of the Templo Expiatorio de la Sagrada Familia, which he took over from his teacher, became his life's work and is still unfinished, reflecting Gaudí's plans which were never fully completed.

Gehry, Frank Owen
*28.02.1929 in Toronto

Frank O. Gehry, originally named Frank Ephraim Goldberg, studied in Los Angeles. His early buildings, created in the late 1950s, appear to be Cubist. In the late 1970s he began to design buildings in an additive and broken style. In doing so he used simple materials from building supply stores and consciously created the impression of unfinished buildings. The renovation of his own house in Santa Monica (1978) is a prime example. Its plywood boards, chain link fencing and corrugated steel siding became essential to the L.A. school of Deconstructionist architecture. He became famous for the California Aerospace Museum in 1984. The artists Richard Serra and Claes Oldenburg encouraged him to strive for more sculptural spatial forms in his architecture. In the 1990s his style became more rounded and fluid. This tendency becomes evident for the first time in the museum he designed for the Vitra plant in Weil am Rhein (1989). In this building the individual spatial compartments can be recognised from the outside, thus the stairway as a large, free-floating, curvaceous form. Since these complicated spherical spaces – often determined by the interior light fall – can hardly be represented in normal blueprints Gehry employed CAD programmes. After he realized that computers could provide him with the same data that machines used in cutting the forms required for pouring concrete, his buildings became increasingly amorphous.

Giulio Romano (also G. Pippi or G. Giannuzzi)
* 1492/1499 in Rome
† 1.11.1546 in Mantua

Giulio first worked as a painter and architect as Raphael's protégé, but he soon turned to Mannerism and sought an expressiveness that had been avoided during the High Renaissance. Instead of being harmoniously balanced, the formal elements were distributed in almost arbitrary fashion (Palazzo del Te), unorthodoxly juxtaposed (his own home), or placed in endless rows (cathedral, all in Mantua).

Grimshaw, Nicholas Thomas
* 9.10.1939 in Hove

Grimshaw studied at Edinburgh and London. Like N. Foster and R. Rogers he belonged to the so-called London School of hi-tech architecture. From 1965 to 1980 he worked in a practice with Terry Farell on prefabrication and standardisation. (Citroën works in Runnymead, 1972). Favourite motifs in Grimshaw's architecture are visible means of construction and the montage of the façade. Particularly spectacular was Grimshaw's British Pavilion for Expo '92 in Seville, whose air-conditioning system used a waterfall façade in order to cool the interior. Solar cells on the canvas sails provided enough energy to keep 300,000 litres of water in motion.

Gropius, Walter
*18.05.1883 in Berlin
†5.07.1969 in Boston
Gropius studied in Munich and Berlin. In 1911 he began building the Faguswerke in Alfeld an der Leine. The style is early Functionalist, but he then turned to Expressionism (Haus Sommerfeld in Berlin 1919 – 1922, the Glass Chain). In 1918 he became the director of the Arts and Crafts School in Weimar and the founding director of the institution that grew out of it, the Bauhaus Weimar (1919), which in these early days was orientated toward the Werkbund and Expressionism. The influence of De Stijl and the early Soviet avant-garde led Gropius to International Style and the Bauhaus building in Dessau appears, in its Functionalism, to be a successor to the Faguswerke. Gropius worked mainly in Berlin after 1928, when he turned the direction of the Bauhaus over to Hannes Meyer, whom he was later to criticize polemically. In 1933 Gropius immigrated to London (Impington Village College together with M. Fry), and then to the USA, where he taught at Harvard University, from 1937 to 1952, integrating young architects into The Architects' Collaborative (TAC).

Hadid, Zaha
*1950 in Baghdad
Born in Iraq, Zaha Hadid studied at the Architectural Association School (AA) in London from 1972 to 1977. After graduating from AA she joined Rem Koolhass and Elia Zenghelis at the Office for Metropolitan Architecture (OMA). Since 1980 she has been running an office of her own, also teaching at various institutions. Her winning the first prize in the competition for The Peak in Hong Kong paved the way to international acclaim. Since then she has won several competitions. Zaha Hadid's designs are being displayed at exhibitions all over the world because of their extraordinary way of presentation.

Hardouin-Mansart, Jules
* 16.04.1646 in Paris
† 11.05.1708 in Marly
The pupil of F. Mansart, he was appointed Royal Architect in 1675, then First Court Architect in 1685, and Chief Court Architect in 1699. In his day, he dominated the entire art of building in absolutist France. His Classicist style derived from Le Vaus, from whom he assumed in 1678 the direction of building the Palace at Versailles (Hall of Mirrors with the painter Lebrun, the Grand Trianon and the Chapel). Similarly, the planning of the town of Versailles goes back to him. In Paris he planned the Places Victoire (1684) and Vend_me (from 1698), and built les Invalides. The decorative style of his later work laid the groundwork for the Rococo.

Hertzberger, Herman
*6.07.1932 in Amsterdam
Hertzberger studied in Delft and is one of the founders of Dutch Structuralism, along with Jacob Berend Bakema and Aldo van Eyck, with whom he published the magazine "Forum" from 1959 to 1963. Its basic tenet states that human beings have archetypical and individual needs and desires that should be considered by the architect or which builders should ascertain. The architect should only provide a shell into which the user can give input. This anthropological approach leads to buildings that form different levels of communication and various degrees of private space. This reflects the "Forum Group's" attempt to counteract the monopolization of functions by post-war architecture. Large connecting roof surfaces are characteristic of the buildings he designed in the 1990s.

Hildebrandt, Johann Lukas von
*14.11.1668 in Genoa
†16.11.1745 in Vienna
Hildebrandt trained under C. Fontana in Rome. In 1701, he became Court Master Builder in Vienna. He then became First Court Master Builder in 1723 after his competitor Fischer von Erlach died. Hildebrandt's speciality was profane buildings, initially palaces for the nobility, which brought him fame through their round or polygonal rooms and unusual and festive stairways, and the assignment for the Belvedere Palaces. His influence did not just reach to Hungary, Bohemia and Silesia, but into Würzburg in northern Bavaria, where he was brought in to help in constructing Balthasar Neumann's Residency. Here his activity is noticeable on the garden facade (upper part of the central pavilion) and inside the Court Church and Garden Hall.

Holl, Elias
*28.02.1573 in Augsburg
†6.01.1646 in Augsburg
Holl came from a long line of Augsburg master builders and was trained by his father. During a journey he made to complete his education, he was impressed by Palladio's buildings in Venice. After returning home – where he became the Master Builder of the City of Augsburg in 1602 – he attempted to imbue his own work with their clear sense of structure. While the Zeughaus façade (1602 – 1607, built according to a plan by J. Heintz, the elder) still exhibits a Mannerist abundance, the Stadtmetzg (1609) already appears more classically balanced. The plans for the city hall illustrate a development from a Palladian palace to a more local, urban structure with vertical axes. The Thirty Years' War led to a stagnation in Holl's productivity even before he was removed from office, as a Protestant, in the wake of the Restitution Edict of 1629.

Horta, Victor
*16.01.1861 in Ghent
†11.09.1947 In Brussels
Horta studied in Ghent and Brussels. His early work was historical, but with the Hôtel Tassel (1893 – 1897) he changed his style by modelling iron into floral forms. He was more inclined to chose the stems of plants for his linear embellishments, while in Art Nouveau the general tendency was to favour flowers and leaves. His use of glass and iron can be seen in the tradition of E.E. Viollet le Duc. Another source of

inspiration came from the English Domestic Revival style (asymmetry). Like W. Morris and H.P. Berlage, he saw architecture as a social responsibility. The facade of the Maison du Peuple, created for the Socialist Party in Brussels (1896 – 1899, destroyed in 1964), is seen as a prototype of the curtain wall. In 1912 Horta became a professor, and in 1927 the director of the Brussels Academy. In the 1920s his style became more Classical Revival (Palais des Beaux-Arts, Brussels, 1922 – 1928).

HPP Hentrich-Petschnigg & Partner KG

This Düsseldorf-based architectural firm was founded in 1935 as Hentrich-Heuser. Known for its innovative, contemporary designs, it has been responsible for numerous important projects since the 1950s, including the Europa Center in Berlin, the Ruhr University in Bochum, Düsseldorf's Tonhalle concert hall, the Olivandenhof in Cologne, the Central Railway Station in Leipzig and the Detlev-Rohwedder-Haus in Berlin, now the home of the German Federal Finance Ministry.

Iktinos

Iktinos was the most important master builder in Athens at the time of Pericles. He is also reputed to have built the Telesterion and the Temple of Mysteries at Eleusis. According to Vitruvius, he also wrote a treatise on the Parthenon.

Imhotep

Imhotep was Master Builder under the Egyptian King Djoser (3rd Dynasty, around 2650 BC) and was later revered as a god of healing.

Isidoros of Milet

Anthemius' collaborator on Hagia Sophia also devoted himself chiefly to geometry. He is not identical with Isidoros the younger, who in 558 AD increased the height of the dome of Hagia Sophia.

Ito, Toyo

* 1.06.1941 in Seoul
Ito studied in Tokyo and initially worked for Kikutake. In 1971 he opened the practice URBOT, which since 1979 has gone under his own name. Although he began as a Metabolist ("White U" in Tokyo, 1976), his architecture (neighbouring residential building "Silver Hut," 1984) soon began to concern itself with the transitory nature of building.

Jahn, Helmut

* 1.01.1940 in Zirndorf near Nuremberg
Jahn studied in Munich and Chicago. In 1967 he joined the practice of C.F. Murphy, becoming his partner in 1973. In 1981 the practice was renamed Murphy/Jahn Associates, and since 1983 he has directed it on his own. Jahn's buildings aspire on the one hand to simplicity (storeys), and on the other to striking forms (roofing).

Jean de Chelles

Jean de Chelles built – according to the inscription – the new transept façades for Notre Dame in Paris, beginning on 12 February 1258. The southern façade was completed by Pierre de Montreuil.

Jefferson, Thomas

*13.04.1743 in Shadwell, Virginia
†4.07.1826 in Monticello, Virginia
The third president of the United States of America (1801 – 1809) and author of the Declaration of Independence, Jefferson, was also important to his country as a Neoclassical architect. In Paris, where he was the minister to France from 1785 to 1789, he was impressed by early Classical architecture. In 1809 he founded the University of Virginia in Charlottesville and, as its first chairman of its "Board of Visitors," he designed its buildings. The State Capitol of Virginia (1785 – 1789) was inspired by the classical Roman Maison Carreé in Nîmes.

Johnson, Philip

*8.07.1906 in Cleveland, Ohio
Johnson, who originally studied history and philosophy at Harvard, was the first director of the New York Museum of Modern Art (MoMA), from 1930 to 1934. In 1932 he published "The International Style," along with Henry-Russel Hitchcock. The book gave the style its name. They also organized a corresponding exhibition. From 1940 to 1943 he studied architecture at Harvard University under Walter Gropius and Marcel Breuer. From 1946 to 1954 he was again the director of the MoMA. His buildings were initially influenced by Ludwig Mies van der Rohe, with whom he built the Seagram's Tower in New York (1958). In the 1960s he turned away from the Modernism of the post-war period (New York State Theater, 1960 – 1964 along with R. Foster). In the 1980s he espoused Post-Modernism (Pittsburgh Plate Glass Company along with Burgee). In 1979 Johnson was awarded the Pritzker Prize. After the exhibition "Deconstructivist Architecture", which he put on in 1988 together with Mark Wigley, he changed to Deconstructionism.

Jones, Inigo

Baptised 19.07.1573 in London
† 21.06.1652 in London
Jones first visited Italy at a time when he was solely working as a painter and stage designer. He revisited the country in 1613, when he became acquainted with the architecture of antiquity, as well as with Palladios and Scamozzi. In 1615 he became Surveyor General of the King's Works and soon built works clearly inspired by Palladio. These buildings not only brought the High Renaissance to northern Europe, they also created Palladianism in England, which proved resistant to many other influences and frequently served as inspiration for new Classicist currents. The Puritan Revolution of 1642 put an end to Jones' career.

Juvarra, Filippo

* 16.06.1678 in Messina
† 31.01.1736 in Madrid

Juvarra was apprentice to C. Fontana in Rome and initially worked as a stage designer, before being appointed in 1714 court architect in Turin. In two decades he produced here a vast oeuvre – from new town districts to creations in the applied arts, all in a refined Late Baroque style. This led to him being fetched by Philipp V. to Spain in 1735. He built for the King the garden façade of the La Granja de San Ildefonso near Segovia, and the New Palace in Madrid, which was only modified after Juvarra's death and completed by Sacchetti.

Kahn, Louis Isidore

* 20.02.1901 on Osel (Estonia)
† 17.03.1974 in New York

Kahn studied in Philadelphia, and worked there for Paul P. Cret. In the 1940s he joined forces with George Howe, who was important for the New Building style in the USA, and Oscar Stonorov (Carver Court Housing in Coatesville, Pennsylvania, 1941-1944). Together with Ann Tyng, he created buildings inspired by Richard Buckminister Fuller's geodesic domes (City Town Municipal Building, Philadelphia, 1952-1957). The Serialist aspect – along with the clearly recognisable monumentalist form – also continued to dominate his Brutalist buildings (Parliament building in Dakka, 1962-1976).

Klenze, Leo von

*28.02.1784 in Schladen
†27.01.1864 in Munich

Klenze studied in Brunswick and learned with Gilly in Berlin. In Paris he was a colleague of Percier and Fontaine and then of court architect Jérôme in Kassel. In 1816 he received the commission to build the Glyptothek in Munich (until 1831) and became head of court construction under Ludwig I of Bavaria. The buildings from him and F. von Gärtner characterized Munich. However, he was also involved in the rebuilding of Athens for Otto I of Greece and constructed the New Hermitage in St. Petersburg (1839–1852). Whereas the Walhalla (1830–1842) near Regensburg is based on the Greek temple type (Classicism), the Leuchtenbergpalais (1817–1819) in Munich can be classified as Italian Neo-Renaissance.

Klerk, Michel de

*24.11.1884 in Amsterdam
†24.11.1923 in Amsterdam

De Klerk trained under the eclectic Ed. Cuypers. From 1910 to 1911, he was on a study visit to Scandinavia and northern Germany: After that he was involved in J. M. van der Mey's construction of the Scheepvaarthuis (Shipping Offices) in Amsterdam. He was already described as a genius during his own lifetime and admired, this in contrast to Berlage, whom he considered too technically oriented. He is also looked upon as the founder of the Amsterdam School. On de Klerk's death, the setting up of the second, stricter phase of the Amsterdam School was put back.

Koolhaas, Rem

*17.11.1944 in The Hague

Rem Koolhaas grew up in Indonesia and worked as a journalist and script writer (e. g. for Russ Meyer). He decided to become an architect during the 1968 student revolt in Paris. He studied at the A.A. in London and, later, with Peter Eisenman in New York. Koolhaas is one of the most important contemporary architectural theorists and received the Pritzker Prize in 2000 in recognition of his architecture and ideas as contributions of great importance for the new century. Along with Madelon Vriesendonk, Zoe Zenghelis and Elia Zenghelis he established the Office for Metropolitan Architecture (OMA) in 1975. In his book "Delirious New York" (1978) Koolhaas explains that the city that has developed organically (in contrast to one that is planned and functional) provides a positive model for the "culture of congestion" with its extremes and determined pursuit of multifaceted excessiveness. On the basis of ideas like this he was awarded the post of chief planner for Euralille (Lille, 1988) where he attempted to put his theories into practice and applied them to the interior of the enormous Grand Palais (1991 – 1994) that he designed. This commission and the redevelopment of a part of the Rotterdam harbour, as well as the revitalization of the former bedroom community of Almere, forged the perception of city planning reflected in his book "S, M, L, XL" published in 1995.

Kurokawa, Kisho Noriaki

* 8.04.1934 in Nagoya

Kurokawa studied in Kyoto and Tokyo and worked for Tange. As the leading Metabolist (Manifesto 1960), he championed an architecture using hi-tech elements, which could be transformed and extended. Later this also came to include traditional elements (Hiroshima City Museum of Contemporary Art, 1984-1988).

Latrobe, Benjamin Henry

*1.05.1764 in Fulneck, Yorkshire
†3.09.1820 in New Orleans

Latrobe trained under S. Pepys Cockerell and emigrated to America. In 1803 he became Inspector of the Public Buildings of the Federal Government. He was America's first internationally recognized classicist architect. In addition, as early as 1799 he had constructed a first Neo-Gothic building in the U.S. He completed the Capitol in Washington and renewed it in 1814.

Le Corbusier

*6.10.1887 in La Chaux-de-Fonds
†27.08.1965 in Cap-Martin

Le Corbusier, a pseudonym for Charles-Édouard Jeanneret, started an apprenticeship as an engraver in the town in which he was born and where he also built the Villa Vallet as early as 1905. It was only in 1908 that he began his training with August Perret, becoming acquainted with new methods of construction quite early. From 1910 to 1911 Le Corbusier worked for Peter Behrens in Berlin. In Hagen he presumably met the artist Lauweriks, who may have inspired his modular approach to architecture. With his Maison-Domino system, Le Corbusier reduced the idea of construction to just rigid floors and free-standing pillars. His radical ideas on an "Esprit Nouveau" resulted not only in his five theses on how building should be carried out, but also in plans for the almost total reconstruction of Paris (Plan Voisin). In building Chandigarh (India, 1951 – 1955), he was able to put his ideas on urban planning into practice. In individual buildings he designed in the 1950s, more plastic elements become increasingly prominent (Ronchamp).

Ledoux, Claude-Nicolas
*21.03.1736 in Dormans-sur-Marne
†19.11.1806 in Paris
Ledoux trained under J.-F. Blondel. He was initially active for four years in the Provinces of Burgundy and Champagne, where he constructed village churches, schools and bridges. In 1766, he went to Paris and designed many classicist palaces for the nobility (Hôtel de d'Halwyll 1766). His project for the new salt works and surrounding ideal new town at the Salines de Chaux, at Arc-et-Senans (1775–1779) anticipates the monumentality of geometric compositions of the architecture of the French Revolution. From 1780 onwards, he designed sixty tollhouses at the gates of Paris, which also appear as if they are composed of geometric basic forms. Later he planned architecture parlant in its pure form. The river flows through the house of a river watchman; the house of a tyre maker has the form of a tyre. The French Revolution brought Ledoux's career to an end.

Le Vau (also Levau), Louis
*around 1612 in Paris
†11.10.1670 in Paris
Le Vau was already called the Royal Architect (Architecte du Roi) by 1638, following his apprenticeship with his father and a trip to Italy. His talent was displayed in particular by his designing of interior rooms (Hôtel Lambert in Paris with C. Lebrun, the Court Painter of Louis XIV). The Vaux-le-Vicomte Palace for the French Minister of Finance was his major work. The latter's successor, Colbert, engaged him to finish the Cour Carrée of the Louvre (from 1659). After that he was active in reconstructing the Palace in Versailles. The Louis XIV style he influenced is looked upon as the highlight of Baroque Classicism. More baroque in the Italian interpretation is the facade of the present-day Institut de France in Paris (from 1663). This swings out to the Seine concavely, enveloping the church in the process.

Lewerentz, Sigurd
* 29.07.1885 in Sandsö Bjärtr
† 29.12.1975 in Lund
Lewerentz studied in Göteborg and worked for Theodor Fischer and Richard Riemerschmid, with whom he also wor-

ked on the garden town of Hellerau. His oeuvre is very small. The design for a cemetery chapel in Bergaliden in Helsingborg (in 1914 together with Torsten Stubelius) was the basis of his entry for a competition for the forest cemetery that he was to build with Asplund.

Libera, Adelberto
*1903 in Villa Lagherina near Trent
†1963 in Rome
Libera studied in Rome. For a short period he was a member of the Gruppo 7 and played a decisive role in M.I.A.R., which represented the architecture of the modern in Italian Fascism. He constructed the Palazzo dei Picevimenti e Congressi (1937–1942) for the Esposizione universale di Roma, at which very diverse buildings were realized. He also constructed the Olympic Village in Rome between 1957 and 1960.

Libeskind, Daniel
*1946 in Lódz
Libeskind, who immigrated to the United States in 1960, studied architecture in New York and architectural history in England. He is one of the leading Deconstructivists. Even before his first building, the Felix Nussbaum Museum, was completed in Osnabrück (1996 – 1997), Libeskind had become famous for his design of the Jewish Museum in Berlin (1989 – 1998), another building that was still under construction. Both of these buildings are based on concepts drawn from French literary structuralism (M. Foucault). The latter attempts to view language as a complex system of individual elements and to analyze the relationships and interdependencies within this system. In designing the museum in Osnabrück Libeskind makes references to historical developments in the city related to the Nussbaum's life as a painter and to Jewish life in the city overall. The building thereby becomes the nexus of a number of historical developments and a starting point for their exploration. Libeskind sees the building's jagged form as result of its function of including references to immaterial aspects of the city's landscape.

Loos, Adolf
*12.10.1870 in Brno
†23.08.1933 in Kalksburg
After an apprenticeship in Dresden, Loos was in Philadelphia from 1893 to 1896. He worked in various professions there and was impressed by construction engineering. Thereafter he settled in Vienna and became influenced by O. Wagner. In 1898 he distanced himself from ornamental art for the first time in his essay The Potemkin City. Publishing Ornament and Crime (1908) brought isolation from the architecture scene. On the outside, his buildings appear cubically simple. However, on the inside, they do frequently search for representative expression through their choice of precious materials. This type of surface aesthetics links him with the Viennese workshops. Loos' proposal for the Chicago Tribune skyscraper (1922) was a gigantic column with entasis. It really should not just be interpreted as an ironic statement on the neo-style of the skyscrapers, but shows itself more as the highpoint of classicistic tendencies in his work. After he was

head of the Viennese residential office (1920–1922), he then went to Paris (1923–1928) where he influenced Le Corbusier but had little success. In 1924, he moderated his theories in Ornament and Education, but by this time he had already become a model for the Neues Bauen movement.

Ludwig II of Bavaria
*25.08.1845 in Munich
†13.06.1886 near Berg at Starnberger See
Ludwig II, King of Bavaria (1864–1886), is considered a sensitive character with conservative underlying attitudes, in contrast to his father Maximilian II. Ludwig increasingly turned away from political events and towards the arts and culture. Apart from the work of Richard Wagner, he was also interested in his magnificent buildings, which supplied him with a fairy tale world. At the start of the 1880s, he showed signs of paranoid schizophrenia. On June 8th 1886, he was certified and declared unfit to govern. Five days later he was found drowned. The circumstances of his death were never finally cleared up.

Luzarches (see Robert de Luzarches)

Mackintosh, Charles Rennie
*7.06.1868 in Glasgow
†10.12.1928 in London
Mackintosh was educated at an arts and crafts school. In 1889, he became an employee at Honeyman & Keppie (Glasgow Herald Building 1893) and later a partner (1904–1913). He got to know Herbert MacNair there. Together with their wives, sisters Margaret und Frances MacDonald, they became known as The (Glasgow) Four. Just as important as Mackintosh's buildings are his furnishings (Glasgow tea rooms for the anti-alcohol movement of Catherine Cranston). Again and again, cut out or deepened squares stand out, ones that form a regular pattern on the surfaces. The decor always follows the basic pattern and mostly underlines this. Mackintosh also became known on the continent through his furniture (Vienna 1900) and the competition for "The House of a Friend of the Arts" (1901). The villas (Windyhill 1899–1901) stand out thanks to a refined interchange of light and dark rooms. In 1914, Mackintosh left Glasgow and moved to Suffolk, London and France. There the brilliant architect busied himself as an average painter.

Maderna (Maderno), Carlo
* 1556 in Capolago on Lake Lugano
† 30.01.1629 in Rome
Maderna was apprenticed to his uncle Domenico Fontana. From 1598 he constructed the Palazzo Mattei di Giove, still in the Renaissance tradition of the Palazzo Farnese, but subsequently his style became increasingly Baroque (Palazzo Barberini, 1628). As master builder for the Church of St. Peter he completed the nave, porch and façade, and drafted the first plans for (Bernini's) Piazza St. Peter's and high altar.

Melnikov, Konstantin Stepanovic
* 3.08.1890 in Moscow
† 28.11.1974 in Moscow
Melnikov studied in Moscow prior to the October Revolution, and subsequently became professor at the WChUTEMAS – the Soviet counterpart to the Bauhaus. He was the most important architect of the Soviet avant-garde, and rose to fame after building the national pavilion at the Paris Exposition des arts décoratifs (1925). This light, Constructivist structure contrasts strongly with his heavy, block-like workers clubs. The change in style around 1930 towards architectural historicism, which grew up around the competition for the Soviet Palace, left Melnikov virtually unable to work in the field. From then on he dedicated himself to typography.

Mendelsohn, Erich
*21.03.1887 in Olsztyn, Poland (then Allenstein, East Prussia)
†15.09.1953 in San Francisco
Mendelsohn studied in Berlin and Munich. The sketches he made during the First World War make him one the earliest representatives of Expressionism in architecture. His drawings exhibit great dynamism in the route of the façade. Mendelsohn became well known after constructing the Einstein Tower. His forms become more moderate with buildings for commercial clients (Mossehaus Berlin with Neutra, Schocken Department Stores in Stuttgart and Chemnitz). After emigrating in 1933, Mendelsohn built the De la Warr Pavillon (Bexhill-on-Sea, 1934–1935) in Britain. Simultaneously he was already constructing buildings for Palestine, where he moved in 1939 (University in Jerusalem from 1936). In 1941, he moved to the U.S. after a dearth of orders. There, too, he also had no luck initially. It was not until 1946 that he was able to construct diverse buildings for Jewish communities (St. Louis).

Michelangelo Buonarroti
* 6.03.1475 in Caprese
† 18.02.1564 in Rome
Michelangelo was apprentice in Florence to the painter Ghirlandaio, as well as to the sculptor Bertoldo di Giovanni, and received his first commissions from Lorenzo de Medici at an early age. In 1508 he was commissioned by Pope Julius II. to paint the ceiling of the Sistine Chapel: similar to his sculptures, the depicted figures are conspicuous for their enormous musculature. His first work as an architect was in 1514, when Pope Leo X. commissioned the façade of the Castle of St. Angelino in Rome. Although architecture assumed increasing importance in his work, Michelangelo always viewed himself as a sculptor. His buildings mark the transition from the High Renaissance to Mannerism (anteroom of the Biblioteca Laurenziana, 1524-1534) and sometimes anticipate the spatial principles of 17th century Baroque (Cappella Sforza in Rome, 1560). When he took over the work on St Peter's, he had part of the work done by Sangallo pulled down in order to create a more powerful composition.

Mies van der Rohe, Ludwig
*27.03.1886 in Aachen
†17.08.1969 in Chicago

Mies van der Rohe trained under B. Paul and P. Behrens. The first buildings he designed on his own show themselves as clearly influenced by Schinkel. In fact, although he became a leading representative of post-war architecture using steel and glass, we can still recognize Schinkel's influence in most of his buildings (New National Gallery in Berlin, 1963–1968). From 1930 to 1933, Mies van der Rohe was Director of the Bauhaus. Under his leadership, the institute was increasingly aligned according to aesthetic sensual principles, whereas his predecessor H. Meyer had emphasized functional building and serial production. In 1937, Mies emigrated to the U.S., and from 1938 onwards was a teacher at the current Illinois Institute of Technology. Alongside villas (Farnsworth House, Fox River) he also designed many skyscrapers (Seagram Building). In addition, his steel pipe furniture in successor M. Stams is still one of the most popular models even today.

Milet (see Isidoros von Milet)

Mique, Richard
* 18.09.1728 in Nancy
† 8.07.1794 in Paris

Mique was apprenticed in Strasburg and Paris to Jacques-François Blondel. At first he worked as Court Architect to King Stanislaw Leszczynskis in Nancy (Porte Stanislas), and in 1775 he became Court Architect to the French Monarch. Mique introduced Rococo (Louis-seize) to Versailles (theatre at the Petit Trianon, Temple de l'Amour, Belvèdére). His designs for Marie-Antoinette's "Hameau" gave it a seemingly rural air, typical of the late, sentimental Rococo. Mique died under the guillotine during the French Revolution.

Montreuil (see Pierre de Montreuil)

Morris, William
*24.03.1834 in London
† 3.10.1896 in London

Morris was not an architect in the narrow sense, but he did have a great impact on architecture as a craftsman and an art theoretician. Influenced by the theories of the Neo-Gothic John Ruskin, he criticized the effects of industrialization from both a social and an aesthetic angle. He said that man and product had become defamiliarized from each other. He wanted the return of the workshop business from the Middle Ages. His utopia, News From Nowhere, showed a world in which everyone just created what he wanted. In 1861, he helped found the company of Morris, Marshall, Faulkner & Co. Here, Morris tried to implement his ideas in the production of furniture, wallpapers, and the like.

MVRDV
Founded in Rotterdam in 1992

MVRDV is a name drawn from the initials of the office's founders' surnames: Winy Maas (*1959), Jacob van Rijs (*1964), and Nathalie de Vries (*1965). They all studied in Delft and then spent time working for OMA (Mass, van Rijs), Ben van Berkel (van Rijs), and Mecanoo (de Vries). Among the most interesting buildings by MVRDV is the "Villa VPRO" in Hilversum and housing for the elderly with greatly extended residential levels in western Amsterdam.

Neumann, Johann Balthasar
Baptised 30.01.1687 in Eger
†19.08.1753 in Würzburg

Neumann trained first as a metal founder and – from 1711 in Würzburg – as a gunsmith and pyrotechnist. He participated in the Turkish War as a military engineer and, after further studies in Paris and Vienna, became in 1719 architectural director to Prince-Bishop Franz von Schönborn, and was responsible for Würzburg Palace (advised by de Cotte, Boffrand, von Welsch and von Hildesheim). His palaces (Bruchsal, Brühl) distinguish themselves by a dynamic vocabulary (staircases) combined with French Classicism, and his sacred buildings (Nerresheim) by a fusion of spaces derived from G. Guarini.

Niemeyer, Oscar Soares Filko
*15.12.1907 in Rio de Janeiro

Niemeyer studied in Rio de Janeiro and was a student of Lúcio Costa's and of Le Corbusier's. Along with Costa, Affonso Eduardo Reidy, Roberto Burle Marx and Le Corbusier he constructed the Ministry of Health and Education building in Rio between 1936 and 1943. Under Costa, who was responsible for the overall plan, Niemeyer built a large part of the government district in the newly established capital city of Brasilia between 1956 and 1961. The more plastic approach in evidence here was already employed in the casino and the Sao Francisco de Assisi Church in Pampúlha.

Olbrich, Joseph Maria
*22.10.1867 in Opava, Czech Republic (then Troppau, Silesia)
†8.08.1908 in Düsseldorf

Olbrich learned in Vienna under C. Sitte and K. von Hasenauer. He worked in the office of O. Wagner together with J. Hoffmann. In 1897, they founded the Wiener Sezession together with K. Moser and G. Klimt. From 1898 onwards, Olbrich was able to approach more closely their target of synthesizing the arts in the Darmstadt artists' colony. As with the Sezession building, the buildings here are also initially formed from simple shapes, but coalesce with more complex ones. With the Tietz department store in Düsseldorf (1906–1909), the latent Neo-Classicism of his earlier buildings (Darmstadt Exhibition Building) breaks through.

Otto, Frei
*31.05.1925 in Siegmar

Otto, who studied in Berlin and Charlottesville (Virginia), is mainly involved with the design of lightweight tent-like structures. Working with Rolf Gutbrod, Otto designed the German Pavilion for the Expo in Montreal (1967, found today as the Institute for Lightweight Structures in Stuttgart). Based on the requirements of the given building, Otto tries to reduce the surfaces to a minimum and push the static possibilities of the supports and membranes to the limit. He has created numerous exhibition buildings and is in demand world-wide as a specialist (a hotel and conference centre in Mecca, 1974; ministerial council building in Riad, 1978 – 1982). Otto is also concerned with construction under extreme climatic conditions, as in the case of the "city in the Arctic" which is covered with a pneumatically supported outer skin (1970 – 1971).

Palladio, Andrea
*30.11.1508 in Vicenza
†19.08.1580 in Vicenza
Palladio, actually Andrea di Pietro della Gondolas, based his creations on the studies of the writings of Vitruvius and the antique ruins of Rome. Initially, he built in and around Vicenza. After 1560, it was mainly in and around Venice. His buildings, including numerous villas, are influenced by the pure volumes and ground plans. He clearly emphasizes these by reducing building decoration. These clear forms help him achieve a dignified monumentalization. It was eagerly taken up as Palladianism in England, France and the Netherlands in particular. In 1570, he published his theoretical treatise Quattro libri dell' architettura, one of the most important architecture tracts.

Parler, Peter
* 1330 in Gmünd
† 13.07.1399 in Prague
Parler came from a renowned family of Late Gothic monumental masons and master builders, whose name derived from the word "Polier" or site-foreman. His father, Heinrich von Gmünd (born around 1300, Heinrich Parler the older.), worked in Cologne (cathedral) before becoming in 1351 master builder for the Church of the Sacred Cross in Schwäbisch Gmünd. Peter was appointed in 1353 by Carl IV. to continue the work begun by Matthias von Arras on St. Vitus' Cathedral in Prague, where he built further buildings. His son Johann was in all probability later involved in the work on St. Stephan's Cathedral in Vienna.

Pei, Ieoh Ming
*26.04.1917 in Canton
At the age of 17, Pei emigrated to the U.S. and studied initially at the MIT, then in Cambridge (Mass.) with W. Gropius. In the following years he worked with various partners (R. Affleck, H. Cobb, J. Freed). His work contains two main motives. The East Wing of the National Gallery of Art in Washington shows itself to be a massive cube that is broken. The Louvre Pyramids in Paris (1983–1993) are filigree but clearly enclosed steel constructions. Many of his other buildings contain a mixture of these basic elements (Rock 'n' Roll Hall of Fame in Cleveland).

Perret, Auguste
* 12.02.1874 in Brussels
† 25.02.1954 in Paris
Perret, son of a building contractor, studied at the École des Beaux-Arts in Paris and, together with his brothers Gustave and Claude, founded in 1905 the construction firm Perret Frères. His most important works (all in Paris) are based on skeleton frame construction and reinforced concrete, but the methods for the façades differed: whereas his house Rue Franklin is faced with tilework, the Garage Rue Ponthieu (1905) is dominated by glass surfaces, and the church Notre-Dame du Raincy (1922/23) uses prefabricated concrete elements. The Musée des Travaux Publics (1937) – with its columns and use of porphyry and marble aggregates in concrete – clearly shows Perret's tendency to Neoclassicism.

Piano, Renzo
*14.09.1937 in Genoa
Piano, who studied in Florence and Milan, began working for Kahn. From 1971 to 1977 he was in partnership with Richard Rogers, with whom he built the Centre Georges Pompidou in Paris. Even in his earliest buildings, like the Free-Plan House in Garonne (1969), his interest in the technical side of architecture is evident. Because of his high-tech approach to architecture, he received a commission in 1985 to renovate the Futurists' only building – the Fiat plant Lingotto in Turin. In the meantime, he had developed a subtler, more elegant style in building the museum for the de Menil Collection (Houston, 1981 – 1986). This style can again be found in the design for the Fondation Beyeler (Basle, 1990 – 1997). Piano combined both of these styles in designing the passenger terminal for Kensai Airport on a man-made island near Osaka (1988 – 1994).

Pierre de Montreuil
† 1267 in Paris
According to the inscription on his gravestone, Pierre de Montreuil completed the work begun by Jean de Chelles on the southern transept of Notre Dame in Paris. The rounded triangles and tripartite tracery of the Rose Window from then on dominated the Rayonnant Style. The dominant niche forms and depressions, the numerous triangular gables on the façades, are the epitome of Export Gothic, which was to be adopted in Germany. Before commencing work on Notre Dame, Pierre de Montreuil built the Lady Chapel and the refectory of Saint-Germain-des-Près. From 1247 he worked as master builder on St. Denis.

Pugin, Augustus Welby Northmore
*1812 in London
†1852 in Ramsgate
The son of a French immigrant, Pugin was initially the specialist for Gothic building details under J. Nash. As the most important agitator of Neo-Gothic he converted to Catholicism in 1834, after the Catholic Emancipation Act from 1829 had triggered a construction boom with Catholic places of worship. He considered buildings aligned on antiquity as unchristian. In 1836, he published Contrasts, comparing the architecture of the 14th and 15th centuries with the descent in taste in the 19th. In 1851, he was involved in the Great Exhibition in London as Commissioner of Fine Arts. The strong representation of Neo-Gothic there ignited the resistance that was to lead to the Arts and Crafts Movement.

Raphael, actually Raffaello Sanzio oder Santi
* 6.04.1483 in Urbino
† 6.04.1520 in Rome
Raffael was apprenticed to Perugino in Perugia, but soon moved to Florence where, under the influence of Leonardo and Michelangelo, he became the third major painter of the High Renaissance. In 1508 Julius II. commissioned him to paint the stanzas in the Vatican Palace, and in 1514 he succeeded Bramantes as master builder of St. Peter's. Although almost nothing of this project has been preserved, he was able to realize the façade of San Lorenzo in Florence (1514) and the Palazzo Pandolfini (1516).

Ribera, Pedro de
* Around 1683 in Madrid
† 1742 in Madrid
De Ribera worked from 1719 for the City of Madrid, and became in 1726 municipal architect. Here he came to dominate the Late Baroque art of building.

Richardson, Henry Hobson
*1838 near New Orleans
†1886 in Brookline, Mass.
Richardson studied at the École des Beaux-Arts in Paris. There, a form of Neo-Baroque was just coming into fashion, one merging its massiveness with Neo-Romantic elements. Distinct volumes, emphasis of materials (rustication) and clear compositions characterize his often-monumental public buildings (Trinity Church, Boston 1874-1877). With his English-influenced villas, on the other hand, often only the basements are massive and the upper floor is more lightly formed in shingle style und half-timbering. His form of neo-Romantic triggered a reaction in Europe (Berlage). Richardson's Marshall Field Wholesale Store (Chicago 1885–1887) was a starting point for Sullivan's architecture.

Riedel, Eduard
*1813 in Bayreuth
†1885 in Starnberg
Riedel studied in Munich and Rome and trained under F. von Gärtner. He built the Bavarian Nationalmuseum (1858–1865) in Munich (before Neuschwanstein).

Rietveld, Gerrit Thomas
* 24.06.1888 in Utrecht
† 25.06.1964 in Utrecht
Rietveld trained as a cabinetmaker and began building Frank Lloyd Wright style furniture for Robert van't Hoff in 1915. In 1917 and 1918 he designed his famous red and blue chair, one of the most well known works of de Stijl, a movement to which he belonged after 1919. Later Rietveld was interested in housing construction, although not as much in individual designs as in basic design types.

Robert de Luzarches
De Luzarches is named the first architect, the "magister operis" of the cathedral in Amiens, in its labyrinth. Later he (or Thomas de Cormont) worked on Sainte-Chapelle in Paris, which borrowed the forms of the chapel at the vertex of the sanctuary in Amiens.

Rogers, Richard
*23.07.1933 in Florence
Rogers studied in London and in New Haven, Connecticut. He is one of the most famous representatives of High-Tech Architecture. Along with his own wife, Su, Norman Foster and Foster's later wife, Wendy, he became part of the Team 4 in the 1960s. Their buildings reveal a mixture of both architects' styles: Foster's austere simplicity and Rogers's emphasis on technical aspects. This High-Tech Architecture reached its pinnacle with the Centre Georges Pompidou in Paris (in cooperation with Renzo Piano, 1971 – 1977) and in the London Lloyd's Building (1978 – 1986). At the European Court in Strasbourg (1989 – 1994) two round building segments are supposed to represent justice marking the return of "architecture parlante".

Rohe (see Mies van der Rohe)

Romano (see Giulio Romano)

Rossi, Aldo
*3.05.1931 in Milan
†4.09.1997 in Milan
Rossi, who studied in Milan, is recognized as the founder of "Rational Architecture" and received the Pritzker Prize in 1990. Rossi's theory operates on the premise that there is an archetypal form that has evolved over time for every building project. By means of formal reduction, the architect has to find this archetype in the basic stereometric forms underlying the many stylistic variations. Hence, the "basilica" is an archetype for church buildings, regardless of whether it is found in the stylistic variation "Romanesque" or "Gothic." Even his early works (The Memorial Fountain on the City Hall Plaza in Segrate, 1965) demonstrate the formal reduction that he describes in his book "L'Architettura della Città" (The Architecture of the City) published in 1966. Rossi's "Teatro del Mondo," built for the Biennale in Venice in 1980, made references both to the floating theatre of the city (Carnival) and to the form of Shakespeare's Globe Theatre.

Ryang, Duk-Kyu
* 1938 in Seoul
Ryang studied architecture in Seoul. In the mid-1960s he began working in Austria for architectural firms that included Carl Auböck and Otto Carl Uhl in Vienna. In 1968 he was awarded the Mautner-Markhof Prize by the City of Vienna for his work. Subsequently he moved to Germany, where he has worked for HPP Hentrich-Petschnigg & Partner KG of Düsseldorf since 1976, taking over the management of the company's Cologne office in 1996.

Saarinen, Eero

* 20.08.1910 in Kirkonummi

† 1.09.1961 in Ann Arbor

The son of Eliel Saarinen, Eero studied sculpture in Paris and architecture in New Haven. Until 1950 he worked in his father's practice. He came to fame for his design for the Jefferson National Expansion Memorial near St. Louis (1948), but it only came to be realized after his death (begun in 1963). The 192 metre (630 ft.) tall arch is based on a project by Libera. The highpoint of his pluralistic oeuvre are his sculpturally expressive concrete shells, as in the Kresge Auditorium at the Institute of Technology in Cambridge, Massachusetts (1953-1955).

Saarinen, Eliel Gottlieb

* 20.08.1873 in Rantasalmi

† 1.07.1950 in Bloomfield Hills

Saarinen studied painting and architecture in Helsinki. He worked here in the tradition of the Arts and Crafts Movement and the Neo-Romanic of H. H. Richardson, which strived to replaced State Classicism. Typical of this is the World Exposition pavilion (Paris 1900), which he designed together with Herman Gesellius and Armas Lindgren. The three architects worked and lived together, until Saarinen made a solitary departure with his work on the Helsinki railway station. After winning second place in the competition for the Chicago Tribune skyscraper, Saarinen emigrated in 1923 to the USA. Here he built his masterpiece, the Cranbrook Academy of Art in Bloomfield Hills, assisted by his wife, Louise Gesellius, and Carl Milles as sculptors. With this academy under his direction, Saarinen was also able to realize his plans for urban development.

Sangallo the younger, Antonio da (actually Antonio Cordiani)

* 1485 in Mugello near Florence

† 3.08.1546 in Terni

The pupil and nephew of Antonio da Sangallo the older, he became in 1516 Raphael's collaborator on St. Peter's and four years later assumed from him the architectural direction. His plans for the church were not realized, but he did build the Scala Regia and the Cappella Paolina in the Vatican Palace. Back in 1510 he had begun building the important Palazzo Farnese, which was completed after his death by Michelangelo, Giacomo Vignola and Giacomo della Porta.

Scharoun, Hans Bernhard

*20.09.1893 in Bremen

†25.11.1972 in Berlin

Scharoun studied in Berlin. From 1915 to 1918, he was deputy head of the construction advisory office for reconstructing Eastern Prussia, and then a member of Die gläserne Kette as a free architect. Despite the utopias of that time, he was a follower of the organ-like architecture as espoused by H.Häring. This perceived neither Expressionism nor Neues Bauen to be styles, wanting instead to develop specific forms from the functions of a building. In the second half of the twenties, Scharoun's style also became more real (Siemensstadt Urban Development Plan in Berlin, 1929), but expressive tendencies remained visible (Haus Schminke in Lobau, 1930-1933). After the Second World War, he was preoccupied with the complete reconstruction of Berlin (including the Berlin Philharmonie, 1959–1963) but also realized many public buildings elsewhere (Embassy in Brazil, 1963-1971; City Theatre in Wolfsburg, 1965-1973).

Schinkel, Karl Friedrich

*13.03.1781 in Neuruppin

†9.10.1841 in Berlin

Schinkel trained under D. Gilly and studied in Berlin. He then travelled to Italy and Paris between 1803 and 1805. After that, he worked as a set-designer thanks to a lack of orders as a painter. The architecture styles that interested him become visible in the buildings of his paintings: Classicism and Neo-Gothic. Most of his buildings can be allocated to the former. One example for the latter is the Werdersche Kirche in Berlin (1824–1830). However, Schinkel also submitted classicistic and neo-Renaissance plans for the church. The latter building made people aware of the rational design of red brick, and the Bauakademie (Building Academy) made them aware of skeleton structures on buttresses. Schinkel had come to know rational factory building on his journeys to England and Scotland (1826). His influence became noticeable in all of Prussia as state architect (from 1810) and director of the Prussian Office of Public Works (from 1830).

Schoch, Johannes (Johann, Hans)

*around 1550 in Konigsbach, Baden

†1631 in Strasbourg

Schoch constructed the present-day Chambre de Commerce in Strasbourg, even before he was named a town mason in 1590. After having already designed Gottesau Palace near Karlsruhe in 1588, he became the court architect to the Elector of the Palatinate under Friedrich IV in 1601. From 1601 to 1607, he constructed the Friedrichsbau of Heidelberg Castle, based on the Ottheinrichsbau, whose plasticity already points towards the Baroque.

Sinan

* 1489/1491 or 1497 near Kayseri

† 1587/1588 in Constantinople

Sinan, a trained carpenter, was a Christian by birth. At first he built military complexes for Süleyman the Magnificent during the latter's campaigns, but soon received his first commissions for sacred buildings. In 1538 he became the director of the Central Office for Architecture and thus was responsible for the entire architectural work of the Ottoman Empire (477 individual buildings). With his 157 mosques he drew on Early Byzantine architecture to develop the vocabulary of form and shape used in Islamic sacred buildings (Hagia Sophia).

SOM

The SOM practice was established in 1936 by Louis Skidmore (1897-1962) and Nathaniel Owings (1903-1984), and received its name when in 1939 John Merrill (1896-1975) joined the team. Originally SOM was based in Chicago and drew on the Chicago School. In 1937 a New Yorker joined the practice; since the 1980s it has also had branches outside of the USA. In the years after its foundation, the practice has had over 1,000 employees. SOM is among the foremost representatives of the New Building style in the USA. During the Second World War they built the secret town of Atom City (Oak Ridge, Tenn.). Typical of its high-rise buildings is the New York Lever House (1950-1952, design: Gordon Bunshaft): slab-shaped, with a transparent facia and a low, podium-like section at its base. Similarly, the SOM style left its mark on a low-built company headquarters complex (Connecticut General Life Insurance, Bloomfield, Connecticut, 1954-1957), which is distributed about a park. In the 1980s the practice turned to Postmodernism (Canary Wharf development in the London Docklands, 1985-1991).

Starck, Philippe
* 18.01.1949 in Paris
Starck, who studied in Paris, came to architecture via design. He became well known after redesigning François Mitterand's suite at the Elysées Palace in 1982. He was also able to realize the integration of design and architecture in Tokyo with his work for the Asahi Brewery, which incorporated the flame motif typical of his design. In 1991 he put up the entire rue Starck in Paris. He has worked as a designer for Disform, Idee and Alessi, to name a few, and has even designed noodles for Panzani (1987).

Suger (Sugerius)
* Around 1080
† 13.01.1151 in St-Denis
Suger was born in the vicinity of the Abbey of Saint-Denis near Paris, and entered the abbey as a child. In 1122 he was elected abbot. Although he was not an architect, he had a decisive influence on the appearance of the building, as is handed down to posterity in Libellus de conversatione ecclesiae S. Dionysii and De rebus in administrationem sua gestis. In 1118 and 1121 Suger acted as ambassador for Louis VI. of France – whose biography he wrote. Later, he not only exerted a strong influence on Louis VII., but represented him as Regent during the crusades of 1147-1149.

Sullivan, Louis Henry
*3.09.1854 in Boston
†14.04.1924 in Chicago
Sullivan only studied at the MIT for a short time. He then worked with Jenney, and with Vaudremer in Paris, and finally jointly with Dankmar Adler. Sullivan was the most important representative of the Chicago School. He became totally opposed to historicism and demanded a clear construction. However, as his buildings show, he did not by any means reject decoration. This offered a starting point for F. L. Wright, who also renewed these and did not wish to see them abolished. In contrast, Sullivan's comment that "form follows function" took on a life of its own and was thereafter misused to reject every non-functional form.

Tange, Kenzo
* 4.09.1913 in Imabari on Shikoko
Tange studied in Tokyo and worked for former Le Corbusier employee Kunio Mayekawa. The competition for the Hiroshima Peace Centre (1949) brought him to public awareness: the hall combines the Western International Style with an Eastern conception of space. With this he coloured postwar architecture in Japan, where previously the New Building style had been in vogue. Tange's plan for Tokyo (1960) also inspired the Metabolists, whose fundamental idea consists of interchangeable room modules.

Taut, Bruno
*4.05.1880 in Königsberg
†24.12.1938 in Ankara
In 1912 Taut became a consultant to the "Deutsche Gartenstadtgesellschaft" (German Garden City Society) and planned two very simple developments, "Reform" in Magdeburg and "Am Falkenberg" in Berlin (1913 – 1914). With the simultaneous construction of three exhibition pavilions made of metal and glass, in Leipzig and at the Werkbund Exhibition in Cologne, he became one of the founders of Expressionist architecture. The glasshouse, in particular, became the prototype of the sort of "crystalline" design for which the poet Paul Scheerbart had made a strong case as well as provided inscriptions. With the books "Alpine Architektur" (Alpine Architecture) and "Die Stadtkrone" (The Crown of the City), his correspondence with what came to be known as the "Glass Chain" and the magazine "Frühlicht" (Early Light), Taut established his reputation as one of the leading authors on this style. During the November Revolution in 1918 he agitated for the establishment of a working council on art: a kind of workers' council for artists. With an increasing number of commissions, Taut – like many other Expressionists in the 1920s – turned more toward rational concepts of building. As the city building commissioner of Magdeburg (1921 – 1923) he propagated the use of colour – sometimes quite a lot of colour – in architecture. As the architect for the "Gemeinnützigen Heimstätten-, Spar- und Bau-Aktiengesellschaft" (Non-Profit Homestead, Savings and Building Society, Inc.) his buildings became more and more simple. In 1933 he immigrated at first to Japan and, in 1936, to Turkey where he was involved in the construction of university buildings in Ankara.

Terragini, Giuseppe
*18.04.1904 in Meda
†19.07.1943 in Como
Terragini studied in Milan and was the most important representative of the Modern Movement in Italy. In 1927 he opened an office in Como along with his brother Attilio. He was one of the founders of the Gruppo 7, which tended toward the Modernism, as well as the Classical Antiquity and Italian Fascism. With his Casa Giuliani Frigerio in Como (1939), his style became more dynamic, particularly in comparison to the House of Fascists in Como. The former can be seen as a reference to the Futurist Antonio Sant'Elia. Terragini and Attilio built a memorial to the war dead in Como in 1933 on

the basis of Sant'Elia's designs. Terragini's practice of drawing on Classical ideals while executing building in and according to modern forms was to become an inspiration to Aldo Rossi and the New York Five.

Thornton, William
* 20.05.1759 in Jost van Dyke (West Indies)
† 28.03.1828 in Washington
Thornton, originally a doctor in the West Indies, became an American citizen in 1788, and the following year designed the building for the Philadelphia Library Company. In 1793 he won the competition for the construction of the Capitol.

Tralles (see Anthemius of Tralles)

Utzon, Jørn Oberg
* 9.04.1918 in Copenhagen
Utzon studied in Copenhagen under Kay Fischer and Asplund. Afterwards he worked for a short period for Aalto and Wright. The Indian architecture of Central America influenced his idea of separate podium-like substructures and roof-like superstructures, as seen in the Sydney Opera House. Additionally, his buildings are influenced by topographical or regional factors, which he always transposes, however, into modern forms, as in the Parliament building in Kuwait, which resembles an enormous Bedouin tent in concrete.

Van Alen, William
* 1883 in New York
† 14.05.1954 in New York
Van Alen initially studied in Brooklyn before a scholarship in 1908 enabled him to study in Paris. He returned in 1911. In partnership with H. Craig Severance (until 1925) he created commercial buildings that conveyed a historical effect. His use of stainless steel introduced one of the typical features of Art Déco architecture.

Vanbrugh, John
* 1664 in London
† 26.03.1726 in London
Vanbrugh was initially a playwright and soldier, before the Duke of Carlisle asked him to design Castle Howard (1699). In 1702 he became the Surveyor General of the Queen's Works – without having had any training or experience in building. His career as an architect was solely due to the assistance of Nicholas Hawksmoor. Vanbrugh was later dismissed by the Tories, but he was able to return to the office after the death of Queen Anne. Similar to Wren, his buildings are inspired by picturesque Flemish models.

Vau (see Le Vau)

Velde, Henry Clemens van de
*3.04.1863 in Antwerp
†25.10.1957 in Zurich
Van de Velde started as a painter in the wake of the impressionists, Gauguin and the Pointillists, and was a member of Les XX. He became engaged in architecture and arts and crafts following a physical and psychological collapse in 1890. Here, the Arts and Crafts Movement in England served as a model for him. In 1896, he furnished four rooms in the Paris gallery of S. Bing. Their name, L'Art Nouveau, was used for the style. In 1899, he moved to Berlin, where he associated in the surroundings of the art magazine Pan. In 1901, van de Velde moved to Weimar as advisor for industry and arts and crafts. In 1902 he became a lecturer at the new arts and crafts school there, which he then led from 1906 to 1914. The institute was the direct predecessor of the Bauhaus. In this period, they already carried out the work in line with the ideas of the Werkbund and they reformed the teaching. Van der Velde's furniture and buildings continuously exhibit the curved lines of Art Nouveau, but they also have clear constructions in their whole volumes, allowing the architect to become a link to geometric Art Nouveau.

Vignola, Giacomo da (also Jacopo Barozzi da Vignola)
*1.10.1507 in Vignola
†7.07.1573 in Rome
Initially, Vignola trained as a painter in Bologna. Under the influence of Serlio he quickly turned to architecture, training under B. Peruzzi and A. da Sangallo the younger on the St. Peter's Cathedral. After stays in France and Bologna, he entered the service of the Farnese in Rome in 1546. Their Palazzo in Caprarola (from 1559) combines both the defensive and the representative building aspects of French castles. In 1564, he became Michelangelo's successor as the leading master builder of St.Peter's Church. Apart from his buildings, above all Il Gesú, his architecture tracts are among the most important from the Renaissance and Mannerism (Regola delli cinque ordini dell' architettura, 1562).

Vignon, Pierre Alexandre
*1762 in Lagny
†1828 in Paris
Vignon studied under C. N. Ledoux. He started his career by constructing barracks in Paris and in 1790 was chosen to build the arsenal. In 1793, he was named senior architect of the Republic. Vignon became known through his classicistic extension of the Church of the Madeleine in Paris. In 1806, Napoleon I engaged him to alter the already started Church building to a temple of glory. The building was still not finished when Vignon died. It was completed by J.-J.-M. Huvé and dedicated in 1842, once more as a church.

Viollet le Duc, Eugène Emmanuel

* 27.01.1814 in Paris

† 17.09.1879 near Lausanne

Viollet le Duc refused to study at the École des Beaux-Arts. Inspired by Victor Hugo, from an early age he was more interested in mediaeval architecture. He published his researches in the Dictionaire raisonné (ten volumes, 1853-1868). He was responsible for numerous restoration works. In his Entretiens sur l'architecture (2 volumes, 1858-1872), he states that the rationalism of construction (engineering construction) is the basis of every form of building work, and simultaneously recommends that new buildings should not adhere slavishly to historical styles, but merge into something new (eclecticism).

Vlught, Leendert Cornelis van der

*13.04.1894 in Rotterdam

†25.04.1936 in Rotterdam

Van der Vlught, who studied in Rotterdam, worked in Michiel Brinkman's office and, after the latter's death, became partners with his son, Johannes Andreas Brinkman. He had previously built a number of projects in a simple Cubist vernacular, such as the Villa with the portentous name, "Linia recta" (Latin for "straight line") in Zuidhoorn in 1925 and the MTS school in Groningen in conjunction with Jan Gerko Wiebenga.

Walpole, Horace (Horatio)

*24.09.1717 in London

†2.03.1797 in London

Horace, the youngest son of Prime Minister Robert Walpole, was himself an MP from 1741 to 1768. He made his name as an author, though. His first novel The Castle of Otranto (1764) was very successful and the starting point for the genre of the Gothic novel. He also presented an art history work with his Anecdotes of Painting in England (Vol.4, 1762–1771). He gathered an extensive art collection for his own house Strawberry Hill, which established neo-Gothic as suitable for non-sacral buildings as well

Walter, Thomas Ustick

*4.09.1804 in Philadelphia

†30.10.1887 in Philadelphia

Walter learned with Strickland. He expanded the Capitol in Washington, DC, and constructed the jail in Philadelphia (1833–1835), including Egyptian elements in the process.

Webb, Philip Speakman

* 12.01.1831 in Oxford

† 17.04.1915 in Worth (Sussex)

Webb was apprenticed to G. E. Street, and through his acquaintanceship with W. Morris and a commission to build Morris a residential house, he became one of the most important architects of the Arts and Crafts movement. The buildings of the Middle Ages were deemed exemplary: craftsmanship was the order of the day and a means of assuaging the problems of middle-class social existence. But since the Gothic style was brought into disrepute by Neo-Gothic industrial products (London World Fair of 1851), it was to be interpreted in its simplified, rural form. The Arts and Crafts Movement was brought to the attention of Continental Europe by H. Muthesius' publication, The English House.

Wren, Christopher

*20.10.1632 in East Knoyle, Wiltshire

†25.02.1723 in Hampton Court

Wren initially turned to the natural sciences and had chairs for Astronomy in London (1657) and Oxford (1661). His architectural career started in 1663 when he was appointed to the commission responsible for restoring St. Paul's Cathedral in London. On a trip to France in 1665–1666 he received decisive impulses through the buildings of Mansart and Le Vau. He was appointed the general architect for reconstructing London after the Great Fire of 1666. In this role he was responsible for constructing 52 churches within the city, ranging stylistically from Gothicist (St. Dunstan in the East) to Italian Baroque (St. Vedast; St. Bride). The St.Paul's Cathedral building shows itself as French Baroque-inspired Palladianism.

Wright, Frank Lloyd

* 8.06.1869 in Wisconsin

† 9.04.1959 in Phoenix

Wright trained in Madison as an engineer. In 1888 he began working for Sullivan, above all in the construction of residential dwellings. In 1894, the Winslow House in Illinois marked the first of his prairie houses, which were above all characterised by open ground plans (formed by the addition of the rooms rather than by a strict rectangular outer wall) and gently sloping, wide protruding roofs (Robie House in Chicago 1908). Wright's buildings not only met with interest in the USA, but also in Europe – such as by the De Stijl group. Indeed, when in the 1920s Wright moved on from the rural-looking prairie houses and – inspired by Europe – turned to concrete buildings, he met with more recognition in Europe than in the USA. His Imperial Hotel was one of the few buildings to survive the great earthquake of Tokyo undamaged. Only with the construction of the Guggenheim Museum in New York was Wright able to establish himself again in the USA.

Zumthor, Peter

*26.04.1943 in Basle

Initially, Zumthor trained under Tischler, before then studying interior design in Basle and architecture in New York. After that he was active in preserving historical monuments in the Grisons. His buildings are mostly simple in their outline, but often have a very striking surface removing all rigidity through their construction or material (such as stacked wood at the Swiss Expo Pavilion at the Hanover 2000 Exhibition.) M. Botta labelled him a "mystic" because of his concentration on the material.

Glossary

Abacus	–> Capital (also antique calculator)
Aedicule	frame, often around a door or window, similar to a –> Temple front
Ambulatory	–> Nave
Amphi-	Greek = on both sides, around
Anchor	plate –> Masonry
Apse, Exedra	projecting, usually semicircular, part of a building
Arabesque	ornamentation containing stylised plants and vines
Architecture	the art or science of constructing buildings. (Originates from Greek arkhitekton (= chief builder) via Latin architectura).
Architrave	–> Entablature
Arcade	–> Floor Forms
Arch	the simplest type is the rounded semicircular arch, which dates back to Roman times. The Greeks only used flat or straight arches (–> Architrave) for bridging openings. The Islamic horseshoe arch forms more than just a semicircle. During the Renaissance arches consisted again of a haunch and a crown, while in the Gothic period pointed arches had been formed by two segments joined at the top. The straight sides on the inside of an arch are the jamb. Slanted sides are formed by corbelliing. The springing point above the impost is where the bend starts at the top of an arch there is a keystone or a crown. (arched roofs or ceilings –> Vault)
Atlas	–> Columns
Atrium	the central room in ancient Roman houses; later the room where guests were received
Balustrade	railing composed of short posts or pillars (balusters)
Baptistery	building used for baptisms (sometimes involving submersion of the entire body)
Base	–> Columns
Basilica	–> Building Forms
Bay	a compartment in a building set off by columns or buttresses –> Nave
Boss	–> Masonry
Building Forms	the hall is a large room with four walls. In churches of this form the nave contains a central vessel and aisles of the same height. In a basilica, the central vessel has a higher ceiling than the aisles.
Calotte	semicircular dome without a drum –> Vault
Capital	Latin capitellum = little head, top of a –> Column. In addition to the capitals found in the clas sical –> Orders, there are also notable cushion capitals developed in the Romanesque period, as well as bell-shaped Gothic forms. The flat slab on top of the capital is called the abacus.
Campanile	free-standing bell-tower
Cella	–> Temple
Celestory	–> Floor Forms
Cenotaph	Greek = empty tomb. A construction feigning to be a tomb for memorial purposes
Chapel	small church or part of a church, for example, radial chapels
Chapter House	–> Cloister
Cloister	–> Monastery
Choir Screen	–> Choir
Choir, sanctuary	Area reserved for the clergy, sometimes separated by a choir screen or choir rail from the nave of the church, it can reach through to it liturgically. In architectural terms, the choir is the area behind the transept and sometimes forms an apsidal chevet. Some choirs are surrounded by an ambulatory. Radial chapels consist of several apses side by side that are sometimes smaller on the sides. English churches are sometimes extended by a Lady Chapel. If there is a choir at both ends of the church, then it is described as a double-choir structure.
Colonnade	the space between columns covered by an –> Architrave
Composite	–> Order
Construction	Latin = built, tectonic
Corinthian	–> Order

Cloister	–> Monastery
Columns	load-bearing part of a building. Piers often have a rectangular footprint, columns a round one. In addition, classical columns wax and wane as they rise (entasis) from the base to the –> Capital. The shaft of a column can be fluted. Other shafts abut columns and can provide support for the ribs in vaulted ceilings. These vaulting shafts can be grouped in compound shafts that in turn may rest on compound piers. A pilaster is a pier projecting only slightly from the load-bearing wall, a Medieval form of pilaster is the lesene (without capital). A masculine figure in place of a column is called an Atlas. This reflects the Egyptian Osiris pillar: both mythological figures stand on the Earth and support the Heavens. In certain systems alternating columns and piers are used in rhythmic succession. The lotus column, palm column and papyrus column are named particularly for the shapes of their capitals.
Cornice	–> Entablature
Couronnement	–> Tracery
Cross Forms	a Greek cross +, a Latin cross †; a St. Andrew's cross X
Crossing	–> Nave
Crypt	area below the choir, evolved from the martyrs' graves often located under the altar of early Christian churches
Curtain wall	–> Skeleton Construction
Cymatium	–> Entablature
Deambulatory	–> Ambulatory
Dome	–> Vault
Doric	–> Order
Dormitory	–> Cloister
En-delit	–> monolithic columns or shafts
Enfilade	French = to thread, suite of rooms one leading into the other
Entablature	in antique architecture, the entablature lies on the columns as the –> Flat or Straight Arch and supports the gable. Below, the architrave bridges the distance between the columns. Above the architrave one finds the frieze (consisting, in turn, of alternating fields with three vertical grooves [triglyphs] and for images [metopes]). This is topped by a crowning cornice. Other cornices that serve to define the façade horizontally are called cymatation and feature ogee moulding characterized as cyma recta or cyma reversa.
Exedra	–> Apse
Flat or Straight arch	Arch
Floor Forms	The Medieval Basilica is characterized by various levels. On the ground floor, Arcades, a row of columns bridged by arches, separate the main vessel from the aisles. On the level over the arcade, there was either a gallery, or – if it was only wide enough for a walkway - a triforium. The celestory, located on the level above, lets light in. Dwarf galleries are found on the exterior. Arcades are also found on the lower level of a building's exterior, a raised platform above such a gallery is called a tribune.
Fluting	–> Columns
Frieze	–> Entablature
Gable	–> Roof
Gallery	1: long formal hall 2: exhibition room 3: –> Floor Forms
Golden Section	harmonic division of a line (A) so that the longer part (B) stands in the same proportional relationship to the shorter (C) as does (A) to (B). The formula is A:B = B:C
Hall	–> Building Forms
Hypostyle	temple containing interior columns; typical of Egyptian hypostyle halls is an illuminated central nave.
Icono-	concerning images; iconography: the identification and description of icons; inconoclasm: the rejection of icons, as in the Iconoclastic Controversy in Byzantium during the 8th and 9th centuries ; inonology: the interpretation of icons
Impost	–> Arch
Inlay	coloured ornamentation of surfaces by means of inlay work using contrasting materials
Ionic	–> Order
Jamb	–> Arch

Kiosk	–> Pavilion
Lantern	–> Vault
Lesene	–> Columns
Longitudinal-Plan Building	building organised along a longitudinal axis in contrast to a –> Central-Plan Building
	Machicolation opening in fortress-like building through which liquids, etc. could be poured over assailants
Masonry	In contrast to –> Skeleton Construction, masonry is based on stacking load bearing material. It is differentiated according to the material (mud or clay brick) and the process by which they are produced and laid. Whereas rubble stone masonry from unhewn stone is very irregular, ashlar or squared-stone masonry is very regular. In the case of cyclopean masonry the faces are only roughly hewn and hewn only very selectively in the case of rusticated masonry. Opposite walls can be supported by means of wall ties, beams extending from the one to the other, and anchor plates. Masonry can also be support by peripheral ring anchors surrounding the masonry on the outside.
Mausoleum	orig. magnificent tomb of King Mausolos (377–352 BC) in Halicarnassus, today tomb buildings
Monastery	an independent complex of buildings designed to house religious communities withdrawn from everyday life. In Christian monasteries, the most important buildings are grouped around the cloister (court with covered gallery). These are the chapter house, in which monks assembled, the dormitory (Latin = sleeping room), the refectory (dining-hall) and the monastery church on the northern side of the complex .
Monolithic	from one stone
Nave	longest section of church building, sometimes flanked by –> Bays and intersected by transepts. In the –> Basilica, the celestory of central vessel rises up above the aisles. At the crossing, where the transept intersects the central vessel, there is often a tower. The extension of the aisles around the –> Choir is called the ambulatory (deambulatory).
Necropolis	Greek nekrós = dead person and polis = city, prehistorical or antique cemetery
Obelisk	tall four-sided pillar, tapering toward the top and ending in a point, originally the cult symbol of the Old Egyptian Sun God
Openwork Gablet	–> Roof
Orders	antique canon of the –> Column Proportions, the accompanying –> Capitals and –> Entablatures. The simplest order is the Tuscan. It has a smooth shaft and a round moulding as its capital. The Doric Order is similar, but has –> Flutes, as do all subsequent orders. In the Ionic Order, the capital consists of –> Volutes, and in the Corinthian the decoration is modelled on acanthus leaf garlands. The Composite Order combines the Ionic and Corinthian.
Parapet	low wall around the top of a building, often serving decorative purposes
Pavilion	small ornamental building in a garden or park. Also known as a Kiosk in Islamic and Asian regions.
Pendentive	–> Vault
Peribolos	–> Temple
Peripteral	–> Temple
Peristyle	an inner court surrounded by a portico of columns in antique buildings
Pier	–> Columns and –> Buttressing
Pilaster	–> Columns
Portico	open porch defined by columns similar to those of a –> Temple front Secular Architecture buildings for non-religious purposes
Projection	component extending out further than the surrounding elements
Pronaos	–> Temple
Pylon	entrance door to Old Egyptian buildings chacterised by two massive corner towers, today a massive towering wall mass
Ribs	–> Vault
Ring anchor	–> Masonry

Roof	A saddle roof consists of two pitched surfaces. Gables can be set in triangular openings in these surfaces. The use of open-work gablets as a decorative motif in Gothic architecture evolved from them. In a hipped roof both of the sides and both ends are pitched. All four of these surfaces are the same size in a pavilion roof.
Rosette	stylized rose
Rustication	–> Masonry
Sacred Building	a religious building as opposed to profane ones
Sanctuary	–> Choir
Screen	a partition or curtain
Shaft	–> Columns
Skeleton Construction	in contrast to massive –> Masonry, skeleton construction entails only the construction of a framework that can either be filled in with materials that do not bear a load or enclosed behind a facade (curtain wall). The Greek –> Temple and timber-framed houses are early forms of skeleton construction using architravs and supports or posts and beams. Socle pedestal on which a column, statue or building is set Buttressing the system of supports including the pier buttresses, flying buttresses and pinnacles that distribute the load and thrust in Gothic churches
Span	–> Arch
Tambour	–> Vault
Tectonic	from Greek tektonikos = to do with building; teaching of the components of a building –> Masonry and –> Skeleton Construction
Temple	holy site for practising a religious cult. The development of architecture was considerably influenced by the antique temple forms – which were set on a podium sometimes in the form of a crepidoma. The core of such temples is the enclosed cella. Its vestibule is the pronaos. Temples are differentiated according to the order of the columns: if they are located only on side of the entrance, then it is prostyle. If they are only between protruding tongues of wall then it is templum in antis. The peripteral is surrounded by columns (in pseudo-peripteral, only the lateral demi-columns protrude forward slightly from the cella wall). This portico of columns is called the peribolos. The round temple is a special form called a tholos or a monopteral if it is without a cella.
Tracery	the subdivision of windows using stone bars and geometrically ordered webs. The lower part of the tracery window consists of shafts (mullions), the crown above it is called couronnement
Transept	–> Nave
Transverse	Arch Vault
Tribune	–> Floor Forms
Triclinum	dining room in an antique house
Triforium	–> Floor Forms
Trompe l'oeil	French = to trick the eye, illusion of real objects in painting
Tuscan	–> Order
Tympanum	an arched pediment over a portal bridged by an architrave
Vault, Dome	a continuous vault is called a barrel vault (also tunnel or wagon vault); when two such vaults intersect they for a groin vault which opens onto four compartments. The number of compartments determines the form (sexpartite; 7/12). A cross-rib vault is where the groins are provided with joists. Joists between the severies (–> Bay) are transverse arches. More complex rib arrangements lead to net or stellar vaults. The dome is half a sphere. A lantern is an attempt to obtain secure illumination via the crown. A circular structure on which the dome is set is called a tambour (often containing windows). Pendentives or squinches mediate between the quadratic substructures and the round domes. A spherical segment is a half dome.
Vaulting Shafts	–> Columns
Vertical Elevation	head-on view of a structure, or part of a structure, sometimes depicting –> Floor Forms
Volute	ornamental form which features spirals directed inward like rams' horns

Index of names

Index of places

Photo credits

A. Bartel/architekturphoto	214
A. Bednorz	172,222, 290, 320, 344
Bitter + Bredt	392
L. Boegly/Archipress	182, 386
C. Boisvieux/Bilderberg	100-101, 136
K. Bossemeyer/Bilderberg	94
Z. Braun/Archipress/Artur	404
F. Busam/architekturphoto	394
R. Bryant/Arcaid	384
S. Cambouline/Archipress	310 © VG Bild-Kunst, Bonn 2001
N. Clutton/Arcaid	278
N. Clutton/architekturphoto	300
S. Collins/PICTURE PRESS	114-115
Connor/OKAPIA, München	148
P. Cook/Archipress	338 © FLC/VG Bild-Kunst, Bonn 2001,
	334 © VG Bild-Kunst, Bonn 2001
D. Dagli Orti	20, 32, 38, 40, 50, 52, 66-67, 72, 74, 78, 82-83, 86, 88, 96, 110,
	112, 142-143, 152, 154, 162, 166, 178, 180, 184, 202, 232, 236
Uwe Dettmar/Bildarchiv Mohnheim	188
C. Dixon/architrekturphoto	370
M. Engler/Bilderberg	90, 194-195
G. Erlacher/architekturphoto	296
H.G. Esch, Köln	402-403
F. Eustache/Archipress	314, 324, 326 © FLC/VG Bild-Kunst, Bonn 2001,
	332,342 © VG Bild-Kunst, Bonn 2001,
	346 © VG Bild-Kunst, Bonn 2001, 396
F. Fischer/Bilderberg	390
Flac/OKAPIA, München	372, 382
K. Frahm/artur	336
D. Freppel/Archipress,	2-3, 358-359
O.M. Gambier	348 © VG Bild-Kunst, Bonn 2001
R. Guntli	104
R. Halbe/arthur	322
Heeb/LOOK	272
J. Heller/artur	218
Hilblich/AKG Berlin	292
H. Horacek/Bilderberg	196
Hornac/PICTURE PRESS	226
W. Janzer/Archipress/Artur	376
K. Johaentges/LOOK	268
KaKi/OKAPIA, München	242-243
Kirchner/OKAPIA, München	282
A. Kunert/architekturphoto	410
M. Laemmerer/OKAPIA, München	30
J. Liepe/Bildarchiv Preussischer Kulturbesitz	34, 48-49
R. Lohbronner	134-135
M. Loiseau/Archipress	264-265
T. Mayer/Das Fotoarchiv	368

Texts by the following authors:
Hubertus Adam (121, 123, 125, 129, 141, 259, 263, 279, 293, 295, 305, 309, 315, 319, 347, 371, 389, 393, 405, 411),
Oliver Elser (313, 365), Markus Golser (71, 73, 161, 163, 171, 193, 209, 219, 221, 229, 231 233, 237, 249), Dietmar Kölbel
(18-19, 21, 23, 25, 27, 29, 31, 33, 37, 39, 53, 55, 57, 65, 84-85, 87, 91, 95, 97, 99, 102-103, 105, 107, 109, 111, 113, 115,
117, 119, 127, 135, 137, 195, 215, 223, 227, 239, 241, 243, 245, 256-257, 261, 277, 297, 369, 373, 379, 381, 383, 385,
397, 407), Andrea Mende (131, 133, 139, 165, 167, 173, 177, 197), Jochen Paul (225, 265, 275, 303, 307, 311, 321, 323,
329, 331, 333, 341, 349, 351, 353, 359, 363, 377, 391), Sebastian Raedecke (288-289), Manuela Schubert (144-145, 147,
149, 151, 153, 155, 395, 399), Ulrike Schulze (169, 200-201, 203, 207, 211, 213, 217, 251), Sebastian Schwarzenberger (35,
41, 43, 45, 47, 49, 51, 59, 61, 63, 75, 77, 79, 81, 89, 93, 179, 271, 281, 285, 299, 301, 325, 327, 335, 337, 339, 345, 355,
361, 367, 375), Chris van Uffelen (68-69, 158-159, 175, 181, 183, 185, 187, 189, 191, 205, 247, 253, 267, 269, 273, 283,
291, 317, 343, 357, 401, 409).

Architecture Highlights

© 2001 DuMont Buchverlag, Köln
(DuMont monte UK; London)

Project direction and realization: Autoren & Management Dr. Andreas Pöllinger/Dr. Silvia Kienberger, München/Berlin
Copyeditors (German): Chris van Uffelen, Thomas Paul, Michaela Angermair
Photo editor: Elisabeth Alric-Schnee
Layout, graphic design and lithography: Regg Media GmbH, München
Cover illustrations: © R. Richter/Architekturphoto, © Pictures/OKAPIA, München
Translations into English: Dr. Maureen Roycroft Sommer, Malkem Green, Ian Cowley, Guy Laurie, Burke Barrett
Copyeditors (English): Frank Auerbach, Burke Barrett
Overall production: Brepols, Belgium
Printed in Belgium

ISBN 3-7701-7086-5